TAZEEN

The Checkout Girl

My Life on the Supermarket
Conveyor Belt

FRIDAY
INSTANTS

The Friday Project
An imprint of HarperCollins*Publishers*
77–85 Fulham Palace Road
Hammersmith, London W6 8JB
www.thefridayproject.co.uk
www.harpercollins.co.uk

First published by The Friday Project in 2009

A catalogue record for this book
is available from the British Library

ISBN 978-0-00-732772-0

Typeset in Minion by G&M Designs Limited,
Raunds, Northamptonshire

Printed and bound in Great Britain by
Clays Ltd, St Ives plc

Mixed Sources
Product group from well-managed
forests and other controlled sources
www.fsc.org Cert no. SW-COC-1806
© 1996 Forest Stewardship Council

FSC

FSC is a non-profit international organisation established to promote the
responsible management of the world's forests. Products carrying the FSC
label are independently certified to assure consumers that they come
from forests that are managed to meet the social, economic and
ecological needs of present and future generations.

Find out more about HarperCollins and the environment at
www.harpercollins.co.uk/green

For Cogs everywhere

PROLOGUE

Except for a short stint in a superstore as a student many years ago, my experience of supermarkets had been the same as most people's; I'd rush in to complete the dull but essential chore that is the weekly shop, I'd have no time for checkout girls and their small talk. I'd rebuff offers of help tactlessly, make demands as though they were machines programmed to serve me without complaint, and promptly forget their names and faces seconds after rushing out. Little did I know that, behind the identity badges, unflattering uniforms and quiet smiles were individuals taking note of my every quirk, comment and foible.

Never again will I shop the same way. And neither will you.

When I began my six-month career as a checkout girl, the country was reeling from the possibility that we were headed for a full-blown recession. President Obama's election brought new optimism around the world but could not disguise the doom and gloom that lay ahead. The credit crunch and financial instability were one thing, but in the early autumn of 2008 things were about to get rocky for every man, woman and child in this country – as we slid into the worst recession the world has seen for decades.

Until that point the main casualties of the financial crisis were the banking institutions – Northern Rock, Lehman

Brothers, Citigroup, Fannie Mae and Freddie Mac, along with mortgage lenders and insurance companies. Most ordinary people were still watching developments from a safe distance. However, unemployment figures were creeping up, redundancies and job losses were looming and food prices were on the rise.

As a mother running a busy home and working in a volatile industry I had started to count my own pennies. My grocery shopping was now leaving my wallet disconcertingly light. I'd push my trolley to the car park while staring at the receipt, aghast that the food in my bags now cost well in excess of a hundred pounds: I knew I had to make cutbacks. It was after one such shopping trip, clutching my hefty bill, that I turned back to look at the checkouts and it dawned on me – *this* was the front line of the recession, where the reality of the downturn really hit home. And that's how I embarked on my quest to see what a billion-pound hole in our economy would really mean for us all.

Someone, with not much time for reporters, once told me that 'Journalists always report from the outside in and so only ever see the story from a superficial vantage point.' My episodes of immersive, experiential or undercover journalism have allowed me the privilege of reporting from the inside out. This requires a degree of individual sacrifice, intrusion, duplicity and commitment that usually leaves me slightly unhinged. However awkward it is personally, thankfully it serves the purpose of shedding light on the truth in a way that turning up with my notebook, pen and press pass never could do. This is that truth.

Why did I choose Sainsbury's? Actually it chose me. Last autumn, jobs in retail were hard to come by and I searched and applied for a number of positions in various supermarkets before this vacancy cropped up. I had to complete an in-depth online assessment and attend an interview: I got the job. In my first month, as the crisis deepened, I was convinced that, like many other retailers, the supermarkets would eventually fall victim to the downturn. I couldn't have been more wrong. I sat at my checkout, week in week out, for six months observing first-hand how the nation was adapting to the onset of what would soon be described as the worst global recession since the 1930s. At first, customers were spending hard and most appeared unruffled by the storm brewing ahead. And then as the year drew to an end, I saw a shift: money-saving tactics kicked in, savvy food choices were being made, offers were hunted down and customers were watching the pennies carefully – the recession was starting to bite. I witnessed for myself how the average British family was suffering, as people opened up to me about their money troubles. And some didn't stop there; I listened, mouth agape, as customers launched into full-blown confessions about their personal lives, divulging their most private thoughts.

To us they are just cogs in the supersonic wheel of our supermarkets, but Checkout Girls and Guys – or Cogs, as I secretly referred to them – have incredible stories to tell and intriguing interwoven lives of their own. Behind the tills, in the shopping aisles, across the customer service desk, beyond the doors leading to the back of the store and upstairs in the canteen and locker rooms, family dramas are played out, love affairs and friendships flourish and sometimes wilt. Here, several members of one family work together, along with friends who grew up together, neighbours, former school friends and flat-mates. At times it's like a small, cosmopolitan village, at others like a big, bustling, multi-racial family. And on a daily basis they welcome us as shoppers right into the heart of their community while unwittingly becoming spectators to *our* personal and financial dramas. Against all my expectations I walked straight on to the set of a gripping soap opera in which all of us have a walk on part. The Cogs I met were in Sainsbury's, but they are in every supermarket and in every town – and they are watching you. This is their story.

The Checkout Girl

Saturday, 8 November 2008

So here I am. Day One. My hair's tied back, my shoes are low-heeled and sensible but even though I've got my orange name-badge on, I'm still me. That may be because I haven't been given my bright blue polyester polo shirt and high-waisted, wide-bottomed, narrow-legged, creased-down-the-front trousers yet.

At Sainsbury's, becoming a checkout girl or 'Cog' requires a two-day training course. Staff recruitment is serious business here, and as I wait in the canteen I'm given a quick summary of what we'll learn today: the supermarket's raison d'être, history, financial status, aims and objectives, health and safety rules and, most significantly, its guiding mottos:

'Do you want your bonus? Then, always smile, take the customer to the product and offer an alternative. Above all, be friendly.'

The mantras are many in number and imprinted on beige-cream A4 pages, crumpling a little at the corners, stuck all the way up the stairwell. And right next to the clocking-in and (equally importantly for all supermarket workers) the clocking-out machine is a poster signed by shop-floor staff all promising to 'smile more', 'be more helpful', and 'treat the customer like someone special'. These are the Cogs' countless messages pledging allegiance and promising to be better at their jobs. It reads like a giant farewell card written by signees at gun point.

Our trainer finds it impossible to refrain from bragging about how well this store is doing.

'The credit crunch has not affected us,' we are told. 'We are set to take a million by the end of this week,' she crows, smiling smugly. 'We've already taken £16,000 on clothes today.' Her grin is now wider than a Cheshire cat.

We have to sign the contract on the spot and hand it back immediately. When I ask if I can get a copy, I am brashly told, 'You'll get one once Personnel have signed it,' with no indication given of when that might be.

Sickness policy: There is no sick pay for six months and if you are ill you only get statutory sick pay.

Holidays: You need to book that *now*.

Overtime: Whether you like it or not, you're going to have to put in extra hours and swap shifts. 'It's a matter of "You scratch my back, and I'll scratch yours."'

Breaks: One hour unpaid lunch for checkout staff if you do a full day. But depending on the number of hours worked this could be a fifteen-, twenty-, thirty- or forty-five-minute paid break. On top of lunch? Instead of lunch? I'm not clear and she doesn't provide clarification either.

The locker comes at a deposit of £5, so technically that's an hour from your pay docked already. And don't even think about clocking in until AFTER you've been to your locker and are ready to head on to the shop floor.

Sainsbury's is at the top of its game, she tells us. However, Tesco *has* inconveniently pipped it to the No. 1 post, and Asda, with its marriage to Walmart, has shoved Sainsbury's into third place.

'I don't think we'll ever be No. 1,' says our trainer wistfully. 'We compete with those two on price, but M&S and Waitrose on quality.' Whispering for effect, she adds, 'I shop at Marks and Spencer when I want something special, but some people actually come *here* for the same reason.'

We are told about the mystery customer who shops in the store to test the full Sainsbury's experience. Today I learn that this supermarket's philosophy is almost entirely defined by the Mystery Customer Measure (MCM), and the bonus that could line everyone's pocket if they give the store the thumbs-up. He or she will come in twice a month and sample every single aspect of the store – the petrol station, the café, the toilets, the shop floor, customer service, checkouts. If the store gets an average rating of 80 per cent or more over a full period, everyone gets a small bonus. 'We've had a couple of 80-plus per cents,' we're told. There are also additional incentives known as 'shining stars' for staff to go that extra mile to please customers. If the mystery shopper (or in fact any customer) mentions the name of a particularly helpful member of staff then a £10 voucher is awarded to the named employee. 'Justin' – Justin King, Chief Executive of Sainsbury's – 'has been so generous this year,' we are told. 'Above and beyond all the normal store cut prices, he's given us an extra 15 per cent discount to shop with this Christmas. We're being paid to take it away, basically.'

We spend the next few hours familiarising ourselves with the store layout and learn about the multiple ranges: Basics (cheap and cheerful), Taste the Difference (high-end foods), Different by Design (non-foods luxury range), TU (bargain-basement clothes), Be Good to Yourself (healthy range), So Organics (organic food). But getting to know my fellow Cogs is the most enjoyable part of the day. We are all struggling to swallow the corporate spiel we're being spun. I have to admit that I had preconceived ideas as to who these people were, and they are certainly not what I expect: ex-professionals, trainee professionals and soon-to-be professionals. They include a law graduate who is going to travel for two hours each way to work the night shift, a middle-aged woman with a long and illustrious career behind her who, in tough times, cannot find another job. And then there is Rebecca, who I love after exactly zero point two minutes; a vivacious, petite redhead in her mid-thirties who battles to disguise her sarcastic deadpan sense of humour. She is training *and* working all week long *and* has taken on weekend work following a dramatic pay cut. She has two teenage sons to put through college soon so 'needs must' she tells me privately. Throughout the day, we catch each other's eye when we should be paying attention and fight to stop ourselves from collapsing into a heap of giggles.

By the end of Day One, I've learned that those at the bottom of the rung have about as many rights as the frozen chicken sitting in aisle 33. And that, if I'm to believe what I'm told, the recession is as far from this particular branch of Sainsbury's as the TU range is from haute couture fashion. But I look at my new colleagues and can't help thinking that, for as long as the country is in economic meltdown, here on the supermarket floor is where the recession is really going to make its mark. The real victims are the new breed of supermarket staff created by this financial crisis.

Sunday, 9 November 2008

Induction Day Two does not transpire. Our trainer has sustained a neck injury and so we end up spending a day on the shop floor. A trolley full of health and beauty products, abandoned at the till, is pushed in my direction. My first task is to take each item back to its rightful home on the shelves, and soon going around in circles has me dizzier than a tail-chasing dog. It takes me a wet-behind-the-ears forty-five minutes to realise the best approach is to sort the trolley into different categories according to shop layout rather than pushing it back and forth up the same aisles again and again. When I attempt to return some chocolates to their home in aisle 24 I'm overwhelmed by an urge to shovel the entire packet into my mouth.

Next up, the customer service desk. After a few hours of agonising repetition I know that this is not the place for me. The refund, refund, refund nature of the desk means it's no more than a factory. Chatting is out of the question and the customers are more irritable than Sir Alan Sugar after a round with his apprentice wannabes. By the end of the day, Anne-Marie's unwavering courtesy, patience and total professionalism – in the face of hostile, grumpy and impatient customers – are awe-inspiring. She doesn't crack once, works without pause and still manages to be polite and courteous not just to the customers but also to me, with my annoying questions. Occasionally I manage to show a customer to their longed-for product in the right aisle after walking in circles for several minutes with the customer in hot (confused) pursuit. The rest of the time I'm jotting product barcodes on receipts and devising reasons for why the goods were returned. I take note of the number of times people come over with bills where an item has been charged twice at the tills in error. After three hours doing this I am told that on Sundays you only get twenty minutes for lunch, so off I go muttering under my breath.

When I return there is still spare salt to rub in my wound. My new friend, Rebecca, and I are given what looks like a million leaflets detailing the in-store promotions – 50 per cent off toys, 25 per cent off wine and 25 per cent reduction on TU clothing. We have to hand these to customers entering the shop. I spend the first ten minutes enthusiastically greeting every customer with an all-American 'Hi!' and the pressure to treat each shopper like a mystery customer is so intense that I find myself taking a seven-year-old to the card section and smiling obsequiously, you know, just in case. The zeal fades quickly though when there are no smiles, barely a hello in return, and without exception, no eye contact. Thankfully, I'm asked to return to customer service to help out. I can't wait to be behind the desk again, but feel rotten for leaving Rebecca distributing leaflets. I tell her we'll do a swap in ten minutes. After five minutes of guilt-ridden angst I find an excuse to get her back to help. Once she's made her escape she's willing to do whatever it takes to avoid leafleting and spends the next couple of hours loitering in the clothing department. Never again will I refuse a leaflet crumpled into my hand on the street and nor will I frown when I discover I've been handed five rather than just the one.

And then suddenly there they are. The words I'm dreading emerging from my own mouth and I'm hearing them after being here for less than two days. A young man is taken off checkouts, placed at customer service for five minutes and then promptly sent straight back to checkouts. 'I hate this place,' he mutters as he walks away.

* * *

Towards the end of my day, at 4 p.m., I'm asked to check if anyone wants help with packing. I run from till to till asking the checkout assistants if they need my help. They all smile politely and decline. I've asked most of them when one finally has the good sense to say, 'Well, that's up to the customer, isn't it?'

Once I've recovered from my idiocy, one lady takes me up on my offer saying, 'Only if you're good at it.' 'It's one of my life skills,' I respond. She laughs, not realising that in this job it's the only one that counts.

Later I help a young mum pack. She seems to have decided to clothe her entire family in the TU range. Struggling to find the right amount of money, she takes one T-shirt off the bill. Seconds after she's said goodbye to me, I spot her at customer service returning the lot.

Rebecca repeats at least half a dozen times today, 'I've got to get a job at Waitrose.' But how will it be better? I find myself wondering.

Monday, 10 November 2008

I put my uniform on for the first time. I haven't worn polyester since the eighties so it takes some adjusting to. When I look at myself in the mirror, I want to ask where the pasta sauce is. Unsurprisingly, Husband falls about in hysterics. Once he has composed himself he tries to take a picture. He's laughing so hard the picture is blurred.

Today is till training. A solemn-faced, gum-chewing supervisor trains a few of us including Rebecca and Adil, from the general merchandise department, who has spent months avoiding his turn on the tills. During those six hours we learn about the slide, scan and pass technique that we're told

Sainsbury's has developed to avoid staff getting back pain and attempting to sue the supermarket. We have to aim for seventeen items per minute (IPM); 'If you don't maintain it, we'll find out,' says our plain-speaking till trainer. All our actions are accountable; CCTV, electronic monitoring, assessments, secret observation, clocking in and out, customer and colleague feedback. With cameras in every nook and cranny there is no escape. 'In places you least expect them,' the trainer tells us ominously. Let that be a warning to us all. If they are doing their job, by now they must have caught me putting things back on the wrong shelves, sneaking off to the loos to send text messages, secretly sampling food and gossiping with Rebecca in quiet corners. In the bathroom there's a sticker on the door with the contact details for a whistle-blowing helpline: *If you see something wrong then say something right. One number. One website. Riskavert.co.uk/rightline.* When she leaves us for a minute, Rebecca and I start singing Rockwell's 'Somebody's Watching Me'. Yet, despite the ethos and attire, this isn't the eighties and the message is clear: no one gets away with dragging their feet.

Our trainer talks coupons, reduced-price items, fruit-and-veg prices, cards, sub-totals, split payments, cash payments, fraud, removing security tags, till maintenance, voids, mistakes, price checks – by the end of it my brain sizzles from information overload. When it comes to Nectar cards, customers get two points for every £1 spent. After you've got 500 points, you get £2.50 off. By this calculation you have to spend £250 before you get a couple of pounds off. When I look at my own receipts I still can't make head or tail of it.

At Boots you get four points for every pound spent and each point is worth one pence. Isn't that a better rewards scheme than Nectar?

Adil is a super-bright young politics student who works here part-time. He gives me the lowdown after three years in the job: 'This Sainsbury's branch never used to take induction quite so seriously but things changed after the store failed a number of times on customer service. Sainsbury's know they can't compete with Tesco on value so they're trying to compete on customer service.'

From an employee point of view, though, everyone I've talked to so far speaks highly about working here. 'If you're nice to everyone, everyone is nice to you,' I hear, over and over again. I also overhear one young staffer tell another how intimidating they find their manager. All the managers are pretty intimidating; they charge down corridors, sour-faced and with little time for pleasantries. My direct manager, Richard, is the exception.

I'm to go back on Sunday for Day Two of my induction. Already I feel like I'm working here full-time.

Thursday, 13 November 2008

I am yet to have my 'Think 21' training – selling alcohol, fireworks and other age-restricted goods – so until then it's the shop floor for what I now call 'reverse shopping'. Sainsbury's staff call it 'shopping' – picking up the goods dumped by customers at the tills. Never again will I have a last-minute change of heart leaving a poor Cog to put the unwanted product back. The one three-quarters-full trolley I have takes me two whole hours. After staring aimlessly upwards in a vain attempt to find an aisle that looks like it might be home to the items in my trolley, I find myself going distinctly doolally. I spend more minutes than is healthy carrying cans of Air Wick air freshener, Fairy Liquid bottles, baked bean cans, 3-for-£15 DVDs, a size-16 leopard-print blouse, an over-priced cuddly reindeer and 2-for-1 cookie selection boxes. Despite asking for guidance, no shelf can be found for the truly homeless – the Peppa Pig umbrella, a bag of mixed nuts and raisins, the rogue Christmas light and Pantene shampoo for thick and glossy hair. They go back to the trolley by the supervisors post and next time I look they've vanished.

Adil gives me a heads-up on the mystery shopper.

'They will always ask for something at the other end of the shop to see if you will just point them in the right direction or actually take them there – which is obviously what you need to do. That's inside information – use it well.'

I get my chance today. A smartly dressed, well-spoken lady in her sixties approaches me while I'm loitering in the household cleaners' aisle and asks me if we have any Christmas biscuits other than the ones in the aisle across from us.

'Yes we do, at the other end of the sto—' A moment's hesitation and I know what's expected of me. 'I'll take you.'

I'm not a hundred per cent sure I'm taking her to the right spot, but if I look confident enough I *may* just pull it off. As we walk from one end of the store to the other, I do the maths. She is definitely retired, which makes her a prime candidate for mystery shopping. I'd better do some talking.

'Are you doing your Christmas shopping?'

'Oh yes.'

'I wish I had the foresight to do mine so far in advance.'

'Oh, you're probably too busy working. I know what it's like. Before I retired' – BINGO! – 'I used to work for Sainsbury's … in IT as a project manager.' DOUBLE BINGO!

She tells me she was there for ten years. I take her to the aisle, show her the biscuits, ask her if she needs anything else and leave her to it.

Back to the trolley and more reverse shopping. A middle-aged man asks if I can help him find a particular brand of toilet roll. I show him and ask if there's anything else he wants. He grunts what may or may not have been a no. Even my toes curl when I cringe.

If I'm trying too hard, one of my fellow newbies isn't trying at all. Young, dark-haired and plump, she sidles up to me with a customer close behind her.

'I've only been here two weeks and this chap is asking if we have any walnut whips. Do we?' she asks.

'I've only been here a week – I don't know.'

'I don't know what to do with him. Should I tell him to go to another shop?'

'Maybe take him to customer service or a till captain?' I suggest.

She wanders towards him and fobs him off.

Meanwhile, as I'm trying to locate the rightful home of Garnier hair conditioner, a Korean family stop me. It's Dad, Mum and their teenage daughter.

'We need something for her hair,' says Dad. 'What you recommend?'

'Oh boy, I'm no expert but I'll try.'

'You know more than me, I'm sure,' grins Dad.

'What are you after – shampoo? Conditioner?'

'Make her hair straight. It's wavy.'

'You want serum for her hair?'

'No sticky, for straight.'

'Oh, so you want sticky stuff to make it straight.'

'No for straight, like this.' He indicates using his hands that he wants her hair straight. And his English seems to have got progressively worse.

'OK, so you want to make her hair straight, right?'

Dad looks at me with exasperation. 'No.'

I look at her hair and it's wavy and kind of frizzy. Why am I talking to her *dad*? This must be mortifying for her. I look her straight in the eyes.

'You have wavy hair and it's sort of flyaway, so do you want something for frizzy hair?'

Dad jumps in, 'No, for the straight, to make it.'

I ask her again: 'What are YOU after?'

'I don't know,' she whispers.

'Do you want shampoo … conditioner … mousse?' Come on, girl, give me something. Anything.

She says nothing. They get fed up with me and send me on my way.

Before my shift started I did some grocery shopping. I picked up a packet of Country Life spreadable only to see a sign when I clocked in stating that it was being pulled off the shelves and we weren't to let any customers buy it. I point this out to another Cog and she tells me to let customer services know. At the end of my shift when I take my butter back, they simply say it would not be scanable if it was withdrawn. They give me a refund and return to their conversation.

I catch my reflection pushing a trolley today and, for a second, think it's someone else.

Friday, 14 November 2008

An item I pick up frequently at the tills is washed and ready-to-eat baby leaf spinach; another is ready-made steak pie. Both items are a reminder that the cook in the kitchen ought to try cooking. Customers are also putting in an impressive performance of pretending to purchase foods they have just sampled for free: they put it in their trolley at the samplers table and, once at the checkout, it gets swiftly dumped.

By the end of today's shift I've broken every new rule I've been taught. I start putting things back in the wrong place, stop to peruse newspapers, sneak off to the loo to make a phone call. It feels good. And then I count down the hours in slots of ten minutes. That doesn't feel so good. Fortunately, I manage to conjure up a new plot to get off the shop floor; I ask to shadow a checkout assistant. And that's how I end up chatting to two checkout girls who speculate that I must be around nineteen. When I tell them how much older I am, they're gobsmacked.

The older of the two Cogs, who is closer to my age, is alarmed that I've had my kids later in life. She had hers twenty years ago. Like all the other Cogs here, she is truly charming. I'm discovering a strong sense of camaraderie. People generally look out for each other here. It's really quite startling. In this line of work, people are actually NICE.

Today, as on my previous few shifts, I witness staff doing their personal shopping just before they leave the store to go home. And now I know why. It's the ultimate test of self-resolve to spend so many hours around food, clothes, toys, DVDs, gadgets, computer games – all the trappings of modern commercial life, and all placed to maximise their appeal. Not being allowed to touch, taste or sample any of it, makes me long for them even more. I find myself stroking clothes, squeezing fruit, inhaling deeply at the bakery – and then lingering longingly in the confectionery aisle while chocolate samples are being handed out to customers. Doing your shop at the end of a shift is the equivalent of finally gorging on a giant cream cake after being forced to stare at it on an empty belly for hours. Oh, it feels glorious.

Saturday, 15 November 2008

The first thing that happens on my shift blows apart my theory about customer service being wasted on the Brits. I help a woman to the car with her two trolleys' worth of shopping and as we walk she tells me that she had stopped shopping at Sainsbury's because it had become so expensive. But after one shopping trip to Morrisons, she promptly returned. 'I don't know what they do to you guys here, but everyone is so helpful and nice that I would never go anywhere else again.' She admitted it was still pricier, but she was prepared to dig deeper so people were nice to her.

I spend about three hours doing reverse shopping, picking up hangers and security tags. When I'm ready to weep with boredom, I blag my way on to shadowing on checkouts again. This time with the lovely Maya. She's been in the job for eleven years and says she took it as a temporary escape from the drudgery of her housewife life. She hasn't looked back because it's the one job she can just leave at the door. She says that the place has changed tremendously during her time, particularly on the checkouts.

'We used to have packers, and someone doing all the running around, and there was none of the customer interaction – that's all down to us now.'

Maya tells me the busiest days are when offers are on and at the weekends – although Dial-a-Ride (old people on a mini-bus) Tuesdays are also very busy. She points out that on those days it's very slow in terms of IPM on which we all get scored. She is, however, fantastic at charming the most uptight of customers, and they cave in quickly.

At the end of the shift there is an impromptu security search – involving the lifting of collars, checking under badges and the removal of socks and shoes. As I empty my pockets, my notes and pen emerge and my heart skips a beat. I'm terrified they'll ask to look at my notes, but they don't.

Sunday, 16 November 2008

So far no references have been taken up – and I've been at the store for about a week. What's become clear to me in that time is that here 'colleagues' (as everyone calls each other) are not only loyal to one another but incredibly loyal to the store too, even though they work their fingers to the bone. I've identified two groups of colleagues. The students, age range 16–23, work hard, earning money to get themselves through college; they mingle with the other students and shrug almost everything off with one-, sometimes two-syllable words. The other group is made up of older women in the 30–50 age group; they've had their babies, are done with housewifery, and want an easy job that gives them a bit of spare cash. They want to make some friends and work but are qualified to do little else. However there is also a third group emerging – a crop of credit-crunched professionals supplementing their incomes after suffering a pay cut or redundancy. Educated, articulate and with few other options, they find it humiliating and belit-tling and do it for no other reason than the cash. Despite being qualified and experienced, the recession has hung them out to dry.

We all congregate for delayed Day Two of our induction – and some of the others look brow-beaten. I think they've had a tough week. We're told about 'the rumble'. Every day from 11.30–12.30 and 15.30–16.30 'everyone, and that means everyone' goes to one department and helps them get their goods on to the floor. I want to ask who is left on checkouts, security and customer service, but don't dare.

Again it is drummed into us that customer service is our TOP priority. Our main aim, we're told repeatedly, is to be as helpful as possible – and to always offer an alternative so that customers don't leave empty-handed. I keep schtum about the elderly gentleman who came in hunting for maternity pads for the daughter who had just given birth. I sent him off to Mothercare. We're also told to imprint the acronym 'REACT' in our minds every single time we deal with a customer – Receive the message, Empathise, Ask questions, Consider options and Tell them the result. We're reminded that it's paramount that we keep ourselves looking clean, tidy, have our hair tied back and frequently wash our hands. There are unkind giggles when they talk about someone with a bad BO problem.

Today I also found out that the Mystery Customer Measure makes up only a small amount of the bonus and is based on the availability of produce, and the amount of wastage. The less we waste, the higher our score.

I also discover other trade secrets, the kind that some customers have become aware of – food rotation (longest life at the back) and price reductions just before the end of the day (which explains why so many customers pile in during the evening).

According to the trainer, our uniform is changing. At the moment it's blue and orange, but from April next year it will come into line with the rest of Sainsbury's and we'll be wearing purple and orange. I'm assuming though there'll be no escape from the polyester.

The most important part of today is our 'Think 21' training. We have to ask ourselves if anyone buying age-restricted goods looks under twenty-one. If in doubt, ask for ID. I never carry any age-specific ID and wonder how many people do. The trainer tells us people will try to persuade and cajole, get angry and joke their way into making us sell restricted products to them. But the consequences are no laughing matter: prosecution, a criminal record, a fine and disciplinary action. During the course of the training, I decide to adopt two rules of thumb: if they look like they could work in the store under the student category – ask for ID. And if they have wrinkles, they are probably old enough.

And if we're not frightened enough by the consequences, we're told about 'Jake Edwards' who sold alcohol to an under-age customer. Unfortunately for him, trading standards were testing the store. He faced a criminal charge, had to go to court, lost his job and, worst of all for him, was unable to travel to New York with his girlfriend on holiday. There are gasps all round.

Next on the training agenda is shoplifting. Another acronym – SCONE – explains the tactic used by shoplifters. They Select, Conceal, Observe, No payment, Exit. No one else points this out, but it's obvious to me that shoplifters are taking advantage of Sainsbury's desperate attempts to please its customers by working in twos. While one distracts the shop assistant with questions, the other Selects and Conceals.

And on the list of most desired items by shoplifters are the usual suspects – alcohol, CDs, beauty products and … meat. At certain times of year, lamb is apparently so expensive, a shoplifter will sneak it under their jumper with a view to selling it on later. I ask repeatedly how and where this black market in lamb operates. There is no response.

Then there is the 'red route' which we are all expected to walk during our shifts – via electronics, DVDs and CDs and past the beers, wines and spirits before heading up to the canteen for break-times. 'Keep your eyes open and look out for shoplifters.'

Sainsbury's is trying to up its green credentials. At the moment they play good guy to M&S's bad guy on the plastic bag front. People are furious about having to pay for plastic bags there. Sainsbury's keeps bags behind the tills until someone asks, but sometime next year bags will be gone from behind the tills, then they will have to be paid for, and eventually they will disappear altogether.

Thursday, 20 November 2008

Two weeks after I started, I am finally on checkouts. At first I just shadow and then I'm thrown in the deep end. I am slow and make mistakes, and most of time I'm too intimidated to apply Think 21. But as with my first attempt at parasailing, after the horror of being flung several hundred feet into the sky subsides, the adrenaline kicks in – and I'm high as a kite. I chat to strangers with the confidence of a teen drunk. My small talk is gauche and unrefined but it hits the mark for the few minutes every man, woman and child spends at my till. Through my checkout comes a recent widower who is struggling to shop alone, a young mum, her terrible toddler and a lot of impulse buys, an older mum accompanied by tetchy teenagers with many 3-for-2 offers, and a couple of middle-aged men with an extraordinary amount of chocolate.

At 3.30 p.m. there's a brief hiatus around the school-run time. Some of the till captains don't like staff sitting around doing nothing, even for a moment – Samantha is ready to take me off and send me on a reverse shopping trip when it gets busy again. During the afternoon I'm handed yet more mystery customer paperwork to read. It reiterates that we have to be nice, polite and chatty.

The first offer of overtime comes my way today and I turn it down. Overall it's quieter than I expect. 'Around the corner, a new Asda has opened up,' a customer tells me. Another checkout girl tells me it's quieter this year than last.

That evening I watch a documentary on BBC2 about the beneficiaries of the credit crunch – the discount supermarkets. Lidl and Aldi claim customers can do their weekly grocery shopping with them for half the price it would cost them elsewhere. The secret of their success is no frills, stocking their own brands, making the packaging similar to well-known brands and selling non-food items. The king of Aldi says he keeps prices low by only stocking one type of cornflakes: he thinks customers in other supermarkets are simply paying for the privilege of looking at six varieties.

Giants in the supermarket world must be anxious about the fact that 55 per cent of us now visit discount supermarkets. We've known for a while that Tesco is trying to fight back; Sainsbury's is keeping itself in the running by price-matching them. Fortunately for the higher-end supermarkets, customers do still like premium brands. However, after watching the programme I'm convinced that if people do start cutting back, Sainsbury's are really going to lose out. Their focus on quality and customer service rather than lower prices seems counter-intuitive as the recession grips.

Thursday, 27 November 2008

After my first few days on checkouts, the patience of the till captains has run dry. One of them, Barbara, barely makes any eye contact and rarely answers my questions. I've learnt that her steely exterior and no-nonsense attitude coats a tough-love approach – she wants newbies to learn by being thrown in the deep end. I've watched her charge around the store like she owns the place and, as she's been here for aeons, she probably does.

Susie's friendliness is skin-deep – she's tired of my inane questions. To start with she would smile kindly even when I asked for the third time how to do a split payment. She's always polite and has a gentle, amiable manner which makes her popular with the Cogs. Recently though her grin has started to look strained when I beckon her over. I've come to dread having to call for any of the supervisors.

On the up-side, the aisles are filled with the sound of neighbourly love. An elderly lady is shopping for an infirm neighbour, a young woman has left work early to shop for her dad laid up with flu, one man is helping his blind brother shop.

* * *

Today news breaks about the collapse of Woolworth's and I eavesdrop on a couple telling another customer how devastated they are by the news.

'It's a part of our culture and landscape. I grew up with the shop and so did my kids.'

'Yes, but do you know what the worst part is? Supermarkets will now be able to charge whatever they want.'

One person with no concern for price hikes is a well-maintained woman in her forties. Her two shopping trolleys carry what she tells me is her fortnightly shop. It takes forty-five minutes to put it through and costs just under £600. When I give her the grand total she doesn't flinch and hands over her credit card with a voucher for 75p off her fabric conditioner. I ask if she has a big family but she says there are only four of them. Other colleagues around me are staring at her food going along the conveyor with wide-eyed awe. Standing right behind her, and in my line of sight, is a colleague with arched eyebrows mouthing incredulous expletives.

Friday, 28 November 2008

I'm on a basket checkout today and mince pies, Christmas decorations, gifts for loved ones are all starting to pass across my till now. There's not so much time for chat – due to the huffing and puffing of impatient customers congregating in the queue here because they want to get out as quickly as possible. I know they don't want to make small talk, but there is a supervisor hanging around nearby and I wonder if she is assessing me. And so I talk.

As during my previous shifts, I find myself chatting to customers about the price of things and affordability. At least a couple of times a shift, this line of chat is followed by hushed, embarrassed queries about vacancies at the store. Today a woman in her fifties asks straight after telling me how expensive she is starting to find grocery shopping. An hour or two later, another shopper about to start training as a police officer asks me about Christmas vacancies. I'm convinced that £6.30 an hour won't go very far for the likes of them, but I've got to be wrong.

Despite the number of people complaining about the price of things, almost eight out of ten customers, with a big basket or trolley full of shopping, tell me they had just popped in for one thing. One guy tells me he's a sucker for the subliminal marketing and product placement. Almost every customer comes to my till laden with reduced bakery items, cut-price clothes and cheap booze. And then gasps at the total.

One customer tells me today that the Morrisons in town is heaving because of the discounted whisky. 'It's much cheaper than yours – and it was much busier in there.' He's got a point. For a store that claims not to be bitten by the credit crunch, it doesn't feel all that busy. There are definitely busy times, but usually there tend to be no more than three to four customers waiting on basket tills and one or two on the trolley tills. And when it's quiet, it can be very quiet.

There is a fundamental difference between the customers coming to basket tills compared to the trolley ones. Baskets seem to attract men in the 30–50 age group who offer grunts rather than actual words in reply to my (usually futile) attempts to chat. They only ever purchase a couple of items, one of which is, invariably, Lynx deodorant.

Truth be known, I'm scared witless of this type of customer and usually give up at the first hurdle. But today, when a grumpy thirty-something comes my way, I decide I won't let him go without a fight. He cracks and before I know it he's telling me that he has no plans for the weekends in the lead-up to Christmas, otherwise he won't be able to afford festivities this year. Somehow, though, he's convinced it's going to be his cheapest Christmas yet. 'There are going to be priçe-cuts galore over the next few weeks. PC World, Curry's, M&S, John Lewis – they're all either in trouble or having big sales early, so as far as I'm concerned it's a win-win situation.'

Although he turns out to be very pleasant, if I am too slow for the blokes in this age group they bellow like animals preparing for battle. When I need help from a till captain, one charmer shouts from the back of the queue, 'I only got in this queue because I thought it'd be quicker.' This is met with a rumble of approval from the other men waiting in line. One man throws his basket down and storms off.

And then a young Asian guy wearing a shirt that is so tight the button sitting at mid-chest level looks like it may pop and fly straight into my eye puts two bottles of Bacardi down on my till. I look at him, take a deep breath and ask for some ID.

'You've got to be kidding!'

'I'm sorry, you look so young.'

'I don't carry ID,' he says, turning himself away from me defensively and rolling his eyes.

'OK, let me just get a supervisor.'

There are loud groans from the queue. The man behind him barks: 'Just serve him – he looks over twenty-one.'

Two women join in the blood sport taking shape before them. 'I'd sell it to him, he looks much older than twenty-one.'

Bolstered by the support of fellow customers, he turns himself back to me and snaps, 'What's the matter with you? I'm old enough.' His frown is now menacing.

'I'm sorry,' I whisper pathetically. 'Take it as a compliment.'

'Look,' he says, pulling up his shirt. 'I've got tattoos.'

I stare at his chest and a large, dark blue scythe stares back at me. And still there is no till captain.

'Just sell it to him.'

'Job's worth.'

'I got two kids. I'm married. I got me own business.'

I repeatedly push the supervisor button and get up on my feet to see if I can get ANYONE's attention.

Eventually the supervisor arrives.

'It's fine.'

He then turns to the customer and in an act of bloke-to-bloke camaraderie says, 'It's all right, I'm from around here.' They both laugh and the supervisor leaves.

As for the now riled-up customer, it's far from over. After paying, I notice he hasn't packed his bottles. I ask if he wants a bag.

'What do you think?' he growls sarcastically. 'It won't be a very good idea for me to go back into work with those, would it?' He aims this not at me but his supportive audience behind.

I bite my lip until I can almost taste blood. I try to explain the scale of the consequences for me but no one is listening.

The only thing that stops the shift from being a total disaster is meeting the trolley boy with an awesome ability to recall any random fact. When I say any – I mean ANY.

Saturday, 29 November 2008

My till-side view of every customer's shopping is a privileged intrusion and lends itself to the worst kind of cod psychology. Take the single woman in her thirties buying the one carrot, a single onion, minced beef, a giant bar of Dairy Milk and a glossy magazine. I can already see her night in with dinner-for-one followed by chocolate and *HELLO!* for dessert. The man with the heavy bags under his eyes quietly purchasing breast pads, sanitary towels and painkillers for the new mum at home is totally knackered. The lonely middle-aged man with a penchant for red wine, who gets through a bottle a night (I know this because he's back every couple of days for more). The pensioner with the sweet tooth, too proud to ask for help with packing her shopping, who will struggle to unpack when she gets home. By the time they get through my till, these shoppers have unintentionally shared some of the most personal moments of their life with me. In many ways I know them better than they know themselves. Sometimes it's fitting to talk, other times I can tell this is their five minutes of peace. Either way, watching their shopping come through my till is invasive enough.

Despite the numerous reports on ready meals and the health implications, I'm still alarmed at the number of people who rely on this as their main meal for the evening. Indian meals are the most popular. I want to blurt out my recipe for a curry that's quick, easy to make, delicious and nutritious. If it weren't for the risk of getting sacked, I'd be distributing it surreptitiously to every customer on laminated cards.

* * *

Today my till is empty for a few moments, and I watch a man in his fifties approach a checkout adjacent to mine that is still serving someone with a huge amount of shopping. I indicate that I am free – and he shakes his head. 'I'm all right here, love.'

He has to wait a full five minutes before he gets served and I soon know why. The Cog at the next till is his favourite checkout girl. He can't wait to talk to her and is positively bouncing on his heels by the time she picks up the belt divider and scans his first item.

He may be too distracted by her blonde hair, big smile and undivided attention to worry about money matters, but others are not so easily fooled. They see the cost of their weekly shop pop up on the little screen right in their eye-line and it's no exaggeration to say that they are but two shopping extravaganzas short of a cardiac arrest. Three customers coming through my till in just the one hour stop dead in their tracks when I announce their bills of £104, £85 and £60.

'In the past my weekly shop would cost £100, now it's much closer to £140. And that doesn't include my daily trips to Tesco, where I'll easily spend an average of £10–15,' says one, sighing as she searches for her credit card.

Another gasps, 'Oh my goodness, I only came in for some potatoes.'

'Why didn't you stop there?' Aside from Sainsbury's marketing working its magic on her, I'd really like to know what possessed her.

'Well, If you've got to have it, you've got to have it,' comes the reply.

The words of one of the other newbies ring loud in my ears. 'Recession or no recession, people do have to eat.'

* * *

My personal distraction today is a problem with childcare. I need to ask for a change in shift pattern. I have my four-week assessment next week and I'm keen to see if Sainsbury's is likely to accommodate my circumstances and if it really is the family-friendly employer it claims to be. My boss has thus far been nothing but charming, courteous and accommodating. The other checkout girls are devoted to him, so let's see how he handles my request. It's a make-or-break situation for me, so fingers crossed.

Spending the entire day at the till watching food, clothes and other goods go through is a bit like watching one long Sainsbury's advert. I've started greedily making mental lists of all the things I MUST get before I go home. So today at the end of my shift I find myself shopping AGAIN. It's the fourth time I'm doing it. I bump into another checkout girl, Michelle, doing exactly the same.

'I can't believe it,' she says. 'It's the end of our shift and we're both still here and SHOPPING.'

'I'm doing it after every shift! I don't get it.'

'Me too, and how easy is it to spend the money we've just earned in just one shop.'

As I make my way to the checkouts, an annoyingly sprightly twenty-year-old, Louisa, who started around the same time as me, is bragging about her first shining star. Bill, the checkout boy next to her, tells her he gets one on every shift.

As I walk away from the brag-fest, I wonder why I haven't got one yet. I'm doing OK, aren't I? Should I up my game?

I go home with an aching upper body. I'm developing check-out arms. All the sliding, scanning and passing is giving me bulging biceps. Madonna, eat your heart out.

Thursday, 4 December 2008

People shout at me today. Actual shouting. One customer yelled at me within ten minutes of my sitting down at the till. Congregating are the usual grim-faced male clientele. They are angry and are sketching out evil plans while they wait. With this much tension in the air I struggle with split payments, mobile top-ups, vouchers and discount cards. It's been five days since my last shift, and I can't remember a thing.

Then my pin pad starts playing up so I can only take signed receipts. I take a couple and today's till captain, Clare, tells me it's OK to continue. I've learnt quickly that anything goes on Clare's shift. I've never seen her rush for anything and she has just the one facial expression – a permanent just-awoken-from-deep-sleepy-slumber look. I like her laid-back approach, but I'm sure she's often giving me the wrong instruction.

When my till crashes, it starts looking as though Sainsbury's is going to be brought to its knees by my incompetence. I raise my head above the till to see if I can get the attention of a supervisor and there is no one in sight. Meanwhile there is unrest amongst the growing mob before me.

It makes perfect sense, of course: place the inexperienced, unconfident, rabbit-stuck-in-headlights Cog on the most complex and pressurised tills at the other end of the store and watch her die a slow and painful death. Well, if nothing else it's good entertainment. I punch and thump my till aimlessly, offering drivelling apologies. And yet no one, least of all me, is going anywhere. Eventually I muster the courage to tell the growing queue that it will take a few minutes to sort the problem out and they should go to another till.

Everyone grumbles loudly and starts to move away. But one man seems to be turning into the Incredible Hulk. Steam emerges slowly from both nostrils and ears, and I'm quite sure he is turning green. Within moments he explodes and bellows: 'FOR GOD'S SAKE – JUST SORT IT OUT. CALL THIS CUSTOMER SERVICE? WHY CAN'T YOU LOT JUST DO YOUR JOBS? YOU GET PAID ENOUGH, DON'T YOU?' Everyone in the store has stopped in their tracks and I see a long line of checkout girls stretching their necks above their screens to get a better view.

I blush, stammer and punch my till for want of something … anything … to do. This is pure unadulterated humiliation and to survive it I force myself into an out-of-body experience. As I listen to the man rant, I watch from above and see the dud till with no supervisor bell attached and my panic-stricken arm pitifully waving in the air attempting to attract the non-existent attention of the non-existent till captains. I've been thrown to the wolves and they are making packet mince of me.

And then, just as I'm preparing to dig a hole in the concrete floor beneath my feet, Tracey, the saviour of countless Cogs before me, emerges like Aphrodite from the sea. Her sixteen years on checkouts has given her admirable patience and rhino-thick skin. She pacifies the raging customer and ushers him towards another till, returning seconds later to fix me.

The till I'm moved to is also half-dead. I wonder momentarily if this is an initiation ceremony and that in some small room upstairs video footage is rolling in CCTV cameras, with managers huddled around it (along with the missing supervisors) all falling about laughing.

I continue to take signed receipts by the dozen until a supervisor shift change, when Samantha tells me I shouldn't be taking these at all. It's a no-brainer – most signatures on the cards have faded. I tell-tale on Clare immediately, knowing that even if it does get back to her she'll be too out of it to care.

Samantha barely acknowledges my blame-shifting. I recall Susie telling me last week not to take signed receipts but I've learnt if you don't tailor your checkout etiquette for the till captain on duty you're asking for a lifetime on the baskets.

My mood lifts a little when the trivia-obsessed Trolley Boy stops off to collect the empty baskets at my till. He immediately makes a beeline for a young male customer and asks him straight up who directed Scarface. The customer shifts uncomfortably and moves closer to the till. Trolley Boy is no quitter, so he questions him on a different film. This time the customer gives him a mumbled answer but makes no eye contact. This is straight out of *Little Britain*. I suppress a giggle as the young man, still seriously uncomfortable, and still without any eye contact, unexpectedly asks Trolley Boy to name Tarantino's last three films. Trolley Boy replies without hesitation, takes the baskets and leaves.

The new VAT reduction means colleagues have been working flat-out to change prices on shelf labels. I'm not sure how many they've achieved, however customers are pleasantly surprised when I announce their total bill. Even a tiny 2.5 per cent can make all the difference – it's true, every penny does count.

Price comparison website MySupermarket.co.uk has been suggesting that this year people ought to shop around to keep their Christmas costs down. Everyone I suggest this to says that they are not going to run around a number of stores just to save a couple of pounds, particularly as their transport costs will mean it ends up costing the same.

Michelle is in today – shopping again. It's her day off but she says she 'needed some bits and pieces'. She comes to my till and tells me how difficult she's finding being away from her twin three-year-old daughters and wishes she had only agreed to do two days. Her childcare arrangements aren't working out; she has a childminder she's not keen on. I suggest she talks to management, but she seems uncertain, makes noises about the probationary period we are on and the risk of losing our jobs. It's a risk I'm prepared to take.

I keep serving beyond the end of my shift. Noting that there are no supervisors coming to close my till, eventually I turn to the growing crowd and say, 'I'm sorry, I'm closing after this customer, can you go around to the other till?' indicating the adjacent basket till.

'NO!' yells a chic, cropped-hair-do fifty-something. 'You are NOT going to do that. I don't care if you are closing or going home, you WILL serve me.' The others in the queue stare blankly to see what I'll do. Before I get a chance to stammer a reply, the man in front of her starts to shoot orders at me. I die a slow death as he first orders me to help the old man in front of me open a bag. He then tuts loudly at my having the audacity to close my till when there are people to serve. He grabs his change from my hand and charges off like I have some unspeakable disease. I want to tell them that, while I am a mere Cog, I also have a life, home and kids to get back to. But in the manner to which I have very quickly adjusted, I say nothing. In the super-market world, the customer is king. And so, with my head down, I serve all ten while listening to them debate my temerity as if I was no longer in the vicinity. The humiliation is complete. Eventually my cranky captain, Betty, comes over to tell me she will send relief and tells me I should have closed my till as soon as my hours were up.

I feel punched in the guts tonight. I've learnt the true nature of the British shopper: they know that kicking up a fuss loudly and aggressively will get results. And having an audience helps, because mobs rule. I stare longingly at the beers, wines and spirits section as I walk back through the shop.

I leave a message for Richard again, saying I need to speak to him. Betty says (unconvincingly) that she will pass it on.

Friday, 5 December 2008

As I drive in, I listen to a radio phone-in about the collapse of Woolies after ninety-nine illustrious years. Callers talk nostalgically about the bric-a-brac, mix-and-match cups and saucers, giant chocolate Dairy Milk bars and pick and mix. Why will they miss this stuff? I ask myself. It's all available in supermarkets, anyway. Maybe that's why Woolies collapsed – the supermarkets can now easily offer everything that made Woolworths unique.

As I walk to the supervisors' post, I say fifteen Hail Marys, two Quranic passages and the Buddhist mantra I picked up in RE in the hope that *some* god, *any* god, may be listening. Let me not be on the basket tills, please.

The first thing that happens is Betty confronts me aggressively.

'Did you take the till key home with you last night?'

'No … I gave it to the guy who replaced me.'

'Well, it's gone missing, and you had it last.'

I say nothing, wondering where this is going.

Another till captain approaches and Betty asks her if she knows where the key is.

'It's hanging in the cupboard.'

Betty says nothing and looks away.

They allocate me my trolley till and, as I walk towards it, Betty tells me there's no chair at my till. I take that to mean that I'm expected to stand for four hours, which is against health-

and-safety rules on checkouts. I manage to locate a chair myself and am soon good to go. Just as I sit myself down, in front of a long line of customers, I fall ungraciously to the floor. After the last couple of days, I know that if I don't laugh I will cry – and so I laugh hard.

I'm starting to get some regulars now. There's a really scruffy-looking guy who comes in wearing threadbare clothes. He's a man of few words but has said enough for me to know he has a gruff voice and a gruff attitude. But he intrigues me with his regular purchase of the *New Scientist* magazine. I bite the bullet and ask him if he's a scientist. He laughs and says, 'Do I look like a scientist?'

'Scientists come in all shapes and sizes.'

'I just like to keep my brain active – that's why I read it. My work is boring manual labour.'

I chat again with the young mum who only moved here from Poland five years ago with no English. She has the strongest Cockney accent I've ever heard from someone who didn't grow up in London.

Human behaviour in the supermarket demonstrates that even the friendliest customer is never *really* your ally and they can turn on you in a heartbeat. An amiable, elegant and chatty older woman with a deceptively uncanny resemblance to Denise Richardson, the Agony Aunt on *This Morning*, has a complete change of personality when she asks me about discount petrol vouchers. I indicate that I'm not sure if we are giving them out. She asks me tersely, 'Well, do you know or don't you?'

* * *

I have my four-week assessment today. Susie brings over the paperwork and starts to give me feedback.

'You're doing really well, really engaging with customers, but I've noticed you lack confidence.'

'Oh really?' I don't like the sound of this. 'How so?'

'You just seem nervous, like you're not confident with customers.' I know she's not aware of the recent incidents so she must mean my general interaction with them.

'Really? I find talking to the customers a doddle. The only time you could call me nervous is over the technical things. But talking to customers, that's the easiest part of the job.'

'There's just something in your manner.'

The assessment is good, though. I get a green, which means that the girl done good. Three reds and you're in trouble, so for now, I'm safe. I add a toadying note on my assessment saying I will try to be more confident. Susie lets me skim-read the paperwork before asking me to sign it. She then fiddles around with it. It seems to me that we are often asked to sign things first with management adding their own notes afterwards.

Then, out of the blue, a supervisor shouts out that, thanks to Jenny we've just got a 100 per cent MCM. I'm not sure what that means exactly, but everyone gives a round of applause.

Michelle is prying again and enquires about my assessment; I play it down. She's finding it hard to get uninterested customers to engage with her. I tell her the trick is to persevere. I know that she's not the only one who finds it difficult; from my till I can often see other checkout girls just silently doing their job. Even Rebecca, who has such a natural magnetic charm, tells me she struggles.

I bump into Katherine at the end of my shift and she wants to talk about the difficult customers I encountered the day before. 'They were so nasty, I felt for you. Some customers just think we are machines and have no life beyond this place.'

Clare, who is slumped in a chair in the corner of the locker room, lifts her head long enough to say sagely, 'In through one ear, out the other.'

Saturday, 6 December 2008

I read today that Tesco's shoppers are dropping it for Morrisons and Asda. Tesco is still doing OK, but the question being asked now is – is the store losing momentum?

After the week I've had, I've lost all momentum. But I brave it and am, thankfully, rewarded with a trolley till. My first customer is an enormous woman with five obese kids and all she buys are five jumbo packets of crisps – that's about a hundred packets of crisps in total. She yells at her kids and they yell at her. It's a joy to behold.

In fairness, a simple shopping trip reduces the best of families to a dysfunctional version of their normal selves. I'm no longer embarrassed by the number of arguments I've witnessed between two unsuspecting adults unaware of the entertainment they've provided for the bored checkout girl before them. And the rows are always over small and ultimately insignificant things: plans for the evening, the choice of dinner for the night, Sunday lunch with the family, the cost of the shop they've just completed, the things they forgot to buy. I read a study that found that couples who shop together for more than seventy minutes will almost always start to row. Seventy-one-plus minutes in a supermarket and they're ready to sign the divorce papers. And when my customers are not squabbling they're just being odd. Some of them plan where they place their groceries on the conveyor belt with military precision, with the intention of ensuring it will be convenient to unpack when they get home. One man today asks me to wait while he spends ten minutes carefully unloading his shop on to the belt. He groups all like items together. As I ring through the items I can see the layout of his kitchen. First the larder with pasta, tinned tuna, baked beans, biscuits and pickles, then the fridge with cheeses, milk, meat and prepared salad. Next, the kitchen cupboard holding the bleach, washing-up liquid, scouring pads, washing powder, fabric conditioner and kitchen towels. It's weirdly inspiring.

I spend much of my shift looking out for Richard, but, as expected, I don't see him. After clocking off I hunt him down. He's in the canteen with the usual posse of pit bulls and I ask for a private word. He takes me to a quiet office and we have a quick chat about my progress so far. Richard is one of a rare breed these days; a touchy-feely manager. I know my request for changing my shift is pushing the limits of new Cog protocol, but I have no option. I explain my childcare problem and he reminds me I had accepted the hours offered, but then promises to look into it. Finally he says:

'We will support you anyway we can – put it in writing, suggest your alternatives, be as accommodating as possible, and Personnel and I will look at it and see what we can do.' His response is heartening; he tells me not to worry and that we will sort something out. He is head and shoulders above all the managers I have had over the years. And I'll bet my last bit of spare change that he's the reason so many checkout girls have stuck it out here for so long. He's considerate, courteous and proof that you don't have to be bad to be good.

I go to Rebecca's till for a quick chat before I leave for the day. The customer Rebecca is serving wants to do a split payment and Rebecca asks me how. Before I can help, the customer jumps in; she's a former Tesco employee. She tells us she was there four years ago, earning £7.50 an hour at the age of sixteen. Rebecca is outraged and asks, not for the first time, 'What am I doing here?'

Before I leave for the day I see a notice in the staff toilet called 'Talkback'. It reads: 'There is a popular misconception that Tesco pay more than we do. It's not true. We also pay for fifteen-minute tea breaks, Tesco don't.'

Saturday, 13 December 2008

Two weeks to go till Christmas. I go in today after the worst bout of flu I've suffered in years. I'm shaky, dizzy and can barely breathe. My chest is congested, but I am too much of a coward to call the absentee line again. I called in sick yesterday and it didn't go down well. The manager at the end of the line interrogated me and left me with the distinct feeling that he didn't really believe I was ill. So today I go in.

I see Michelle as soon as I walk through the doors. She tells me that when she had to call in sick she was reminded, in no uncertain terms, that she was still on probation.

'But when you're sick, you're sick. You're only going to contaminate others.'

'And it's not as if you get paid sick leave here, is it?' she adds.

I take my painkillers, put my head down and get on with the job. I can't think straight so struggle to talk to customers. I opt for cursory greetings, ask about plastic bags and Nectar cards, and send them on their way. Nevertheless, I do end up chatting to another Cog. She tells me she works thirty-nine hours a week at the store plus an extra eleven hours cleaning. 'I've got to pay the bills somehow.' She's only just started at Sainsbury's after finding it impossible to meet her growing monthly expenses.

That's not a problem for the numerous ladies who come to my till with their designer bags. Today I count seven luxury-end bags. But designer bag or no designer bag, everyone loves a bargain. One of these upmarket ladies tells me she queued up to shop at Woolworths' closing-down sale and picked up some knocked-down bed sheets.

Christmas gift shopping has started at the store and *Mamma Mia!* is in virtually every woman's trolley, so I share with them the one nerd fact I've picked up recently: it's the fastest-selling UK DVD of all time. According to Justin King's latest newsletter, Sainsbury's alone sold 200,000 copies in its first week.

He also reminds us of the importance of ensuring availability of stock, delivering great customer service and doing our job well in the build-up to Christmas. He also says the new ads with Ant and Dec and Jamie have gone down a storm.

Just before the end of my shift, I'm asked to close my till early. I'm taken aside and told that I was being assessed today. My heart skips a few beats, but somehow I get a green despite my minimal customer interaction. Ayesha reminds me that the mystery customer is most likely to come in on a Friday and Saturday so I've got to be on the ball. I point the finger at my ill health and add creepily, 'I really do love talking to customers.' Ayesha and Susie make sympathetic noises, but they're not convinced. In a shameless attempt to save my skin I ask them to reassess me soon.

I hand in my letter for Richard and wonder if this impromptu assessment has anything to do with my request to change my hours. Then I head to Rebecca's till for a quick end-of-shift gossip session.

'I've been waiting for one assessment and you've already had two.'

'That's probably because you're so kick-arse at this they don't need to test you.'

'Far from it, it's the most unnatural thing in the world for me. I just don't believe that *they* want to talk to us.' She looks at the middle-aged man she's serving and asks me to dare her to ask him what he thinks about our customer service policy.

'Excuse me, sir, can I ask you something? Would you like me to engage with you?'

'Pardon?' He says looking baffled.

'Would you like me to talk to you, ask you how you are?'

'Well, if you want to, but I'm not that bothered. Why?'

'We're told to, and I wasn't sure if customers want that from us.'

'Well, I always find it odd when you lot ask how we are and when we ask you back you get caught off guard. Or when you offer help with packing and we say yes – you look put out. It shows it's just superficial.'

'But is it nice when we do it? Does it leave a good impression?'

'Sometimes I just want to get out of here as fast as possible. And to be honest, I'm usually in a bit of a coma when I'm shopping. So chat to me, don't chat to me – I'm not bothered.'

Wednesday, 17 December 2008

I miss the place so much this week I go to my local Sainsbury's on a day off. My shop comes to almost £90. And I react in exactly the same way as my customers: shock, horror, 'really??' Followed by frantic bill-checking afterwards. As a result, I resolve to live a little and pop into Morrisons. I buy a packet of frozen peas, frozen vegetables, pizza bases, bread and milk and it comes to just under £7. That *is* cheaper. I need to stake this place out, hunt down items on my regular shopping list, get to know the store despite there being no obvious attraction. If I could, aged fifteen, go out with the sweaty boy with pimples and over-sized glasses, I can do this. OK, so that relationship only lasted for a third of an hour, but it was good to step into my discomfort zone. And if it saves some pennies, I'm up for the challenge. Customer service here really sucks, though. The checkout girl barely looks up. No matter, in these times I'd rather save some pennies than get a pleasant smile.

The *Sunday Times* has run an exposé on workers' rights at Amazon. Endless shifts, long weeks and terrible pay. They get £6.30 an hour, which is the same as Sainsbury's. But the big complaint is about those who are punished for being ill; taking a day off sick results in one penalty point. A worker with six points faces dismissal. Thank goodness I don't work there.

Thursday, 18 December 2008

The first hour today is really quiet. A few people come through the tills, but most of the time I'm just twiddling my thumbs. I read Justin's newsletter and he says that Woolworth's demise has had a knock-on effect because Entertainment UK – who supply Sainsbury's with DVDs, CDs, games and books – is part of the Woolies chain. He talks of stock supply challenges, but states they are now working with three new suppliers. His outlook is eternally upbeat and it's obvious to see why. Sainsbury's prospects look bright, they've cornered their market fairly well and may yet ride out the hard times ahead.

But while the view from the top down is looking good, at the bottom where the wheels of the supermarket turn silently I've noticed a quiet indifference. Most of the newsletters sit unread and the internal magazine is usually only thumbed by me – my colleagues clock in, do their duties and clock out – and my questions about the future of the supermarket and its success are met with lethargic shrugs or bemused stares. 'It's just a job,' I get told.

During a quiet period I get sent to the bakery. Sarita, a young Asian checkout girl, shows me the ropes. She turns out to be a great source of gossip, although I notice some bitterness in her tone compounded by the fact that she never smiles. As we get our hats and aprons on she tells me that two Cogs have been sacked this week – one of them for stealing. It is the stupidest thing to do because there are cameras right above the tills.

As Sarita talks, it becomes clear that she hates being on tills. 'The supervisors have got their favourites and there is a lot of backstabbing – you'll find out.' She says that the customers are 'horrid' and the more she talks about them, the clearer it becomes that she actually *hates* them. Her advice to me is 'just keep your head down and don't get involved ... everybody finds out everyone's business and then interferes. I got some training at the cigarette kiosk and I told one person – by the time I went down everyone knew.'

She says all of this with little prompting or interruption from me. I'm starting to feel rather perturbed by the picture she paints of this place, until it transpires that she's going through a hard time right now because she has just broken up with her boyfriend who works in the store and is the son of one of the supervisors.

'I let business and pleasure come too close together and now I'm paying the price.'

I spend the next thirty minutes packing cookies and noting that the place is a mess. I find myself putting cookies into paper bags and leaving traces of chocolate behind on all the packs I touch. It's not unhygienic, but the packs look really grubby by the time I'm done with them. For the next two hours I seal buns, baps and hot-dog rolls under the supervision of Sarita, only to find an hour later that I'm sealing them in packaging that is not sufficiently airtight to prevent them from going stale, so I redo them all.

I meet Marcus, a third-year Business Studies student Cog. We start chatting and he tells me he doesn't know what he's going to do once he graduates. He's going to stick with this until he figures it out and 'rides out the recession'.

I'm sure I hear my name called but Sarita assures me it's someone else. Later she rushes to get me and says the supervisors are furious because they've put out three calls for me. I race to the tills. 'I couldn't hear you because the music in the bakery is blasting,' I tell Susie while trying to catch my breath. She smiles, not looking remotely convinced.

The first lady through my till is a lady in her late sixties. She complains about her no-good thirty-something son. 'He's trained as a graphic designer but has been out of work for eight years. He's lazy, doesn't help around the house and I'm his financial crutch. And now we've got this recession and I'm more stressed than ever. He's doing some charity work and he reckons that's doing enough. But where's the money going to come from?'

It strikes me that at her age she shouldn't have to worry about taking care of a grown man. Despite her own woes, she's shopping for her ninety-nine-year-old neighbour who is house-bound and virtually bed-bound. 'She's ready to go,' she says to me meaningfully.

An architect comes through my till and tells me that work is still madly busy. 'Credit crunch or no credit crunch, it's just not quiet now, not even with Christmas. If the recession is going to take effect, we'll be the first to be affected. But hey, so far so good. So let's see.'

A man in his thirties tells me he's decided to rent out his home because he can't afford the mortgage; he's found a place to rent nearby instead. With rent rates sky high at the moment, the rental income he's getting is covering the mortgage on the house he owns and some of the rent on the place he's staying in.

The rest of the afternoon passes without event. Thursday is often a staring-vacantly-into-mid-air day. When I look across at the other Cogs, I see them all doing the same.

Friday, 19 December 2008

For the first time in six weeks someone comes through my checkout and, when I tell them the total is £72.97, they actually say, 'That's not too bad.' Her entire shop is from the Sainsbury's Basics range.

Everyone is starting to ask about their reward points. I redeem as little as £2.50 up to a staggering £130 for one couple who have been collecting their points all year. Now the yuletide spending has begun and the Christmas gift shopping is well under way – they're all buying beauty gift packs by the dozen: soaps, creams, bath oils. It's the thought that counts, but if you ask me, it looks like a pretty thoughtless gift. And just as I'm wondering what constitutes a deep and meaningful gift, a woman comes over and piles packets of cake cups, cake mixture, marshmallows, smarties and cake icing on to the belt.

'Are you having a party?' I ask.

'Oh no – this lot are my Christmas gifts. I do food hampers.'

'That's a great idea!' I exclaim.

'I'm making cakes, biscuits, pasta, chicken soup – I'll spend two days cooking, and then I'm done.'

The whole thing costs her £85 – and there are gifts there for about twenty people. Now that's a creative credit-crunching Christmas.

Another lady tells me she's dishing out cash for Christmas. 'There's no thought in it and it takes the pleasure out of giving, but at least they can get what they want.'

A teenager and his mother discuss their Christmas plans with me; Mum's looking forward to a couple of weeks off work with her family. 'If only, though, I could get the kids away from their computer games.'

'Tell me about it,' says the lady behind her. 'The Xboxes, Nintendos, Wiis – so much for spending time together at Christmas.' In both sets of shopping trolleys they have, you guessed it, computer games.

More couples arguing today. And no one cares that I'm watching. One man storms off, receipt in hand, furious at the amount his wife has spent. I watch her follow him, red-faced, pushing the huge trolley and dragging her toddlers behind her.

Richard runs from till to till saying he wants to see us all get into the Christmas spirit from tomorrow.

'I want to see tinsel, lots of tinsel. I want to see reindeer hairbands, Santa Claus, the lot.'

Saturday, 20 December 2008

I'm in the locker room loos tying my hair back with a piece of tinsel when Michelle walks in.

'Are you doing any overtime next week?' she asks.

'No, I'm not. It's too difficult with my kids. Are you?'

'Same here – I just can't. My daughters were ill last week so I had to call in sick. You know, I'm finding it really difficult with them – I just don't know what to do. I really need to change my shifts from three to two.'

'Why don't you talk to Richard? Just tell him how tough it is.'

'I know I should, I should … but … we're still on probation, you know.'

She is obsessed with our probation. I want to tell her I've asked for a shift change but don't.

'If my situation doesn't change, I might have to leave – you know,' she says rubbing her eyes wearily.

Suddenly we realise that there is someone else in the toilets. So she changes her tune.

'Well, maybe I won't have to leave … I'll see you downstairs.' And she runs off.

This is my last shift before Christmas. I turn the corner towards the tills and walk on to a pantomime set. There are elves, female Father Christmases, two-legged reindeers, walking Christmas gifts … One of the supervisors is parcelled up inside a box wrapped with ribbon. Richard is dressed in a Santa Claus outfit with an enormous white beard. The others have all gone with a Sexy Santa theme: short skirts trimmed with tinsel, tight black belts pulled suggestively around the waist, red corsets lined with white fake fur, stockings, tails, reindeer hairbands – it is a Santa's harem.

The local scouts are in, helping with packing (and raising money for charity) and I've got a garrulous Scout leader at my tills. She ends up talking to all my customers so I just listen.

Everyone wants to know about our Christmas hours and I tell them we're open twenty-four hours a day next week. They must all be planning to come in then, because it's certainly quieter today than I expected.

There are lots of unfamiliar faces around and I realise that they're the extra staff taken on for Christmas. Others in the retail sector are cutting back on part-time staff and offering extra hours, but not so at Sainsbury's, and there's been no talk here of redundancies.

At the end of my shift, Richard calls me into his office. He gives me a Christmas card, thanks me for my work and offers me a Quality Street. He asks about my childcare situation, tells me he will consider it in light of the recent sackings, and give me an answer in the New Year. He then talks to me about being off sick. He asks me to go through what was wrong, how I informed them, and reminds me that I don't get paid sick leave. He takes out a piece of paper and draws up a six-point list for every instance of sick leave:

1. Fill out a back-to-work form. And talk through what happens next.
2. Have a chat about why sick. Can Sainsbury's do anything to support you?
3. Verbal warning.
4. Written warning.
5. Disciplinary action.
6. Dismissal.

'Wow!' I find myself spluttering. 'But most people are sick about three times a year. What about the fact that we might pass on what we've got?'

He tells me politely that once everyone learns about these six stages, no one goes beyond the second or third. This, it seems, is Richard's way of pulling us into line.

When I emerge, Michelle is next in the queue. She looks anxious and asks me what it's about. I reassure her it's a Christmas greeting and she relaxes. She comes to my till ten minutes later looking brow-beaten.

'I asked him if I could change my shifts and he said no.'

'Really? He's not even going to consider it?'

'No. He said someone has already asked him, so it's too late for me.' Her soft blue eyes are piercing when they stare.

I say nothing and I'm not sure why. As she walks away I feel uncomfortable. I know that the supermarket has already invested £2000 in training us, I've done OK in my assessments and I'm not scared of negotiating. Michelle is scared witless about losing her job, paranoid about our probationary period and doesn't know how to play the game. It shouldn't be my problem, yet I'm racked with guilt.

Tuesday, 23 December 2008

Today I go to my local Sainsbury's to get my Christmas shopping at 9 p.m. and I'm seething because they've run out of rosemary. I peruse the other shelves and note that many are short of stock. What's the point of being open twenty-four hours if the shelves are empty?

The newspapers are full to the brim with Christmas cheer; there's no escape from recession stories, but I've not yet seen it translate on the shop floor. I am now becoming more certain that supermarkets will survive this recession. I read that nine out of ten retailers are already discounting – Sainsbury's is one of them. Since I've been here, there has been a sell-out half-price sale on toys, 25 per cent off on clothes and equally large discounts on booze.

Saturday, 27 December 2008

I get in early to do some shopping and as soon as I walk in I'm distracted by yet another half-price sale in the clothing department. I find myself rummaging through racks of clothes I definitely do not need. Sainsbury's TU range is really a huge success story. It's the reason the supermarket has broken into the top ten of the UK's biggest clothing retailers, thanks to the number of shoppers, including myself, who combine their food shop with some retail therapy. According to a report in the *Times* supermarkets' clothing ranges make up nearly a quarter of items of clothing sold in the UK. Asda has 10.3 per cent of the market, Primark 9.9 per cent, Tesco 9 per cent and Sainsbury's, new to clothing, has 2.3 per cent of the market by volume. The reason for their success is that they focus on cheaper basic items of clothing. I know this myself, having picked up a £9 cardigan, £18 jeans and £4 indoor boots in recent weeks. I also read in the report that Sainsbury's TU range is believed to have increased by 40 per cent in the last year, making an estimated £300 million in sales. The report says that its top performer is thought to be lingerie, and I can certainly vouch for this judging by the number of bras and knickers that come down my till several times a day alongside the tinned tomatoes and kitchen foil.

* * *

I take a peek at the newspapers at the kiosk and all the front pages are reporting the record-breaking Boxing Day sales. People have been queuing around the block from the early hours and there have been stampedes around the country. On an inside page there's an editorial reporting that, despite the Boxing Day boom, the New Year is going to bring spending cuts, job insecurity and a long recession. It claims that people have started planning cutbacks and aiming to live more cheaply, although I have yet to see it.

The high-octane sales atmosphere is making some shoppers tense. My first customer today grumbles at me about the intense traffic in the retail park nearby – people are trying to get to Comet, Argos and Homebase. 'What's wrong with them? They've all gone Comet mad.' The couple behind him tell me they went to the big shopping centre for the sales but when they saw people arguing in the car park they turned around and drove here instead. Then a middle-aged couple tell me they queued up from 5 a.m. outside Next and are pleased that, while they spent £300, they saved £300 in discounts. He doesn't let the fact that he had to spend £300 to save £300 bother him. But when I ask if he's worried about the recession, a different story emerges. He works for BT broadband.

'There's no such thing as a job for life there any more. They're making redundancies across the board, but I think for the moment my job is safe. Who knows for how long, though?'

Another customer, a mum with a three-year-old, has spent £200 on clothes in Oasis, Principles and Next. 'I'm not letting myself think about the recession today – ask me in a few days.' She pauses. 'But when you've got kids, life is so difficult that you need to spoil yourself, don't you?'

'And spending makes you feel good, even if it's a temporary high,' I add. She nods, but I see a small frown starting to develop across her forehead.

Most people I ask haven't been to the sales yet. They're all saying they just can't face the shops at the moment. One woman in her thirties has the recession very much on her mind. She says she has decided against any sales shopping 'because everyone has got to tighten their belts for the rough ride ahead. Things being as they are, I'm just grateful to have a job.'

I eavesdrop on two middle-aged ladies talking. One is chastising the other for dragging her into Sainsbury's. 'It's only been two days and here we are shopping again, it's sickening.'

When I ask people about their New Year plans, the vast majority say they are going to celebrate at home quietly, while one or two are having small soirées, saying, 'It's cheaper than going out.'

For the New Year penny-pinchers, paying in cash is truly the only way to control spending. Studies have long shown that it's much more painful than swiping a card, and stimulates a region in the brain linked with discomfort which is anaesthetised by credit cards. And that's exactly what one customer is thinking. She plonks her shopping on my belt and announces, 'No more than £21.' When it gets to £20.33, she ruthlessly takes something off the belt and pays in cash, and I crown her queen of thrift.

One man shopping with his six-year-old twins has crackers, a chicken roast, root vegetables, wrapping paper and bottles of wine in his shop.

'Are you celebrating Christmas late?' I blurt out before I can stop myself.

'Tomorrow – seems a good way to save money.' The crackers are the Different by Design range and absolutely stunning – he's picked them up for a bargain £6.

I hear one of my first bona fide redundancy stories today. A customer tells me her daughter was made redundant two months ago and now can't find a job.

'She used to be a secretary at a big estate agent's in town and she's been hunting high and low but there is just no work to be found. She's started looking in retail now and, fingers crossed, she's in the running for a secretarial job at Tesco.'

At last I'm someone's favourite checkout girl. A lively, colourful family I've served a few times have started to seek me out. I see them standing by the checkouts scanning the tills – and when I wave at them, they hurry over with big smiles. *I've finally made it.*

'I was looking for you,' says Mum. 'I was terrified you'd been sacked after we were chatting to you, and the man behind us was so angry.'

'He was fine, don't worry. We certainly don't get into trouble for talking to customers here.'

Her thirty-something son joins them with some extra groceries in his arms. We hold our usual spelling bee competition and he teases me for misspelling a word a few weeks ago. I love this family. There are two generations of them shopping together and Dad, the patriarch, always pays, although not before grunting loudly about the price of food shopping.

There is a big fracas at the front of the store and it transpires that the lottery machine has crashed. Unsurprisingly, there are a lot of angry customers complaining about it around the store. I find myself apologising on behalf of Sainsbury's and feeling like a moron when I'm told, 'Well, it's not YOUR fault, is it?'

Before I leave to go home I pick up my discounted kettle and go to Rebecca's till. She tells me that the person sacked for dipping into the tills is Bill, the young man I heard bragging about his collection of shining stars a few weeks ago. It's raised the level of suspicion amongst management, she says. During a meeting with Richard she witnessed one of the other managers showing Richard a receipt where the checkout girl had reduced something from £25 to 25p and said he suspected 'she's up to something'. 'I get the feeling that the eye of suspicion here is really strong and we all come under detailed surveillance.'

On my way out I hear one of the Cogs talking about her shifts in the last two or three days before Christmas. 'There were queues all the way down the aisles, every single checkout was heaving. Unbelievable ... If I hadn't been here, I wouldn't have believed it.'

The radio goes on as I drive home and the lottery crash is making the news. It wasn't just a local event; computer terminals crashed in shops around the country leaving thousands unable to buy tickets. It's been reported like a national disaster. The only other news is the sales frenzy; half-price cuts, 75 per cent and even an unprecedented 90 per cent off sales. It's an insane scramble to beat the credit crunch. People have been queuing since dawn to get into some shops and there have been fights breaking out over handbags. After the news I listen to a programme about how to save money on food shopping during the recession by cooking more, making a shopping list and paying in cash.

Saturday, 3 January 2009

The New Year starts with grim news for the retail world – shop closures. There are more Woolies shutting up shop and now it's Adams kids wear. I think the winners in all of this will be the supermarkets – they already provide the Woolies style bric-a-brac and low-cost children's clothes. Rumours are circulating that Sainsbury's may buy the Adams brand. One insolvency specialist has predicted the collapse of between 10 and 15 national retail chains by mid-January. Others are saying that at least 15–20 retailers are extremely weak financially and that one shop in ten will close in the coming months.

I'm in the locker room, squeezing my over-sized bag into my tiny locker when Michelle walks in. She's a bit cool and barely says hello before heading down for her shift. I'm puzzled – I hope everything's OK with her girls. Before I get on to my till I have a quick chat with a twenty-year-old student called Nick. I overheard him being reprimanded by a till captain a few weeks ago about a break issue. He tells me he's been here a year – and he isn't happy. He needs time off around his exams and this is proving difficult because he needs a job to get him through college. 'If I don't have a job after I finish college this place will be to blame.'

I talk to a man in his fifties who works as an eye consultant at a hospital. He tells me that jobs are being cut in the NHS and he shrugs his shoulders wearily, telling me he's not sure that even his own job is safe. A checkout girl from M&S comes to my till telling me she never shops at M&S because it's too expensive. She hasn't noticed it getting quieter, although she's well aware that the store isn't doing too well. She has her bags for re-use with her, saying it's a habit she's had to learn after watching customers reluctantly cough up for bags. I'm turning into a bag obsessive myself. The supermarket insists we ask customers at the start of their shop if they are re-using their bags – the red prompt on my screen pops up before every transaction. And that's where it starts to go wrong.

'Do you have your own bags or do you need ours?' I always ask, leaning down below the till in preparation to tear off some.

'I've got my own, thanks.' And then about a dozen or so emerge. For every bag a customer brings back they get a Nectar point. This is the main motivation for most customers.

'How many do you have there?'

'I don't know how many I'm going to use yet, do I?' comes the gruff reply.

So I ask them to tell me at the end. And then they (and I) usually forget. One customer this happens with asks me *after* I hand over her receipt whether I put her bag points on. She is hopping mad that I haven't. I apologise but I *had* asked her to tell me how many she used. She looks at my name badge and storms off.

Right behind her are three generations of women from one family. This is something I see a lot, and today I comment on how sweet it is to witness. We laugh about how a simple super-market shop can push mother–daughter friction to boiling point.

While many are up for a quick chuckle at the checkout, others use me like a drop-in therapy service. A pretty thirty-something blonde tells me the story of her life-long struggle to control her diabetes. It transpires that her sweet tooth gets in the way. I ogle the cakes, chocolate bars and bags of sweets she's purchasing.

'I comfort-eat because things at home haven't always been great, you know?' she says with a sad smile. 'So every time I felt down or tired or stressed I'd just have a piece of cake and I'd feel better. Before I knew it, I went from being quite slim, to quite fat.'

'You're not fat,' I say quickly.

'You're sweet, but I am.'

I'm desperate to take the goodies off the belt, but I'm neither her doctor nor her friend, so I wish her 'Happy New Year' and watch forlornly as she walks away.

One man in his late twenties is getting the weekly shop while his wife is at home tending to his three-year-old, two-year-old and one-year-old. I'm in awe. He tells me with three under-fours the couple no longer have any time for each other and it's affecting their marriage.

'It's all our own fault, because we weren't careful enough. She has these really heavy periods and so she has to take these injections to control her menstrual cycle because she bleeds too much ...'

OK, that is far too much information.

'And what happened was that she was on the pill but I reckon that either the injections were cancelling out the pill or she just forgot to take it and then when we fancied a bit of the ol' Posh 'n' Becks, that was it – wham bam ...'

By now I'm far exceeding my items per minute.

'The thing is that the doctor told us that, with every kid you have, you get more fertile, so the riskiest time to do it is straight after you have your last one. I mean, obviously all that breast-feeding stuff gets in the way, but I'm a man, aren't I. I got my needs.'

He grins and I feel quite queasy. I'm no prude but there is a time and place.

After my shift I see Michelle three times: once at the checkouts, then in the locker room, and then when we do our usual end-of-shift shop – each time she gives me the cold shoulder. On the final occasion I grin and wink at her as we walk past each other, shopping baskets in tow. She barely makes any eye contact and grunts, 'I can't wait to get out of here.'

I head with my basket to Rebecca's till for her take.

'Do you think it's me?'

'Don't be silly, why would it be you?'

'I don't know, she's usually really friendly.'

'Maybe she's having a bad day.'

'Or maybe she's found out I'm the person who has bumped her request for a shift change?'

'But it hasn't been offered, has it?'

'No, but so what?'

'Well, she'd be silly to be annoyed already – he's only considering it. You're being paranoid.'

And with that she changes the subject.

'Look I've got my own problems. I haven't been assessed yet. Do you think it's because they already know I'm rubbish?'

'Well, that's pretty obvious,' I tease her. 'It could be all that not-looking-at-the-customer stuff you do. It kinda gives the game away. Is your screen tuned into satellite TV or something, because every time I walk past you're just staring at it?'

She chuckles. 'No, I'm just staring at the time. It's called clock-watching.'

Hooking up with Rebecca before I leave is the highlight of both our shifts. She's anxious I'm going to leave if I don't get my shift-change request approved. She's right, I may have to.

When I get home I read a newspaper article about a forty-year-old woman who was asked for ID when buying alcohol in Tesco. She berates both the checkout girl and Tesco's alcohol sales policy. The article is one-sided and I'm incensed. I'm desperate to write in and report the insidious way in which customers handle any request for ID. She may have been forty but judging by her photo (which I stare at for a while) yes, I may well have asked her for ID too.

Sunday, 4 January 2009

There's a picture in the paper of Gordon Brown's online shopping arriving in the very plastic bags he has pledged to scrap. He wants to wipe out the ten billion plastic bags given out each year and has ordered supermarkets to cut the number they give out by 50 per cent by this May. I think that's an over-ambitious target. An overwhelming majority of people are still coming to the tills asking for bags even though we keep them out of sight. Some ask for them as if they have no idea that landfills are full of an endless number of non-biodegradable bags. Others, usually the elderly, bring their ones back without fail. But most people seem to leave them in the car.

Thursday, 8 January 2009

As news of Next's and Debenhams' drop in sales hit the headlines, the Boxing Day sales flurry is fast becoming a fading memory. But it's not all doom and gloom; John Lewis has bucked the credit crunch curse and New Look has had a pretty robust performance over the festive period. My shift begins with news of Sainsbury's Christmas sales making the headlines. The shop has beaten the national trend of retail gloom and enjoyed its 'best ever Christmas performance'. Richard's updated newsletter reports that 'sales have shot through the roof' over Christmas and that we all 'provided excellent service at the checkouts, especially those who got into the Christmas spirit'.

It's the astute Basics range that may pull the supersonic supermarket through this recession. Basics has seen a sales rise from 40 per cent a year ago. I'm certainly seeing it at the till as customers come to me, their trolleys laden with an entire shop from this range. An analyst quoted in the news says, 'Sainsbury's appears to be gauging the mood of UK consumers extremely well ... It's capitalising on its perceived offering of quality products, combining aggressive pricing promotions in the hope of capturing consumers' desires to "feel good" in the face of an economic downturn while reducing expenditure.' But he had a bleak warning too; with a vulnerable UK economy, the store was left more exposed than Tesco, which has an international portfolio.

I accidentally scan something twice and the customer I'm serving points this out. He treats me like a moron, smiles at me condescendingly and won't allow me to explain why this happens. The man behind him decides that attack is the best form of defence and says, 'I'm going to watch everything you put through very carefully.' I explain to him that some scanners are very sensitive so things can sometimes accidentally get scanned twice.

'It's fixable and we always look out for it,' I say.

'It's atrocious that Sainsbury's are using such terrible software. You need to get that sorted.'

Katherine is also on the basket tills, so we have a little chinwag. She has received yet another fan mail from one of her customers which she shows me. They love her – she is engaging, down-to-earth and has the sweetest manner. She's only been here six months and does it to get herself out of the house and for the useful extra cash. Her daughter tipped her off about the job. There is a marked supermarket trend for attracting mum-daughter dynasties.

Many customers today ask me for the 'Feed your family for a fiver' recipe cards. For the first time I can see that the recession is starting to take hold, and people are really keeping a close eye on their shopping habits. My shift ends with news of interest rates falling to their lowest level ever. They are now standing at a historic 1.5 per cent, with talk of them dropping even further. No more than eighteen months ago people were anxious they might rise to 15 per cent; in this climate anything is possible.

Friday, 9 January 2009

My shift starts with a pat-on-the-back newsletter from 'Justin'. Sainsbury's may be feeling very pleased with itself, but there's no good cheer amongst the customers I serve today. One man and I talk interest rates and he says he can't believe he has lived to see this day. 'My mortgage in the 1980s shot up to £1,500 a month and I was almost broke from trying to meet the payments. But now I don't have a mortgage so I don't care what interest rates do.' I take that to mean he's not got too many savings either.

Today everyone wants to talk about their redundancies. One chap tells me there are looming job cuts at the kitchen distribution company he works for. They sell and distribute kitchens worth £20,000-plus but 'when all the rich people run out, where's the money going to come from?' With redundancies being announced next week he has put his plan B into action. He's getting his Class 2 licence so that he can 'drive the really big lorries'. He reckons the company, running for almost twenty years, will virtually close down and, even if it doesn't, most people are going to be made redundant. I help him calculate his pay-off.

A sales assistant from Halfords comes in during his lunch break and tells me that they are cutting one of the six full-timers in the next month because 'business is eerily quiet', and a girl who works at Gala Bingo says it's really quiet for this time of year, although she can't tell if it's the cold or the recession. A father-and-son shopping team are up for a chat and tell me the son is in his final year of his law degree. He graduates this year and is worried about finding work. We talk about the Association of Graduate Recruiters warning that students should prepare to stack shelves. I see fear in his eyes and tell him that he wouldn't be alone; there are so many students in this Sainsbury's that they could set up their own college.

A woman I serve in the mid-afternoon is in a fractious mood. I say, 'That's 19.84 please, like the book.' She looks at me blankly and so I say it again and quickly follow it with mutterings about how low-level number-crunching can make you spout nonsense. 'NO! I understood your reference, I just didn't HEAR it,' she barks at me. Another customer growls at a man who accidentally pushes in. I try to pacify them both and fail miserably.

On the upside, I see Danielle, a Cog who is an arbiter of common sense. She's the first person I befriended at the store – within the first two minutes of our meeting she'd bombarded me with advice about how to handle working here. She told me that the supervisors needed to be handled with an equal dose of diplomacy and casual indifference. 'Don't ever let them know they're getting to you, it'll make you feel weak in the long-term.' She's been here for over five years and seems to move from department to department with confidence. She could be a supervisor herself, but seems satisfied just working on rotation. Last week I asked her again for the lowdown on some of the supervisors, and she told me that they just take some warming up. She asks me how I'm getting on with them now and so I lie and say, 'They're fine.'

'You see, they're not that bad. You know, life's too short and you can't take things too personally. If they want to be offish, let them be – you can't let it bother you.'

My favourite trolley boy frequents my till numerous times today and quizzes bemused customers. Most people are happy to humour him. One woman tells me she's been coming here for years and is in total awe of him.

'How can someone have such an incredible memory and literally remember things, huge overwhelming lists, in the way that he does – and yet not move beyond being a trolley pusher in all this time?'

'He's a genius of sorts,' I say – and totally wasted here, I think to myself.

At the end of the day Richard calls me to his office and gives me the news I've been waiting for. I almost hug him. He's granted my change in shift but makes it clear that this is an exception rather than the rule.

'But we're happy to accommodate you because you were direct and approached me as soon as it was a problem.'

'Thank you.'

'Now look, I've been watching you chat to customers and I think you're doing really well. Soooo …'

This doesn't sound like good news.

'… once your probationary period is over we want to train you up for the customer service desk.'

I can't stop my face from contorting into a grimace. The customer service desk is where checkout girls go to die.

'Don't react like that,' he laughs. 'You'll do really well there. You're nice and friendly but also have balls, so I know you won't take any crap.'

When I get back, Louisa, who is also on the basket tills, is desperate to know what Richard wanted. She's easily distracted, so when Betty comes over to ask what shade of blonde Louisa is intending to go next, she forgets what she's just asked.

After Betty leaves, Louisa asks if I've heard about the six-penalty-point approach to sickness. She was on her bike and fell off. She had a pain in her shoulder afterwards so called in sick.

'Richard took me aside and said, "You're on probation, you need to be careful about calling in sick." I was really shocked.'

During some quiet-time I read Justin's latest newsletter. He talks about the competition from discount stores like Lidl, Netto and Aldi, and quotes a report that says discounters are more expensive than the big supermarkets. He suggests we get this message out to customers. His take on why Sainsbury's is doing so well is because customers are getting 'great value for their values'; in other words, he says they're not prepared to compromise on how food is produced and where it comes from, even if they are looking hard at what they spend.

I end my shift with Barbara telling me that someone will relieve me. Five thirty comes and goes and I am still here. After several minutes of waiting, and in the absence of customers, I bite the bullet and close my till. I go over to Barbara and explain this. She roars at me, 'You can't do that, you have to wait. No matter how long they take. It doesn't matter if it's quiet, it could get busy again.' I look towards the till where Louisa is sitting. She's staring into thin air, twirling her curls and chewing hard on the gum in her mouth. Deflated, I turn back to Barbara and apologise. Betty's instruction from five or six weeks ago is ringing in my ears. 'When you are on baskets and it's the end of your shift, just close the till and cash up.'

Saturday, 10 January 2009

The store feels like a deep freezer due to the below-zero temperatures outside. Customers complain about the cold in the store and my fingers are like icicles. I see Michelle and she's back to her usual self, giving me a friendly hello, although I swear that I see a hint of suspicion in her eyes.

There's a lot of white bread coming down the belt today and I don't know if it's the cold or the credit crunch. Either way, it looks like comfort food to me. During the coming months people look set to gain a few pounds, just not the right kind.

One of my first customers is a sweet-as-pie sixty-something couple. They've only just returned to the store after years away. They were deeply scarred by a bad customer service experience but decided to forgive the store, although from the convoluted anecdote they share with me, they certainly haven't forgotten. I know that under Richard's management things have certainly changed, so they are probably back for good.

There's no avoiding the talk of yet more job cuts amongst my customers today. One man works for a charity that takes care of parks and looks after kids' play areas and they're short of money. He and his team have all decided that, rather than lose any jobs, they would all take a pay cut. Another small businessman says his work has gone so quiet he's just sacked everybody who works for him. He's got two kids and his own skin to save, so he sent them all home one day saying, 'Sorry, but there's nothing left to do.' A receptionist at a law firm tells me they've just cut nine people at her law firm of 400. It's all her friends who work at other law firms are obsessing about. One regular works for BNP Paribas and tells me that things have hit rock bottom there. They are about to cut 2500 jobs. While his job is safe, he says it's never been gloomier.

But it's not all bad news. An older dad, who comes in with his newborn son, works in the oil industry and tells me it's 'down but definitely not out', and a nurse and her policeman husband are not worried about their jobs – she works at a doctor's surgery and thinks her job is safe because 'people get sick during recessions, after all'.

Apart from talk about jobs and the recession, customers are all raving about the BOGOF (Buy One, Get One Free) deals in the store. And Sainsbury's have definitely got their finger on the pulse because next Saturday is 'Make the Difference' day. The focus will be on promoting the Basics range. At executive level they claim that more groceries and frozen items are expected to sell as customers start cooking from scratch and spending their cash on cheaper items.

I haven't seen Rebecca for a week and am itching to tell her about my shift change. Just as we are chatting, Michelle nips in beside me. As soon as I see her, I know there's trouble on the horizon – she's planning to pin me down. First she tells us about her recent failed assessment. Richard has told her she needs to talk to customers a lot more and he's not pleased. She tells us it's not easy or natural for her to make small talk. Rebecca agrees.

'Do you know what? I'm going to carry out my own poll and ask customers if they would like to engage in chat with me.'

'Yes, you must – and then release the results of this meticulous empirical research to Justin King. I'm sure he'll take heed.'

We are still chuckling about this when Michelle suddenly asks me, 'So, have you changed your shifts?'

I turn to look at her. She has caught me off guard, but I have no intention of lying.

'Yes, I have.'

'Oh,' she tries to say casually, 'what to?'

'Fridays and Saturdays.'

'Two days! That's what I need. Is it because of your kids?'

'Yes.'

'That's what I need to do. I miss my girls too much and they're too little.'

'Well ... well, he ... he didn't agree to it straight away ... You know, he ... he thought about it for a while ...' I trail off.

'You know, I'm going to ask him again. No, no, I'm going to wait until I'm in his good books, and then ask him.'

I am officially teacher's pet. Rebecca and I exchange a knowing look and I scarper as quickly as I can. It's about minus three degrees outside and I feel for my friend having to take two buses to get home in this cold.

As I drive to pick my children up from my mother's place I listen to Radio 4. The author Mike Gayle is talking about his new book *The To-Do List*. One of his resolutions is to talk to checkout girls more.

Thursday, 15 January 2009

Two weeks into the New Year and I promise myself a new me. Researching and reading about this downturn every day and listening to other people's financial fretting for the past few months has started to grind me down. I've found myself getting fanatical about my own money matters, so for the sake of my sanity I need a new outlook.

With only minutes to go before my shift, I race into the canteen to grab some water and stumble head first into an enormous article stuck on a whiteboard by the entrance. It's the *Evening Standard* heralding Sainsbury's recent success. My thoughts are lingering on my parched throat and the tick-tock of the clock counting down to the start of my shift, but I stop to skim read the article.

A voice behind me interrupts:

'If you're thinking we're going to get the bonus – we won't, you know.'

I turn to see a Cog I don't know too well.

'Oh no, it wasn't the bonus … I was just interested in how …'

'Come on, it's the bonus you're after, it's all right. But you aren't going to get it, you know. We just don't.'

'I thought we all got the bonus?'

'Well, we do, but it is not much for the hours we put in.'

She turns to the Cog she's with. 'It's how it is, isn't it? We do all the hard work and THEY get the glory.'

Down at the checkouts, there's no ignoring the doom and gloom; redundancy tales abound. When I sit down, the Cog behind me is listening as earnestly as she can feign to a customer who's fretting about her daughter's recent job loss and lack of success in finding a new job.

My first customer today is a friendly woman in her twenties with cute cropped hair like Demi Moore circa the *Ghost* years. She works at a recruitment agency.

'The agency has just cut half the people who work there because it's gone so very quiet. It used to be busy and bustling with people coming in and out, but now …' She stops packing for a second to emphasise. 'It's just strangely quiet.' She resumes packing. 'So, muggins here has picked up the workload of four people, can you believe?'

'That must be pretty stressful,' I say, scanning, sliding and listening intently.

'Definitely. And the mood is so depressing. We're supposed to be recruiting – but there are no jobs out there to recruit for.' Not far behind her is an extraordinarily tall man with lots of his own plastic bags and a stomach so big I'm sure he's hidden a dozen or more in there. He used to work for the Royal Mail but he's bored stiff after taking early retirement in April last year.

'Now I'm starting to go out of my mind with the routine of not doing anything. I'd really have liked to go back and work –

even to pick up just a little bit of work. But what work? There is NO work.'

OK so I'm not going to escape the economic drudgery, I've just got to keep it at a psychological arm's length.

It's a Thursday so there are plenty of retirees like my mail man in the store. Weekdays at the supermarket are for the elderly (very old), the mid-elderly (old but somewhat sane) and the stay-at-homers (mums, the unemployed and, more recently, the redundant). They've all got one thing in common – they're keen to beat the weekend rush. With the elderly and mid-elderly there's a lot of packing for me to help with and my items per minute target is pretty much off target. I have to give them the time to catch up, so I slide, scan and pass at snail's pace. It suits me though, as I get to chat and listen carefully. A woman with a giant silver cross dangling from her neck tells me she worked at a big high street bank and left last year, taking early retirement.

'I wish I'd stayed on for severance pay as I may have been cut anyway, with the culling that took place after I'd gone. It was bloody though, I hear.'

'Well, at least you're getting some time off. It must be good to slow down.' I say trying to sound positive.

'Hmm,' she says, packing distractedly. 'It's just boring, you know. I've been off for a few months and I think I'm ready to do something else. It's just that, at my age ... who's going to give me a job?' She's a young-looking fifty-eight-year-old and I tell her that she ought to find something soon.

'Well, I kind of have already,' she says, suddenly brightening. 'There's going to be a new Holland and Barrett up my local high street and they've promised me a job.'

'That's great! See? All is not lost.'

'Yes, but the only thing is, it was supposed to open in September and it still hasn't.' As we talk, it starts to dawn on her that with things being as they are it may never open at all.

Housewives flood into the supermarket on weekdays. They are my favourite breed of customer as they've perfected the art of small talk in ways I can only admire from the creaking discomfort of my checkout chair. They stand by my till day after day, hour after hour, opining and ruminating about the sun, the moon, the stars, and then by equal measure politics, the populace and the price of food. And if you listen carefully they often have practical solutions to problems that the great and the good of this country are currently struggling with. All this while being the linchpins of family life. They are, and I say this sincerely, a fascinating and remarkable bunch.

Dear Gordon Brown,

With every passing year I've found myself becoming more of a girl's girl, so now seems as good a time as any to tell you about my people. These creatures, women in their twenties, thirties, forties and menopausal years, rush to my till day after day – in all shapes and sizes. At first I only half listened to them, my other uninterested ear concentrating on the rhythmic beep of my scanner. If you could hear them talk as I often do, you wouldn't abandon them to the pitiful confines of daytime television, supermarket dwelling and the odd un-gratifying hobby (read: gardening, kids, cooking and interiors), but realise that as a demographic they are under-utilised resource of our time. I hear that you are somewhat occupied with a little economic crisis, but perhaps you could find a way of tapping into them? We may all be better off if you did.

Yours,

A. Cog

One such person makes her way to my till today. A mortgage broker turned housewife. 'The mortgage market is dead,' she declares soon after I instigate conversation about house prices. 'My husband is still working in the same industry, but lending mortgages in the public sector for key workers, civil servants, police, who can all borrow at zero per cent interest. That market is still very much alive and well. The rest of it is dead. Dead as …' she looks at the packet of beef steak I'm about to scan '… dead as this piece of cow in front of us.'

'So when would be good to buy again then?' I ask, passing the dead cow over.

'Two years. Don't buy now, and don't tell anyone you know to buy now. Wait. Because prices are going to fall so low it'll make your nose bleed.' She leans forward and whispers, 'By more than 30 per cent.'

'WHAT? As much as that?'

'Oh, definitely. And if anyone you know is going to buy, tell them only to go for it if they can get 30–40 per cent knocked off, otherwise it's not worth it.'

She says this with such conviction I'm too intimidated to argue with her. And despite my promise to myself, I'm frightened witless by her statistics. It would bring my own home down to almost the price I paid for it seven years ago. And it goes against what we're being told will happen. Reports say we are almost at rock bottom so by the end of the year the only way is up. How can she be right?

If the mortgage prophet isn't terrifying enough, there are others to help fuel the Dread Factor. Take the carpenter. He tells me that, while he is still getting work, he's no longer getting the big jobs.

'It's just little jobs here and there. No one wants to spend big money on renovating at the moment. So I'm just doing repairs and shelves and things. And if I'm really lucky, the odd kitchen-cupboard door.' He winks. Despite his jesting and upbeat manner, I sense a marked pessimism in his words and not least in his choice of groceries; everything he buys is reduced.

As the afternoon passes, the mood gets gloomier. Shoppers today are subdued and, when they talk, they grumble. One customer complains that as a regular shopper she's noticed our food prices have all gone up. She tells me that she also shops at Tesco and finds it much cheaper there.

'I do prefer the food here, but I'm starting to find it very expensive to shop in here.'

Thankfully, elderly shoppers who've lived through more recessions than I've scanned fair-trade bananas don't want to talk about money. They buy their favourite rich tea biscuits, fruit loaves and Red Label tea and smile politely at my faux American attempts to ask 'How are you, today?' True, many *are* half deaf, but often they are unexpectedly lucid. Some of the best repartee I've had has been with a customer in their seventies commenting, usually, on my hopelessly disingenuous customer service style. However, I'm starting to realise how elderly shoppers are increasingly being crippled by the demands of the modern supermarket. They come in during the week and avoid the weekends for fear of being trampled by the rush. I don't blame them, only the brave and foolhardy set foot into a supermarket on the weekend.

Friday, 16 January 2009

Fatima is at the customer service desk. She has a permanent spring in her step and is the polar opposite of Clare. She's been here for six years and has a cosy-big-sister-appeal about her. She took me under her wing within a few weeks of my starting here and pulls me into a bear hug every time I see her. I don't know how she keeps up her all-singing, all-dancing, love-to-serve-you act throughout her shift, and it's exhausting to watch. I think I'm just jealous. She was made for customer service and floats through customers' demands as if they were offering her deluxe spa days out rather than a dressing down for damaged items or receipts that show they've been charged for items they haven't bought. She is the sunniest personality in this place and I stop to talk to her as often as I can in the hope that some of her eternal optimism will rub off on me.

'Hey – how are you?'

'I'm really well. Happy to be here. Lal, la-la lah-la …'

She is so off the wall that it makes me laugh.

'What are you doing on the customer service desk?'

'They've just trained me up and I'm here doing me thing. Lal, la-la lah-la …'

'I know you're not madly keen on checkouts, but this can't be fun either?'

'Y'know, it's all right. Not too bad at all. Can't complain. Lal, la-la, lah-la …'

'Come on – it's all right! How can it be all right if all people are doing is moaning?'

'It's fine, honestly. People aren't as grumpy as you think. Lal, la-la, lah-la …'

Hmmm. I doubt that, somehow. As I wave goodbye and walk past the cold-food aisles, I can still hear her singing.

Betty is in charge when I start my shift. Unfortunately I have to call her over within a few minutes of starting to serve. The customer at my till forgot to pick up some jam and wants someone to get it for her. So I press the supervisor's button and watch as she strides over. I smother a snigger as the waiting customer watching Betty approach remarks to her husband in a hushed voice, 'Blimey, look at the face on her!' When I ask for the jam, Betty looks as if I'd just asked her to wipe my nose. She is, however, a true professional and hurries back with the item in less than a minute.

Betty may have to up her game though, because there is new blood on the shop floor. Hayley is a definite high-flier in the making and has the personal skills to match. During my ten-minute conversation I can see she won't be a supervisor for long; she has a manager's room with her name on it in her sights. She's thirty years old with long curly black hair tied back sensibly in a bun and thick black-rimmed glasses that sit just below the crook of her nose, and she has a truly likeable, down-to-earth way about her. Within a minute of talking to her I can tell she has an old head on young shoulders; as good an egg as the organic ones in the far corner of the store. We exchange a few niceties, talk about the store and people-watching, and share some personal anecdotes about our family lives. She then gives me my coupon and voucher training. Apparently we Cogs have been accepting too many inaccurate ones and it's led to a shortfall in the tills.

'You get this training now, and then if you still make mistakes be it on your own head.' I listen carefully, because customers, I've now learnt, will do anything to save money and often hand over out-of-date vouchers and coupons for things they haven't bought.

As we are chatting, a Hijab-totting customer with a loud voice comes over and asks if we've seen a dummy lying anywhere. Hayley looks at her as if she's crazed. The customer explains it belongs to her baby who's sitting in a pushchair a couple of yards away. I tell her we haven't seen it and after she goes Hayley says:

'You do get some characters in here – it's so multicultural. It can be a bit strange sometimes, can't it?' She looks at me and can see I'm listening carefully, so she adds hurriedly, 'Don't get me wrong, I do really like it.' I get the feeling she may have wanted to say more but decided against it. Nobody's perfect.

I'm deep in my robotic routine when another Cog stops at my till to give me the lowdown on the latest MCM visit. Our mystery friend pounced on us last Saturday apparently, and we failed on the checkouts.

'So the person on the checkout didn't smile or make conversation.'

'Right.'

'So you can't do that. You've got to be smiley and chatty.'

'Right.'

'Because what you did was you just passed the stuff through and didn't smile or chat.'

'Right.' But it wasn't me.

'It's not enough to just say hello and goodbye. You've got to do more.'

It wasn't me …

'Because if you don't do it, it's not good customer service.'

Does she think it was me?

'You know, you've got to chat, ask them about their shopping …'

'Right. So did THAT person not do more?'

'Yes, you just went …' She then does an impression of a bored checkout girl scanning and sliding.

It certainly *looks* like me.

'Well … I mean … not you exactly …' she finally corrects herself. 'The person just did that.'

'So she was kind of going through the motions?'

'Exactly. So you know what I mean?'

'Yes.'

'Good. OK, so don't do that then, yeah?'

'Right … OK.'

She then turns to the Cog behind me and has exactly the same conversation with her.

After this morale-boosting chat, I continue to serve my customers with as much sincere small talk as I can conjure up. Happily, most of my customers are in fine spirits. One regular, who has actually started skipping in and out of the store, is back again. He was living next door to noisy neighbours for the best part of a year; he finally called it a day and moved out about three months ago. The peace of mind it has given him was well worth the huge rent he has taken on – and explains why he's always bouncing around like Tigger on speed.

'How's the flat?' I ask him.

'Oh, it's great. Thanks for remembering.' He grins broadly. 'So wonderfully peaceful. I've been sleeping like a baby.'

'I guess that explains the spring in your step.'

His bill comes to £6.66. It's so tempting, but I fight the urge to blurt out one of my bad jokes. The number game has thus far only entertained me and falls flat with most customers I've had the poor judgement to thrust it on.

He digs into his wallet and says, 'I'm not the devil, you know.'

'Hooray!' I squeal. 'You speak the forbidden language!'

Like two over-grown primary school drop-outs who've just discovered basic maths, we start reciting all the two-, three- and four-digit numbers we can think of with any modern-day symbolism.

Catch-22 (me), 69 (him – he is a bloke, after all), 7.07, 7.47, 9.99, 9.11, 20.12, 19 followed by any two digits, he's a history buff so has lots of four-digit facts that start with 17 and 18. On and on and on we go until our little number party is inter-rupted by a rather bewildered customer.

When I head back to the locker room at the end of my shift, there are grumblings echoing up and down the stairs about the mystery customer results. Other Cogs clocking out are not amused.

'We all work so hard, no one is that robotic.'

'What does the mystery customer want, blood?'

'It's unfair, and now we're going to be watched closely again …'

And so on. Connor, one of the very few checkout guys, shares his gripe with me.

'What are we supposed to do? People don't want to talk.'

Checkout guys are mostly young students aged between sixteen and twenty-three who have not yet mastered the art of fine conversation – particularly not with the full range of customers we are required to serve. Even the girls in this cate-gory struggle, and it's an unfair expectation. I didn't realise how much one has to finesse one's dinner-table conversation for it to be plausible and have an iota of sincerity – and then to have to tailor it to suit each customer – it's a huge task. Rebecca tells me one young Cog who sat behind her last week asked every customer who passed through her checkout where they go for a night out. 'That was basically her idea of good small talk. She was even asking old people.'

Saturday, 17 January 2009

Down at the till captains' post, Michelle is telling Susie that she's feeling poorly. Susie is sympathetic and says she can go home if she's not up to it – which, by my reckoning, is very reasonable. I'm not convinced that Michelle really is unwell because as she turns a corner away from Susie, she glances back at me as if seeking assurance that she has pulled it off. She doesn't want to be here – and it's becoming quite obvious. I don't think she's going to last.

It's so busy today, I can hardly breathe. Shrieking tots accompanied by over-wrought parents, disapproving couples in their fifties and sixties muttering to each other about toddler tantrums, and highly strung male shoppers gather at the basket tills. In every aisle there are trolleys so full that food is tumbling down the side.

Every customer has their own theory about why the place is heaving.

'People have just discovered they've got more money than they thought they had now that the expense of Christmas is over.'

Another says: 'It's because people are not eating out or having takeaways as frequently, so they're spending more money on eating in – and they're cooking! Makes sense, doesn't it?'

Yes it does. But even eating in is costly. A young couple having French onion soup and lamb burgers for dinner have bought soufflé for dessert. They also buy other food that needs to be cooked from fresh. They end up spending £157.40.

The word of the day is 'Basics'. Basics range, Basics vouchers – and customers are being told about it (by the likes of me) and encouraged to buy it (by Cogs handing out coupons). It's cheap and cheerful but, according to Sainsbury's, still 'sourced with integrity', and it's selling. One twenty-something young man who is nifty in the kitchen is buying basic lamb mince. He gives me his recipe for simple burgers which he swears smell so good that they will 'make your mouth water till you beg for mercy'.

Mix the meat with a touch of mustard, finely chopped onions, chopped peppers, a handful of oats and your own preferred seasoning. Finally a bit of salt and pepper, roll, flatten and fry. Within ten minutes, I promise you perfect burgers.

It's not all good food and good cheer though. A Royal Mail employee comes to my checkout today. He's distraught that there are cuts on the horizon.

'They want one person to do several jobs.'

'That's just the way it seems to be now, doesn't it?' I say, not unsympathetically.

'That doesn't make it right though, does it?' he snaps.

'No, no, of course not.' He's misread me, but no matter, I'm long accustomed to misunderstandings at my till. A sixty-second conversation that attempts to delve too deep will drip with misinterpretations, and in any case I've become an expert at apologising and back-tracking.

One customer comes in especially to buy something from the Tchibo range 'before it becomes history'. Tchibo's demise has been well reported in the papers; it's a German coffee brand that sells coffee as well as other consumer goods. It's now scaling back business in Britain due to the recession and its presence in supermarkets will be gone this year. The Tchibo range has always struck me as a bizarre one – it's the come-to-life version of the mini catalogues slipped inside the Sunday papers that offer a wide range of seemingly useful goods that you think you need but will, inevitably, never use.

Customers today repeatedly offer big apologies for forgetting their bags and it's starting to get boring.

Dear Customer,

I know that you feel pretty lousy about forgetting to bring back one of the dozens of bags you've got sitting in some cupboard in the kitchen. But honestly, stop apologising. It may surprise you to hear that it makes no difference to me. Ultimately it's between you and your conscience. Save the world for your kids currently standing at the till yelling, or leave it to rot – it's your choice.

If it was up to me I'd just leave the bags on the till until you get your act together. But for those of you who forget bags in the car there is no excuse – if you really cared you'd just leave your shopping with one of the numerous happy-to-help Cogs in the store and nip back to the car.

One of my customers told me that in Ireland they have the same ruthless bag policy as M&S – if you forget, you pay. So stop making excuses and offering annoying over-the-top apologies. Just politely ask for a bag. We don't need to talk about it.

Yours,

A. Cog

I have two Romany customers today who give me a hard time. But when the spectators behind try to support me, the check-out-chair socialist in me shushes them gently. The two women with minimal English spend a long time at the till. First they dispute who will pay. This takes a while to resolve. Then they decide to pay for their shopping separately. Next they accidentally muddle the shopping so the nappies, carrot soup and apples end up in the wrong person's shop and then they blame me for it. I sort out their illogical mess with a bit of voiding on the till screen and rearranging on the belt. Waiting customers are not impressed. Then to reward me for my patience both women start to argue with me about the number of Nectar points they have left. Contrary to what many customers think, Cogs have no control over this and can only go with what the screen and the receipt say. I try to explain this to them but they look at me simultaneously perplexed and hostile. This goes on for a minute or two.

'Look, she can't do anything about it so will you just get your shopping and go?' interrupts a woman from the back of the queue. Under normal circumstances I'd be begging for this kind of help, but I feel for how the language barrier has rendered these women incapable of querying a simple point. I turn to the woman in the queue and say, 'It's all right, I can handle it.' I turn back to the women and point to the customer service desk. 'Take it there and let them help you. Me? I can't do anything. OK?' They shrug their shoulders, pick up their shopping and give the waiting customer a steely stare before wandering off. The waiting customers make politically incorrect observations about them and I resolutely refuse to join in.

Not many tills down, I can see Rebecca and Louisa sitting together at the basket checkouts. Louisa has recently had her hair coloured and it seems to make up the main bulk of their conversation. Studying Rebecca's face closely, I can see furrows deepening across her brows.

At the end of my shift I go over to say hello. Louisa gets up to take a toilet break and as she leaves she asks Rebecca to touch her newly coloured hair.

'It feels really light, doesn't it?'

Rebecca touches it with a conspicuous display of indifference while muttering such an unconvincing 'yes' that the customers standing by all laugh. I ask Rebecca how she's coped sitting next to her all day.

'It's OK I guess, until you hear the same story for the hundredth time.'

Now that Richard has sanctioned my shift change Rebecca and I will finish at the same time. I feel deeply indebted to Richard for being so accommodating about my childcare problems. He's a good manager and manages downwards as well I'm sure as he manages upwards. Of all the people I thought I'd meet in a place like this, I wasn't expecting my line manager to win me over so convincingly. So I pay it forward and offer to give Rebecca a lift back.

I'm shopping as usual and take it to a till where the Cog serving is a nineteen-year-old university student called Paulo. He gets called on to checkouts whenever they are short-staffed and hates it. Katherine is teasing him. 'You hate it here because you lose your freedom, don't you? On the floor you can do anything you want.'

'No, no, that's not true.'

'Yes it is,' she laughs, taunting him further, 'and it's worse because you can't talk to any of the girls when you're stuck here.'

'No, no! Katherine …' He smiles and starts to blush.

'Yes, it is – I know what you're up to … out the back … pretending to work … but just checking out the checkout girls … I know.'

This is excruciating and he is now a deep shade of crimson. It's like being teased by your mum and so I force her to stop. She's right, though; this is heaven, if ever there was one, for boys on the make. There are single girls in their teens and early twenties in every nook and cranny in this store; no wonder the boys spend all their time skiving in the back waiting for young Cogs to pass by to flirt with.

As I'm about to walk out of the door I bump into Danielle. She was the first person I met at the store so I have a soft spot for her. We talk about more of my customer service fears and she tells me, 'I told Richard that you would be great at customer service very soon after I met you.'

'Oh, right, so you're to blame.'

'Come on, girl, it's not that bad. You'll be fine. And anyway, you look clever and that's all that counts. Not that you have to be brain of Britain or anything.'

Friday, 23 January 2009

The government is telling us what those of us on the front line have known for months: we are officially in recession. The economy has shrunk by 1.5 per cent, which means wages will be frozen, unemployment will increase and the variety of shops and shopping experiences we have enjoyed for so long will shrink dramatically. News from my employers states that there'll be some restructuring at head office and the loss of 200 jobs. But this will translate into an increase in jobs elsewhere in the business by 3–4000 this year alone. Meanwhile I'm being blinded by notices in the canteen and the corridors about our last mystery customer visit and the big fat 'FAIL' that we achieved. Our percentage score was 79.5 per cent and we have five more visits to get our average up to 80 per cent and nail the bonus. I'm quite sure I'm not the only one who is struggling to care about the bonus that we may receive.

* * *

I'm on baskets and a regular from the car shop across the road pops in during his lunch break.

'How's it all going over there?'

'Not bad, not too bad at all.'

'Really? I thought the car industry was suffering?'

'Not us. I mean it *is* quiet, but there are no cuts and we're still selling, so nothing to worry about.'

Despite my numerous attempts to make him see the dark side, he plays down any talk of the recession affecting sales.

An office worker who pops in for lunch tells me she's also becoming obsessive about the recession. 'I've got really scared by it recently. I think I'm listening to the news too much. Do you know that the economist who predicted this recession is saying that it will take one and a half to two years before things get better?' I see nothing but fear in her big blue eyes.

'Yes, I heard that too, but another analyst said that this time next year the recession will be looking better. So it just depends on who you listen to, right?'

Behind her a dark-haired woman with a German accent joins in the discussion. She works at a car-manufacturing company which makes lights for Chrysler and Volvo cars. She says they've had huge cuts since October and that more job cuts lie ahead.

'It's gone very quiet. I work in sales, and for the time being that's OK. Touch wood.'

Not long after those two customers have left I serve a chap who works at BT. He tells me that, while it's as busy as ever where he works, there are huge cuts ahead.

'They just want more work done by fewer people – same amount of work but having to pay less. There is definitely plenty of work around, but why pay five people to do it when you can pay just the one idiot for it?'

After all the dreary recession tittle-tattle I need some supermarket idle gossip, so I eavesdrop on Sonia and Katherine
discussing one of the fruit-and-veg boys.

'Do you know, right, that I gave him a cuddle. But only …
because I felt sorry for him. He seemed very upset about the
fact that his granddad was ill, so when he asked I thought, all
right then.'

'You DIDN'T! You idiot. I'm sure he's just trying it on.'

'Well, do you know what I saw next? He then asked four
other girls to hug him right after I hugged him – and all of them
on the stairs by the canteen. Can you believe the cheek of it?'
My eyes widen by the second.

'Euch. It's creepy. When he asked me, do you know what I
said? I said, "Get away from me! Try that again and I'll put a
complaint in against you,"' says Katherine.

I admire Katherine's balls. Sadly, I also fell victim to his get-
a-free-grope ploy and complied when he asked. The whole
thing has made my stomach churn a little, so I turn my atten-
tions back to my customers. A teacher wants to tell me about
how she's saving a fortune through 'recession-friendly cuts'
she's made.

'I've stopped going out for dinner and to bars and to the
cinema. And I've started cooking from scratch. And do you
know how much I saved this month? About £400 in total,' she
declares proudly. That's an impressive amount, but I wonder
what she does for fun.

'Well, I certainly don't need to worry about my job because
I'm a key-worker and we're not affected by downturns.'

'So that's a good recession-proof job then?'

'Oh, definitely, and during recessions or when people lose
their jobs they start training to be teachers. The only thing is, all
these people who are in training now will be looking for a job in

a year – they don't know what they are in for. There's going to be so much competition, they're going to struggle to get a job.'

Around two hours into my shift along comes a man with a lot of potatoes.

So I say, 'That's a lot of potatoes.'

He says, 'Well, that's not surprising, there *are* eight of us.'

'Eight of you?' I gasp.

'Six kids, of whom five are boys; the eldest is seventeen and the last one is a two-year-old girl.'

I stop scanning and look him directly in the eye.

'Don't tell me you kept going in the hope that you'd get a girl?'

'It's funny you say that, because that's *exactly* what we did.'

'And now you've the same size brood as Brangelina, minus the team of nannies and the billion-dollar fortune.'

He laughs and starts packing his bags. 'You don't need a team of nannies to make it work, trust me.'

'So what's the secret then?' I ask.

'Well, I work night-shifts and my wife does day-shifts and we've never had need to pay for a child-minder.'

'And I guess neither of you ever sleeps.'

He laughs again. 'That sounds about right.'

Nevertheless, he seems like a very happy sleep-deprived dad of six. He takes his 30 kilos of potatoes and hobbles out.

In supermarket world, the cheery are often followed close behind by the cheerless; heart-warming stories are followed by heart-rending ones.

A man in his sixties comes to my till. Thick-rimmed black glasses sit on his weather-worn face and he's wearing a bright blue cagoule. I ask how he is.

'You don't want to know how I am.'

'Yes I do,' I say, smiling.

'Well … my wife is sick and I spend all my days looking after her,' he blurts out. 'And it's the toughest thing I've ever had to do. I've had a shit day today and all I want to do is go and hide under a rock, but I've got to get food so here I am doing my bleeding shopping. *That's* how my day has been.'

It's not fitting to say anything, so I say nothing. Besides, I'm totally out of my depth and he's on a roll.

'Do you know I've worked for years, and that job was a piece of piss by comparison, I tell you! And the worst bit is that the love of my life doesn't even know that I'm there most days.'

This is the *exact* reason why checkout girls should *not*, under any circumstances, ask customers how they are.

'And do you know how much I get for looking after her week after week, month after month?'

I shake my head, but I know it's not going to be pretty.

'A paltry fifty quid. Fifty quid to not go to work any more. Fifty quid to stay at home and lose every semblance of my former life. Fifty quid to not have anyone to talk to. Fifty quid because I love her and if I don't look after her then who will?'

I've scanned all his shopping but there is, unfortunately, no one behind him.

'Then the other day my mate who works in a post office tells me that a woman with two kids who couldn't speak a word of English picks up fifteen hundred quid every fortnight – fifteen hundred! I've given this country a million pounds in my lifetime in taxes and all I get is fifty quid. And these Romanians and Polish people who have been here just a couple of years get that much more. I mean, I don't blame them, I blame the system …'

And then to my utter horror his voice starts to break and he wells up.

'… it's just very hard to deal with. I don't understand it.' And there it is – a tear slipping down his crumpled right cheek.

I know I have to say something, *anything*. There is, after all, a grown man crying at my till.

'Oh dear, you *are* having a bad day.'

It's feeble, I know, but in the circumstances it's the best I can offer.

'Well, you asked, so I told you.' He picks up his shopping and without a further word walks towards the exit.

Out of sheer terror I don't talk to the next three customers I serve.

Soon a train driver with job cuts on his mind comes to my till. He drives overground trains.

'The recession won't affect me because they always need drivers and people always need to get from A to B. But you should see the cuts they are making at a number of over-ground stations out of King's Cross.' 'They're just getting rid of ground staff, it's been ruthless. And the thing is, we're being told it's because of the recession, but I reckon that was always the big plan for the company that bought Thameslink.'

Not far behind the train driver is a woman in her fifties with no such recession woes. Dressed in a fleece and jodhpurs, her freshly highlighted blonde hair is tied back neatly in a ponytail. She's just about to drive to a local riding school where she will pat her horse on the back and take him out for a ride. She tells me that she came in here because she can't bear to stop off at the Tesco closer to the school as 'it's full of riff-raff. There's a much better clientele in here.' After she leaves, Katherine, who is sitting with me at the baskets, does a marvellous impression of her.

It's so quiet today we've been gossiping and giggling most of the afternoon. Against my better judgement I take a stick of gum she offers that comes with a warning: 'Just don't chew it when a customer or manager is close by.' I take it cautiously, because we've been told it's rude to chew. But if it's good enough for the supervisors, it's good enough for me. I've lost count of the number of times I've seen them all munching sweets. Both Sonia and I are chomping away happily when a manager pushing a trolley passes by.

'You two – with gum in your mouth. Take it out and put it in the bin, please. Now.' Our faces flush and we mutter threats at Katherine as we throw the gum away. My metamorphosis into a Cog is complete.

There is a brief flurry of confused activity when a supervisor comes over asking if we had seen Fatima cash up. Her shift ended a couple of hours ago, but they can't find her cash. Usually at the end of our shifts we empty our tills, pop the money in a canister and send the money up to the office. Her canister is missing. Sonia and Katherine tell Samantha they are sure they saw her put the money away.

As usual during my shift, Betty is on. She comes over to talk to Katherine and blanks me completely. After she leaves Katherine and I exchange notes on her. She tells me Betty is pleasant with her because she's friends with Katherine's neighbour. But Katherine is no fool. 'I know what she's really like. Why be nice to me just because you're friends with my neighbour? Why not just because I'm a nice person?'

* * *

A few minutes before the end of my shift I see Susie talking to a young student called Grace a few tills down. From where I'm sitting I can tell she's just had an assessment. She looks crestfallen by the time Susie has left. When it's time for me to go home, I pick up some milk and take it to her till.

'Hi – how are you?' I ask brightly.

'I'm OK … I had observation today.'

'Oh, really? How did it go?'

'Not well at all. Susie was nice about it but, you know, I wasn't very good.'

'Why? What were you not doing?'

'Apparently I look down too much and I'm not talking to customers enough. But I … I … just don't know what to say to them.'

Grace is seventeen, almost six foot tall with large hazel-coloured eyes and long eyelashes that she tries to hide behind. She's gorgeous, but really uncomfortable in her own skin. I've developed a soft spot for her because I remember too well what it's like to be a gauche teenager – the painful self-consciousness and crippling shyness. The refined small talk we're expected to initiate day in, day out requires the kind of skills that a tongue-tied teenager is a long way from developing. And she has not yet grown the layer of thick-skin required to bounce off the inevitable rejection that comes from customers in no mood to chat. Coming of age is excruciating enough – let alone before a stream of obtuse customers unmoved by a young Cog's best attempts to appear urbane.

'Don't worry about it, OK? Just chat when you can think of something to talk about.'

'Hmm,' she says distractedly, not looking at all comforted by my words.

Saturday, 24 January 2009

Reports on the radio this morning say that it's no longer a recession but a 1930s-style depression. It will be 2010 or 2011 before things start to look better and the economy starts to grow again. The more I learn about this recession, the worse I feel. Thankfully there's no evidence of this dismal news in the store and it is a wonderful escape from the melancholy of the outside world. There is a tangible upbeat atmosphere in the air, and to top it all my favourite family stop by on their way out to say a quick hello.

Rebecca comes to my till and is up to her usual tricks. 'Excuse me, madam, I'm assessing this young lady and wondered if you could tell me what you think of her service?'

'Oh, yes, yes,' says the startled customer, 'she's very good.'

We collapse into a heap of prepubescent giggles. It doesn't take much to amuse a Cog in a place like this. I do, though, appreciate the fact that the general public is always benevolent enough to respond in the affirmative, regardless of how poor or imperfect my service has been that day.

Not for the first time, a customer asks me if they can take someone else's Nectar points. I've become increasingly hopeless at dealing with this so turn to Tracey behind me and ask her.

'Tracey, she hasn't got a card and the customer behind her wants me to put her points on her card – can I scan it?'

'You can do it. Just as long as you are not the one to suggest it. If one customer asks the other – just do it.'

'But we were told in training not to do it.'

'Well, if you don't do it then they'll start getting cross with you. It's not worth it. Just don't ever suggest it yourself, but if they offer each other – it's nothing to do with you – just do it.'

I tell her about a customer I served last week and how I banged on about a rule being a rule.

'I know … it was pretty sad of me. Apparently some other checkout girl had done it, she said, so why wouldn't I?'

'That was probably me,' laughs Tracey.

My next customer is full of the joys of spring.

'Ah,' I say, picking up the birthday card to scan, 'someone's turning eighteen – that's a great age, isn't it?'

A perfunctory smile.

'The weather has been improving, although it's still very cold, isn't it?'

Nothing.

'Oh, these are lovely,' I say about the Petits Filous on the belt. 'One is never enough, is it?'

Silence.

'I never know how to peel a butternut squash, you're left with arm ache at the end, aren't you?' I say, scanning, sliding and passing the offending butternut squash. I cut my losses. She hands me her Sainsbury's staff discount card and the sound of pennies dropping clangs inside my head. She knows the drill – and can't be bothered. Last week I was in her sensible black shoes. I was running late for my shift but I wanted to get some of my shopping done first. The Cog who served me didn't know I worked there and so on she went, on and on. First it was, 'Aw, do you have a kitty cat?' prompted by my cat litter, then 'I like this bread too.' And then, 'Skimmed milk is so much better than full fat, isn't it?' and 'Always better to buy recycled toilet paper than any other,' and so on. I wanted to tell her to shut up and get on with the scanning, but didn't. Quickly, quickly, quickly, I had the urge to tell her, but didn't. Instead I blanked her numerous pitiful attempts at checkout idle chatter. It's faintly ridiculous – one Cog unknowingly chatting up another.

I ask one man about his plans for the weekend.

'No plans, no fun. This is my bill-paying weekend when I pay penance for all the fun I've had this week. It's time to deal with the mortgage and shopping bills. It's also time to remind my family that we are in a recession.'

Another couple tell me about their nineteen-year-old son who works in the warehouse at Sainsbury's. He's training to be an electrician and desperately needs an apprenticeship. 'There is nothing to be found, which is worrying. But there is one piece of good news about the recession: at least now is a good time to be training,' says Dad.

Other customers, especially older men, have a little of the war-time spirit in them. 'Even if we are talking a depression like the thirties, let's not forget they survived it – so will we.'

'There needs to be a correction. There is day and there is night, ups and then downs. If we didn't have this recession I hate to think where we'd end up a few more years down the road.'

'I'm not worried about it. I've seen a couple of recessions and eventually we all get through it. There's a lot of hysteria about. What's the worst that can happen? We'll all tighten our belts for a while. We need to do that anyway – we've got too used to spending too freely.'

With only minutes to go till the end-of-shift o'clock, I'm doing some reverse shopping and notice that every Cog on every till is talking to their customer – even Michelle is so engrossed in chat that she barely notices me when I pick up leftovers dumped at her till. On my way out I've filled my basket with milk, bread and eggs when we bump into each other in the dairy aisle. She cracks a joke about the fact that we are both shopping.

'So have you heard yet – are you staying on?'

'What?'

'Are you staying here past your twelve weeks?'

'Yes, I guess so.'

'You know, after your probationary period – have you passed?'

'Oh, I see.' It's probation talk again. 'Well, I'm not sure if it is twelve weeks yet. But I guess I am staying on or they would have said something. What about you?'

'I don't know, no one has said anything yet. I think so. I hope so.'

It's fair to say she has a pretty complex relationship with this job. On the one hand she loathes it with a passion as it keeps her from her kids. On the other, she's desperate to stay on and lives in fear of not being kept on.

I give Rebecca a lift home and we gossip about the other girls. She has been working every day this week and looks exhausted. When she's not here she is either studying or working in her other job, and I give her some advice on asking for a change in shifts. Despite being as burnt out as she is, she's worried that she hasn't had an observation yet, which she thinks translates into bad news. Much as we mock the work we do, she's as worried as the next person about being out of work. It is hardly surprising, since up to three million people are expected to be unemployed in the UK by the end of 2009. Almost half will be under the age of twenty-five. Average student debt upon gradu-ation is now almost £20,000. University graduates are going to be hit hard by the financial crisis. That's roughly half of my colleagues at the supermarket walking away with huge debts and few job prospects.

Friday, 30 January 2009

On the radio on my way in, the headlines focus on the protests in France about President Sarkozy's handling of the recession and my first customer stands on his soap box for five minutes lamenting the state *our* country is in. I smile politely but say nothing.

'But do you know why people – voters, I tell you – are really angry? This government saved those who wear bowler hats, not those with hard hats. And that's why, despite the fact that I've voted Labour all my life, next time they won't be getting my vote.' He's still going when I start serving the next customer. Even though I'm now sorry I asked, raw anger like his is not uncommon. When he finally leaves, I resolve not to stoke any more fires and don't talk about the recession again for a full hour.

During a moment of peace at my till, there is high drama at the customer service desk. Molly has burst into a flood of tears. She's in her early forties, originally from Italy and tough as old boots – and a permanent fixture at the customer service desk. A few of the supervisors have gathered around to comfort her. Someone pressed the panic alarm and all the managers are at the front of the store. I have no idea what has happened, but from where I'm sitting it looks terribly exciting.

In the shopping baskets today are home dye kits galore. People are now choosing to lean over their own bathtubs, staining their hair various shades of strawberry blonde, deep mahogany and magpie black rather than go to the hairdresser's. 'When you can pay a few quid for DIY hair, why spend £90 at the hair-dresser's?' says one customer with hair so brittle it looks like it may disintegrate any second.

I'm serving an attractive woman in her thirties. She tells me she's recently divorced but has a six-year-old and seven-year-old to keep her 'cheery'. She's struggling with her new-found status, but is trying to keep positive for the sake of the kids. Suddenly a 'friend' rushes over from another till to say hello.

'Hi, Colette, how *are* you?' Her eyes are so wide with conspicuous insincere sympathy, I find myself almost retching.

'I'm fine, Margaret,' says my dignified divorcee. 'Can't complain. The kids are good too.' She's packing intensely to avoid dear Margaret's unblinking stare.

'Yes, yes, you look really well. We're all so proud of you,' says Margaret, not looking too proud at all. The searching intensity of her stare suggests she's looking for a little crack in Colette's regal display of strength.

'You know that Cathy is on her own, too?' she says, fishing for gossip for the next coffee morning.

'Oh, is she?' asks Colette, trying to strike a graceful balance between sympathy and empathy.

'Yes, poor thing. Her husband had an … an … affair.' Margaret whispers this last word, but I still hear it.

It's quite obvious that Colette has now had more than she can take. I decide to intervene.

'Do you need some more bags?'

Colette turns to me enthusiastically. 'Oh, yes please.'

Margaret does evidently have some shame and says, 'I'll let you finish your shopping, Colette. I'll call you next week.'

Her work is done, so off she goes.

Colette's relief is palpable. She turns back to shopping but then spends the next few minutes packing silently, deep in thought.

I serve a couple of customers that come in regularly. One tells me he shops here every day.

'What? Every day of the week?'

'Yup, every single day.'

'Why don't you just come in once a week and get everything you need?'

'Because we run out of food or things perish. You need fresh grub.'

'And how much do you spend each time?'

'About £30, I'd say. Sometimes more.'

Ker-ching.

Another customer I've just served comes back after thirty minutes because he forgot something and adds another £10 to his shopping bill.

'See you again in twenty minutes,' I jibe.

My last customers of the day are regulars. They're a couple who've been married for thirty-four years and are both coppers. They provide such high entertainment value with their good-humoured squabbling that they ought to have their own show. Watching couples bicker is hands down my favourite part of this job.

On the radio on the way home there's talk of 1000 jobs cut on the London underground. And there's a discussion about yesterday's announcement by Asda to employ another 7000 workers and create at least fifteen new stores.

Saturday, 31 January 2009

Today there is increasing unrest about the use of foreign labour. Gordon Brown's 2007 pledge of 'British jobs for British workers' is being used by protestors angry that a refinery is using Italian workers rather than local staff. In the past I'd have had little time for this argument, but in the current climate, with mounting job losses and a fall in vacancies, it's every man for himself. I completely understand the furore.

I start my shift with the usual hunt for a chair that isn't going to collapse the second I sit on it. Betty is on shift and I know if I ask her for a chair it will go down like a ton of bricks, so I go on my own private treasure hunt and find one torn at the seams, with yellow foam poking out from beneath. It's not perfect, but perfectly adequate. During my induction I was told to always look for a sturdy bloke to help lift it over, but today there are none to be found. I weigh up my options – go looking for someone who can help and delay getting on the till, potentially risking the wrath of the already cranky Betty, or risk putting my back out. I opt for the latter and hear a disconcerting crack as I do it.

My first customer is a chap with a wife who has perfected the art of control freakery. He tries to pack the shopping and she moves in.

'Alan, don't put the detergents in with the cereal.'

He picks up the bread and puts it in a new bag.

'You can't put the bread at the bottom, it'll get squashed.'

So he opens another bag.

'Alan, we've got our own bags! We don't need theirs.'

He puts the potatoes in one of their bags.

'Potatoes at the bottom, not on top of the blooming eggs,' she tuts, and grabs the bag from him.

He looks for the card to pay with.

'I'm paying on the credit card today – I want the air miles.'

Hen-pecked husband then leans against the till with his back to us and stands there seething quietly for the remainder of the time. She packs, pays and then pushes the trolley to the car park.

Dear Control Freak Husband/Wife,

I appreciate, more than most, the importance of packing well. Who wants potatoes squashing bread and fish stinking out your delicious desserts? But do you have to humiliate your spouse in front of me? If they don't know how to pack, then have a quiet word in their ear before you leave, not while you are at the checkout. And if it really matters, there are other ways of getting round it. Get them to load while you pack. Get them to go pick up some 'forgotten' item while you pack. Get them to pay while you pack. Best of all, get them to chat to the bored Cog while you pack. Just please, for the sake of your marriage, for the sake of supermarket etiquette, don't keep crucifying them in front of us.

Yours,

A. Cog

I get a recipe for a beef meatballs bolognaise from a lady with more fresh food in her trolley than the fruit-and-veg section at the front of the store.

Roll the meatballs with beaten egg and Italian herbs, fry gently, dunk them in a sauce made from fresh garlic simmered with tinned tomatoes and more mixed herbs; add some salt, a dash of chilli powder, tomato purée and leave to cook for an hour. Hey presto.

A customer with a pace maker tells me how he lost ten pounds in a week with what he calls the British Heart Foundation diet. He had to lose weight quickly before going in for surgery and it worked for him. It sounds like a dangerous crash diet, but he heartily recommends it. I look it up later and, indeed, it comes with a health warning. Needless to say, the BHF has distanced itself from it.

Domestic matters are, as always, high on the agenda in a supermarket. People talk recipes, extreme dieting and, of course, about their beloved pets. An elderly couple have just taken in a beautiful stray Persian cat that has lost his way. They tell me they've adopted him after countless attempts to find his original owner. I tell them that there are websites they can register him at in case the owner is still looking for him. They pretend not to hear me.

I serve a friendly Australian.

'I've just come back from Australia and they're not admitting to a recession, but you know when you go shopping you really feel it. The price of food is through the roof. I wonder how long it's going to take before the price of food here shoots up.' She stares at me as if I may have some inside information. I look back at her blankly. If I knew something like that was on the horizon I'd be buying my food in bulk down at the local cash and carry. Pronto.

Sonia is on the till opposite me. She seems to be on a mission to get shoppers to buy British meat. She tells every single customer about a documentary she watched in which animals for slaughter were kept in terrible conditions. 'Don't get me wrong, I like my meat, but if you had seen this programme you'd know what I mean.' She describes in graphic detail everything she witnessed in the documentary: 'They were caged twenty-four–seven and had this look of crazy wildness in their eyes.' The customers look uncomfortable. 'And they were packed into this tiny little space with most of them looking emaciated, and some were even bleeding.' One customer looks like she's going to throw up. 'And they were so uncomfortable they never slept.' Another feigns polite interest. 'And, if you think about it, if the animal isn't well, then what's its meat going to taste like?' One customer is so bored she doesn't look away from her shopping once. Sonia is not one to give up easily. 'It completely put me off and now I always check the back to see where the meat is from before I buy it.'

I know my recession small talk isn't exactly sophisticated dinner-table conversation, but surely she can do better than this?

Between my credit crunch chit-chat and Sonia's butchering stories, I'm amazed we haven't scared most of the customers away. When all else fails there's always the infamous forgotten plastic bag to talk about. One customer tells me she has a special bag that she always brings with her but without fail leaves it behind in the car.

'I've had it for so long, I feel lost without it. It's so grand that I sit it in the car next to me – in a kind of privileged position. And then I come into the shop and leave it there, untouched, unused, just waiting for my return.'

'So it's like bag royalty,' I muse.

'Yes, a Queen of bags.'

'A virgin bag, in some ways.'

'Yes, a kind of bag lady.'

Her son begs us to stop, but it's still far better repartee than I get from the bloke who comes to my till at least once a day and shouts 'BAGS!' at me.

* * *

One thing I've started to learn after three long months in this job is that the customer is *always* right. The belt where the shopping is placed *after* I've scanned it is more or less always on the move. It's there to transport the shopping from me to the bottom of the till so the customer can conveniently pack their shopping. It's certainly *not* designed for a customer to place their cash on – especially not when it's moving. So, along comes a lady who defies the rules of conventional transaction and puts her money on the moving belt: all £120; in six £20 notes. I watch as they slip down the moving belt and disappear into the innards of my checkout. There's a mad scramble and then they are all gone. Fortunately this till appears to be designed with the idiocy of such customers in mind: under the till is a large open and empty space. All the notes have simply floated to the floor. I manage to rescue them all and when I emerge from the bowels of my till with my hair ruffled and glasses skewed, the customer tells me, 'I'm glad you got them back because you shouldn't have just let them go on the belt.'

It's almost the end of my shift, and in the fine tradition of Cog etiquette I stand up so that a supervisor (often too busy gossiping with co-supervisor to notice) can see it's time to bring me over a *Closed Checkout* sign. Standing, sitting, jumping or waving my arms – none of it has any effect. Huge over-loaded trolleys approach and the sign is still nowhere to be seen. Betty eventually tells me that I have relief on its way. So that means an extra few minutes at the checkout – unpaid.

Dear Supermarket Boss,
    Today my relief came three minutes late. I know what you're thinking – what's three minutes, you skiving Cog? But as you know, my colleagues and I only get paid £6.30 an hour. If we

are late you dock our wages. But if we work an extra ten minutes we get nothing. By the time the lovely Phillipe came down, he inadvertently, through no fault of his own, extended my shift by an extra unpaid fifteen minutes. He clocks in at the start of his shift on time. He makes his way down the stairs, through the shop and over to the till captain who allocates him a till. I think he did well to make it to me in three minutes. However, I still had to finish serving my customer with their trolleyful of shopping before I could hand over to him, and that took an extra ten minutes or so. If my shift ends at 5.30, I should be able to go home at 5.30.

Give us a break. We work hard for your money.

Yours,

A. Cog

Friday, 6 February 2009

It's freezing today so Fatima gives me her amber jacket to keep me warm and tells me she's moving on in a couple of weeks. She, like many of the women at the store, started working here to boost her confidence once her three kids started school. She had them in close succession, a year or two apart, and desperately needed some time to herself. Now that the eldest is about to start secondary school she wants to be at home for them again, 'so that when they come back from school I'm around to keep an eye on them'.

We discuss last week and the mystery of the missing money. 'I just put it in the wrong tub and they all got a little overexcited,' she tells me.

Richard is gutted she's leaving and her last shift is over Valentine's weekend.

'How romantic for you and Sainsbury's,' I say.

And then we both chime, 'Parting is such sweet sorrow,' and laugh hysterically.

After serving a couple of customers I turn to her and say, 'You didn't even stick around for your discount card?'

'Yes, but Adil has one.'

At first I think she means her husband, who is one of my favourite customers, and then it dawns on me she means Adil, the politics student. This place is insanely incestuous. Her youngest brother is a charming, eloquent Cog who works on general merchandise. When I tell her how great a job her family has done with Adil, she beams.

A chap I serve hunts around in his pocket for the right change, wrongly believing that it will in some way make my life easier. Out of politeness I watch him dig around for at least a minute.

'Life's too short to look for the right change,' I say eventually.

'Aah, a checkout philosopher – I like that.'

I'm feeling generous towards my customers today, although not generous enough to give them their cash-back. Again and again I'm so engrossed in our exchange that I forget to give them their requested cash-back. Fortunately, most gently remind me.

Sadly, some of my encounters today are even less auspicious. A face from my not-so-distant supermarket past re-emerges. I look up and standing before me with a smirk on his smug little face is the customer with the tattoos and no ID from before Christmas.

'So I'm not too young to serve now, then?' he asks haughtily.

'Depends on what you're buying, sir,' I reply, not making any eye contact.

'So do I look older now?'

I smile genially although I really just want to thump him.

'You *do* look young. You should have been flattered.'

He puffs out his tattooed chest with pride.

'I always get asked for ID. I can't even go to clubs without it. How old do you think I am? Go on, take a guess.'

'Well ... I mean ... under twenty-one, of course, that's why I asked you for ID in the first place.'

'Thirty-one,' he says.

He wants me to gasp in awe, but I've had about as much as I can take. He gets bored with trying to impress me and leaves.

Behind him is a man with bags on the brain.

'Why should I bother to save the planet when the government is building yet another runway? Why should I bother to bring my bags in when our recycled stuff is lying in a mountain of rubbish because China doesn't want it any more? Why? Give me one good reason – why?' says this rather trying customer.

Another customer is buying a carrot cake with thick icing on the top.

'Why don't you have plastic bags for cakes?'

'I guess because we're trying to reduce the number of plastic bags that customers use.'

'Well, you should have them. Look, if I put my cake in one of your bags, it will topple and all that good icing will just go to waste. M&S do them, after all.'

'They do indeed, but then you have to pay for them.'

There are two other colleagues on baskets with me – David and Magda. They're complaining about the supermarket's customer service policy.

'When I go shopping I just put my head down and get out of there as quickly as possible. I can't be bothered to have a chat,' says David.

An hour or so into our shift, we all notice that Magda is having an observation. It's not exactly surreptitious. The manager stands right behind her and watches her for a good five minutes or so. Not surprisingly, she passes. We all note that she does exactly the same with two other Cogs.

A salesman from Honda cars tells me the car industry is very quiet but is not as bad as the papers would have us believe. 'But now is the time to pick up a bargain, and cars are dirt cheap. Peugeot are offering buy one, get one free at the moment. All people have to do is come down and barter – we're doing good offers.'

Betty drops by before the start of her shift and chats amiably with the Cog next to me. If I don't get to join in, I certainly get to eavesdrop and learn all about the relationship, the work and the domestic arrangements – she is part of a mother-daughter Cog team. I suddenly make an unexpected error during a transaction and turn to ask her for some help.

'No can do, my shift hasn't started yet.' Fortunately, I figure it out.

It's quiet so the Cogs are up to mischief. Some of the younger ones giggle unkindly about a customer they suspect of having had a sex change. After a little while I'm taken off the basket till and asked to tidy Red Nose Day boxes. They are full of red balls that squeal, hang off key-rings or have bespectacled faces with gritted teeth. This last one looks almost exactly like me following a dressing down by a customer, so I promise to buy myself one at the end of my shift. When I return to my till twenty minutes later, Ariana is now on baskets with me.

'Don't forget to ask for your break, otherwise you'll lose it,' she tells me. 'Sometimes they just forget about me – I can't tell you the number of times I've lost my break.'

I've been on shift for four and a half hours without a break. When Ayesha passes by I ask if I can get a break. She looks at her watch and reluctantly says, 'Take a quick fifteen minutes.'

I'm entitled to twenty and after hours spent on the tills every minute counts. Just before I head up Molly comes to take some money from my till. It's something to do with a refund at the customer service desk. She gives her customer a large refund and discovers minutes after he leaves that he was pulling a scam. It's the second time in a couple of weeks that she's made the wrong call. Another Cog tells me, 'They're not happy with Molly.'

When I get back after my break, my chair has disappeared. Magda admits pinching it after Ariana nabbed hers. It's like musical chairs around here. Fruit-and-Veg Bloke walks past the till twice today and I give him the cold shoulder both times now that I'm on to his steal-a-hug scam.

My day-dreaming is interrupted by a man who buys a pregnancy test. It's the only thing in his basket and I'm desperate to ask him one simple question, but there are times when a Cog needs to keep her mouth shut, and this is one. The remainder of my shift is spent messing around with Magda. She's seventeen so always has teenage games up her sleeve. I'm pubescent of mind so enjoy these time-killing exercises. She asks all our customers to guess my age. Customer after customer has me down as a medical student. I suspect this has less to do with my brain power and more to do with the fact that I'm brown and wear glasses.

I see Adam as I'm about to leave the store. He started a few months before me after losing his job in the city. Having spent most of his twenties and early thirties working in middle management, he is far too qualified to be doing the menial tasks I often catch him doing. He's been long convinced that the store has much bigger plans for him. 'I reckon they're thinking they could train me up in different departments so that they can move me upwards as soon as a position is available.' Today he's wandering around in circles in the kids' clothing aisle with a woman's top in his hands. 'Adam, that's a blouse, not a dress,' I say, showing him the label. 'It's a size 12, not age 12.' Every time I see him, he's working in a different part of the store. He's quickly becoming a jack of all trades. Clothing is his latest home, although by his own admission he's certainly no master of it.

I take my shopping to Sonia's till.

'That's £77 please.'

'Should I do what our customers do and go, "Ohmigod, how did that happen?"' I joke, digging into my wallet for my credit card. As I'm tittering to myself, she launches into a full-blown tirade.

'I know! They are so stupid. Why don't they just watch what they're spending? Like it's our fault they couldn't control themselves. It's your money, you control it. No one's forcing you to spend it – it's up to you, you idiot!' It's harsh and she's had a long day, but I know what she means.

As I drive home, there's a news item on the radio about how some supermarkets docked the pay of staff who couldn't make it in to work because of the snow.

Saturday, 7 February 2009

I ask my first customer about how his week has been.

'Terrible, I've been laid off.'

I stop scanning immediately. 'God, how did that happen?'

'I mend machines for the building business and work has just quietened down. It's all I've been doing for the last six years and now I've been laid off, just like that.'

'That's dreadful. So what are you going to do?'

'I might be after your job next.'

'Well, you know retail is where it's at,' I say, smiling – but not in a smug way, I don't think.

'I wouldn't want to work in retail, there's no money in it!' he snaps.

He listens tensely as I offer what I hope is advice with some sympathy thrown in. The more I hear of someone's redundancy worries, the more incompetent I've become at handling them. Platitudes flow easily today but they don't go down well at all. He seems irritated that he revealed his financial despair to me.

If nothing else the buzz around the Basics range in the store should have brought a little smile to his face. It's a big hit with the customers. Two ladies at my till discuss the Basics frozen mixed fruit pack. Before I know it, 'Lynne' and 'Pam' have exchanged numbers, promising to compare reviews on the product. It could only happen in a supermarket.

It's a Saturday so trolleys are full to the brim. I see customers struggling with the supermarket version of Murphy's Law (once all the shopping has been paid for and packed into plastic bags it doesn't fit back into the trolley) and they get annoyed with their own grocery shopping.

I've learnt a lot about myself since working here. I definitely like rules – in a place like this I'd be lost without them. One customer comes to the till without any plastic bags and just one granny trolley (also known as a granny cart, shopping bag on wheels, wheelie trolley, wheelie shopper). 'Can you count this as four bags please?'

'You don't actually have four bags though, you only have one …' I look over the counter trying to decide how to describe the tartan box on wheels '… one of those.'

'Yes, but if I didn't have it, I'd be using four of your bags.'

'Right.'

'And I'm not, I'm using one of my own.'

'So I'll give you one Nectar point then.'

'Yes, but technically it's like me bringing in four bags.'

'But you didn't actually bring in four bags.'

Why am I arguing about this?

'Yes, but this much shopping would have required four bags.'

'If you only bring in one bag – I can only give you one point.'

'So you're not going to give me four points, even though I'd need four bags to take this home?'

'No, because you only have one bag.'

'Job's-worth,' he finally mutters under his breath. I cannot disagree – and I'm not sure what possessed me.

A couple in their thirties have their ten-month-old baby *and* their bags. The wife, who is from Finland, tells me she never forgets her bags. 'Where I come from, there was never a time when I didn't have to take my bags to the supermarket. It's just a way of life there, ever since I was young. It's a habit. Just like I always remember my phone and purse, I remember my bags.'

One customer's bill comes to £20.12. I cannot resist the game of the bored Cog, so I say, 'That'll be 20.12, like the Olympics, please.' At first she looks blank and then: 'Yes, yes. Don't we all know it, too? That's all this government cares about. Not the recession, not the fact that people are losing their jobs or the fact my shopping is so expensive now, but just the ruddy Olympics.'

Marital matters rear their head at the till this afternoon and it makes for great entertainment. A woman with a brunette bob and two young kids asks if she can do a part payment for her bill. She pays £100 on the card and £15 in cash.

'My husband has placed a top limit on our weekly groceries of £100 since the credit crunch kicked in. But it's ridiculous, isn't it? Who can do the shopping for four people on just £400 a month? I've been telling him that it's not possible these days but he's very unrealistic.' If she can't convince him, she'll lie to him and pay the remainder in cash. Her French friend behind has no such budgetary restraints. She buys nothing but organic food. Her husband insists, so her entire shop is from the So Organic foods range and costs £166. She doesn't have a car of her own so is driven back by Mrs £100.

Shopping à deux leaves one couple in need of immediate Relate counselling. She's in charge of the selecting and he's in charge of the packing and paying. But he's not happy. Every item that I scan is met with a variety of expletives, lots of rolling of eyes and a myriad of sideway sneers. It comes to £154.73 and it's met, as expected, with a top-notch profanity.

A daughter snaps at her mum not once but twice for forgetting her Nectar card. Mum blushes and smiles awkwardly to hide the embarrassment. Another bites her mother's head off for not telling me she needs bags. A third grabs the purse out of elderly Mum's shaking hands and rolls eyes as she dips into it to pay. I quietly promise to pop into my mum's just to give her a cuddle.

A woman old enough to *be* my mother is reading about Jeremy Clarkson's apology for calling Gordon Brown a 'One-eyed Scottish idiot' in her paper. 'It's all a bit silly, isn't it? Ever since that Jonathan Ross and Brand man said those silly things, all these presenters are getting harassed. It's all a bit of a fuss about nothing and the media are going to town with it.'

'Yes, I think you're right, there has been a media frenzy,' I say. Buoyed by my response, she continues, 'Like that Carol Thatcher and the whole golliwog thing. That was really silly.

When I was little, we all used to collect those jam jars with the golliwogs on them and we loved them. So you know, that was an overreaction, sacking her just because she called that tennis player one, wasn't it? What's offensive about that?'

And so I say nothing.

Richard is staring at me from a ten-yard distance and he couldn't have chosen a more inopportune time to be observing me: the chap who has just arrived at my till is one tough customer. He throws his shopping on to the belt. Moves swiftly to the packing side of my till. No eye contact. Bags open in rapid succession. I smile and say hello. He gives me a quarter of a smile. I ask how he is. 'Fine,' comes the short, sharp response. I scan. Ask if he's had a good week. 'Fine.' 'Plans for the weekend?' 'None.' Lots of speedy packing. 'This looks good,' I say, picking up chocolate cake. An eighth of a smile – it's getting worse. 'Is it for you and yours to gorge on?' A nod, no more. Blood from a stone. I look up, Richard is still watching. Rethink strategy. 'You're in a hurry, aren't you?' Half a smile. 'I won't hold you up with my feeble small talk.' A full grin, teeth showing. Eureka! 'I know – it must be dull, listening to me drone on and on.' And then … more than one word.

'No, I'm sorry, it's the football.'

'Well, in that case I won't take it personally.'

'No, please, you mustn't.'

He pays and races out. Richard has turned his attention to another Cog. Mission accomplished.

I've got four under-18 Cogs placed around me and they need me to authorise their alcohol-buying customers. Grace is one of these Cogs. After a few minutes she's removed from her till by a supervisor and told to stand behind Jane and observe her.

'What are you doing here, Grace?' I whisper to her over my shoulder.

'I don't know, I've just been told to watch and learn from Jane.'

So what does she learn from Jane?

Jane talks about her boyfriend. A lot. She talks about being dumped. A lot. She asks one customer, 'Why are you lot all such bastards?' The thirty-something man in a suit and tie is not often asked this question by a sixteen-year-old and he smiles uneasily. She reveals details of the act of being dumped. It involved a text message sent by boyfriend, followed by several frantic phone calls from Jane. It's highly inappropriate, but in terms of entertainment value – it's worth all the cash in my till.

Ayesha interrupts.

'It's good you're chatting, but you need to quieten down. You're too noisy. We can hear you all over the store and customers will get irate.'

'No, no – she's fine. She's not noisy at all,' says the thirty-something bloke, now starting to settle into the role of Agony Uncle. Ayesha's out of line; she should have reprimanded her privately – now they both look foolish. With reddening cheeks, Ayesha turns her attention to me.

'How long has this fish been here?' she snarls, picking up the piece of salmon beside my till.

'A customer left it behind about forty-five minutes ago.'

'Why didn't you say anything? It'll have to be thrown away now,' she barks.

'I told Samantha; she said she'd come back for it but never did.'

'Well, you should have called us again.' And with that Ayesha storms off.

Jane continues her unsuitable till chit-chat with the next few customers. Susie stops by to remind Grace and Jane not to start gossiping together. She fails to notice that Grace is but a mere spectator in Jane's Shakespearean melodrama. Jane's eyes are still sore from the crying she's been doing this morning. I know this because she tells everyone who asks. Ten minutes later Jane is sent to Richard's office. Grace and I decide her personal crisis has landed her in trouble. When she emerges, she tells me she was being observed and was told she's doing really well. Thankfully, after a full hour of watching Jane, Grace seems to have learnt nothing. Next time, I'm coming loaded with all the teen angst I can muster up from yesteryear.

It's 5.30 and the end of my shift, but yet again I'm still serving. Ayesha arrives with her *Closed Checkout* sign at exactly 5.30. At that precise moment a customer pulls up with an enormous shopping trolley. Ayesha looks at me and shrugs her shoulders.

Rebecca comes looking for me fifteen minutes later, jacket on, bag in hand.

'What are you still doing here?' she shrieks. 'What time do you finish?'

'Fifteen minutes ago.'

'Oh goodness, you must have wanted to kill me,' says the customer I'm serving.

'Yes … No, I'm kidding. It's not your fault. The sign should have gone up earlier.' And then I add unprofessionally, 'Otherwise we're just working for free.'

'It's the way it is with these big companies,' she says sympathetically.

'Yes. We do all the hard work and they get all the money,' I say, quoting another Cog from earlier in the month.

Friday, 13 February 2009

Richard has granted me the unpaid leave I wanted next month. Whatever I think about this place, he is a premium supermarket kick-butt brand. And I know I'm not the only one who thinks so.

I'm early, so I stroll into the canteen to get a cup of tea. It's just after the lunch hour so there are several uncleaned tables piled high with empty Coke cans, coffee cups and crisp packets. The large-screen television in the corner is blasting its usual dose of *News 24* and a couple of my colleagues are strewn on the sofa gazing lazily at it. At one table in the corner there are a number of Cogs alongside staff from other departments having their lunch. I consider sitting myself down with them but decide against it. Two of them smile at me but don't invite me over. I'm sipping my tea and flicking through a magazine when Lesley comes over.

'How's your dentistry course going, darling?'

I don't correct her. 'It's going fine, thank you.'

She asks after my kids, saying, 'You're like me, you had them young.'

Again, I'm economical with the truth.

'It must be tough; working, studying and raising kids,' she ploughs on. 'I've always wanted to do an Open University course in counselling but just never did it and now my daughter is twenty-one. She works here actually, her name's Kelly, do you know her?'

I shake my head.

'She studied criminal law at college. She wants to be a lawyer, but you know what it's like at the moment. I'm proud of her whatever she does. But I wish I had done something else apart from this when she was growing up. Now, it's probably going to be really expensive ... How much do you think it will be?'

'I really don't know, I'm afraid. But if it's what you want to do, go for it – it's never too late.'

'I could probably afford about £500 a year, but any more than that and my husband would go off his rocker.'

I smile. 'How long have you been married?'

'Twenty-three years. We met when I was twenty-two.' Twenty-three years married, eleven years in this place – no wonder she needs time for herself.

It's the Valentine's weekend and so, in typically unoriginal Cog style, I make it my opening gambit. The customers I don't waste it on are easy to spot: a basket with one giant chocolate bar, a rom-com DVD or two and usually a magazine with Jennifer Aniston on the front cover. Needless to say they don't have any plans for the weekend. As for the couples – they buy mussels with butter cream, chocolate cheesecake and a bottle of red wine. One chap also throws in flowers, a box of chocolates, Taste the Difference vegetables, ready-made salad and a pretty blouse. It costs him just over £30.

'It's my credit-crunch friendly Valentine's night-in.'

Most men are actually buying their Valentine cards while wife is in tow. I scan the card and then the wife picks it up and drops it in the bag without a word. One customer with two boys buys his Valentine's card for his wife and absent-mindedly passes it to her to put in the bag. She looks at it, rolls her eyes and says, 'How romantic!' He tells me he's 'making the effort tonight and cooking'. His cooking involves popping the ready-made Thai meals into the microwave. I tell him the total and he takes his card out.

'Here you go,' he says, handing it over to me.

'No, I don't need it. Just shove it up there,' I say, pointing to the pin-pad.

'Ooh, you've made me blush,' he wisecracks.

Deep sigh.

Dear Male Customer,

Ever since I was a teenager, you've been a taxing breed. Now you are tougher than ever.

The worst of you congregate around the basket tills so I give that the wide berth as much as I can. Those of you that do come to the trolley tills are a mixed bunch and, if I'm fair, I can't complain about you all. Some of you are actually really terrific and indulge my nonsensical musings. But I tolerate a lot from you in return. Monosyllabic responses, grubby hands, schoolboy humour and being talked at endlessly. But there's one thing I really do mind and, trust me, if there was a way around it, I'd have found it.

Your credit card goes in the pin-pad. End of story. That's what I mean when I say, *Put it up there, pop it in, shove it in, push it in …*

It's all cracking stuff, admittedly. But, surprising as it is, talking about sex in the middle of the afternoon with a complete stranger with whom I've shared nothing but the Nectar card you've just handed me doesn't do it for me.

So can you just stop? Now.

Yours,

A. Cog

After the school run, the half-term crowd piles in. They're buying extra juice, sweets, chocolates and crisps. Those without the kids – aunties, uncles and grandparents – are all stocking up for the children coming to stay. And there are more teachers in the queues than at an NUT conference. Everyone has forgotten their plastic bags – in the car. I'm quite sure that there are more plastic bags in the car park than there are in here. I serve Mrs £100 with her six-year-old in tow. Her shop this week is £108.

'You're over budget, I'm afraid. It's £108.'

'God, is it really? I haven't even done my weekend shopping yet.' There is pure terror in her eyes.

'Really? What do you want to do?'

'Well, um … er … I know – I'll pay for the Barbie doll on my card. And I'll just have to see if I can pull it off without him noticing. I lied last week, you know.' And off she goes, home to her unsuspecting husband with the dwindling bank account.

Newspapers coming through my till are reporting that the number of people out of work increased by 146,000 in the last three months to December and is now at 1.97 million – the highest figure for twelve years. Unemployment has increased by 369,000 over the past year and is expected to top 3 million during this recession. I'm seeing evidence of this every day. Just last week, a customer came to my till with a sandwich and a drink. He had tears in his eyes and I asked him if he was OK. He told me he had just lost his job. I commiserated, but he didn't want to talk. Today, a woman who used to do the deliveries for a local florist tells me she lost her job last week.

'They don't need me any more because deliveries are down and the boss is doing it all now.' Her shop totals almost £100.

'I don't know how I'm going to live on £60 Jobseeker's Allowance while doing a £120 grocery shop every week. It just doesn't add up.' She delves into her purse for her credit card. And then leans forward and whispers: 'Are there any vacancies here?'

'I don't know actually. If you have access to the internet, then check there.'

'I've been doing that and popping in and out of shops, but there's just nothing around at the moment. I'm feeling pretty desperate about it all already.' While she's praying for a new job, another customer is hoping to lose hers. She's been working at the Halifax for ten years. 'Right now, there are no redundancies, but there will be in a year's time. I'm absolutely desperate for it because, with my bonus, I'd get a nice little pay-off.'

'And what will you do then?'

'I want to go into teaching and mentoring disadvantaged kids – that's where my heart lies.'

'Well, I can't imagine I'll be saying this often, but I'll keep my fingers crossed you lose your job.'

One woman shows me the pictures in her paper of people queuing around the corner for jobs at London Zoo. And I get another recipe from an elderly couple who are buying soup ingredients for their Valentine's dinner:

Broccoli and Stilton. Fry the onions with celery, sweet potatoes and broccoli. Simmer with several bowls of water with a bag of bouquet garni, vegetable stock and season well. Purée with the melted Stilton cheese.

Katherine is sitting at the adjacent till and she points to her daughter at the till captain's post. Keeping it in the family again on the tills. Katherine's daughter Helen is a sweet-natured, courteous supervisor who always closes tills on time and is never snappy.

An hour before the end of my shift, Katherine leaves and Edith nips into her place. She's usually on baskets but has been freed to sit on trolley tills for what she, unsurprisingly, sees as a pleasant change. We catch up between customers and she tells me about her six kids between the ages of one and sixteen. She works here two full days a week and is studying Economics at university. Nicola Horlick has nothing on her. She is the ultimate super-mum.

Just before the end of my shift I see Michelle. She is in on a day off – again. She pops over with her adorable little girls. She looks happier than the last time I saw her and far younger than her forty-something years. Her shoulder-length blonde hair looks freshly blow-dried and she has on a full face of make-up.

'I never see you any more,' she says.

'Yes, I was thinking that. Have you been sick?'

'No, maybe it's because of your hours.'

That old chestnut again.

'Yes, yes it's probably that.'

'What hours do you do now?'

'Fridays and Saturdays. Six hours each day.'

'That's really good. How did you get it again?'

She no longer disguises her shift-envy.

'I had to change because of my kids – my mother was struggling to look after them.'

Edith joins in. 'Did Richard change it for you then?'

'Yes.'

'So, how you finding it?' asks Michelle.

'It's OK. But it's long. Four hours is a quick turnaround, but if you include the travel time and back, the longer shift feels like a full day.'

'Yes,' they both mutter in agreement.

'There's no such thing as the perfect shift – it's just what works for your life,' says a very sensible Edith.

* * *

118

Seconds to go before the end of my shift and Betty is the bearer of bad news. 'I'm not closing your till – relief is on its way,' she says breezily as she passes by. Huge trolleys are coming my way so I figure if I take my time with the first customer then hopefully relief will be here just as I'm finishing up.

6.35 there's still no relief.

6.40. No relief.

I look up at 6.43, annoyed and ready to throw down the towel. A closing sign has been slipped in quietly at the end of my till while I wasn't looking. I've been duped – again.

Rebecca has come in to do some overtime and is wearing a beautiful red dress in aid of Red Nose Day.

'Hey, lady in red, how are you doing?'

'I feel like dog-poo. Not only did I not get a single Valentine's card but I've just got a D on an essay.'

'Well, you look stunning, so if nothing else I'm sure you'll pull.' And with that I race out into the car park to get home to my own Valentine.

Saturday, 14 February 2009

Richard is handing out the till keys this afternoon while crooning about his Cogs. 'All my new girls are lovely. They're all my princesses.' Only he can pull off a line this cheesy.'

Among the newer Cogs there is unrest. Rebecca, Magda and Michelle are all talking about the twelve-week probationary period. None of us knows yet if we are being kept on. I've figured that no news is good news, but no one's listening. I think they're expecting a graduation ceremony and then perhaps a crown of some kind.

At Grace's till opposite me two shoppers are arguing over the time that one of them is taking. Grace is in the thick of it.

'Calm down,' shouts the customer she's serving. 'There's a problem on my receipt and it's not her fault or mine.'

'Well, just hurry up, will you?'

Grace looks over her shoulder nervously for a supervisor.

'Can you just calm down so she can sort it out. Just stop shouting,' hollers the customer that Grace is serving.

'You stop shouting,' bellows the waiting shopper.

Supermarket wars rock – they're the highlight of my day. There is a long wait and then Susie arrives and takes one of the shouting customers away. Grace looks like she's survived – just about.

Mums and their kids are in. Some with two and others with three. I read an article today that declared that couples need to opt for recession-friendly family planning. So I gauge opinion.

'Once you've got the cost of two, the cost of three is not that much more.'

'I've got two boys and I'd love to have a third child. But it's going to be too expensive during this recession and I can't afford to be off on maternity leave now.'

'Two is better than three, definitely. The financial cost of two is enough as it is – computer games, DVDs, Nintendos, etc.'

'With just my two kids I get free time to myself. I play tennis, I have coffee and don't have to worry about money. Spare cash goes on me, not a third little thing crawling around. Although, I have to tell you, if my husband had been up for it I would have gone for it in a heartbeat. But then I see women at the school gates with a third child in the pram and I just feel sorry for them and their bank account.' She changes her mind so many times, I lose count.

* * *

Hayley sends me on my break a highly considerate three hours in. I bump into Adil and he's unhappy about his hours. Like all the other students, he doesn't get enough time to study but needs the money. I tell him to threaten to leave; it may just do the trick. While enjoying a quiet coffee and chocolate bar, I start thinking ahead to when *I* will leave.

Dear Supermarket Boss,

   I've only been here just over three months but it's been an eye opener. Your workers are fine people. Can I just make some requests for them based on what I've learnt so far?

1. Get them proper chairs. Hunchback of Notre Dame is not a good look.
2. Adjust the hours for students so they don't flunk all their exams and spend the rest of their days here – unless that's your grand plan.
3. I don't care much for bonuses myself, but could you be more generous with them? A couple of extra hundred pounds won't mean anything to you but would make a world of difference to a Cog.
4. Your profits are increasing every day. How's about paying them slightly more than a pitiful £6.30 an hour? Most of them blow that straight after their shift while doing their shopping in your store anyway, so it makes good business sense; the more money they have, the more they'll spend in here.
5. Don't be so strict on the no-chatting-to-other-colleagues rule. When they are serving a customer, admittedly it's not on. But when it's quiet, let them make friends. Otherwise they will curl up and die like the vegetables in the waste crate at the back of your warehouse.

6. Finally, as soon as their shift ends, send them home. I bet they will reward you with greater loyalty.

Yours,
A. Cog

Just before the end of my shift, Susie offers me overtime, *again*. I turn it down *again*. And then Hayley closes my till ten minutes early. I can barely believe it. I *LOVE* her. Rebecca and I drive home together and we talk D grades, Valentine's Day dateless-ness, studying, working, mothering. She's not doing well. On the upside, she's knocking the competition sideways with her customer service.

I switch the radio on after she gets out and I'm told that white-collar jobs will face the biggest cuts during this recession – and that this downturn will be deeper and larger than any of us expect.

Tuesday, 17 February 2009

It's my day off, but I pop into my local Sainsbury's and, after being served at the checkouts by a man in his sixties, I stop by customer service and give his name. She writes it down and I see a star shine just for him. I'm going to start doing this on a regular basis; it's the least my fellow Cogs deserve.

Friday, 20 February 2009

Today's headlines are too dismal to dwell on: an increase in repossessions and the deputy governor of the Bank of England thinks that we're headed for a ten-year recession, making it the worst this country has seen for sixty years.

I pop into the canteen for a quick coffee before my shift and Adam is there, drowning in paperwork. He's being moved around the store but like any former professional he's turning the art of the most menial of tasks into a masterpiece. His key aim is to make himself indispensable. Now he's on newspapers and magazines. He has to make sure they're on the shelf by the time the shop opens at 7 a.m. Today he has one quibble:

'Like everything at Sainsbury's, the worst part about the job is the customers. It makes perfect sense, doesn't it, to pick up a magazine from one place and dump it at the opposite end, leaving a poor sucker like me to silently scream NOOOOO?'

Adam is so terrified of losing this job that he's making himself as flexible as possible – all the positive talk and mock cynicism is a cover-up for the fear of being out of work again. He is too clever to be rearranging pet-lovers' magazines.

When I get down to the tills, I'm sent to the baskets. But the fear has faded. I realise that here, time flies. Sitting and chatting with fellow Cogs means that it is never dull. I notice one of the young newbies is being trained up on customer service by Molly, and she looks terrified. Half an hour later she ends her shift and comes to the basket tills with her shopping. I eavesdrop on her conversation with the older Cog serving her.

'How you finding it, love?'

'It's all right, a bit scary though.'

'Yes, some of the customers can be quite difficult there. They'll buy a magazine and then bring it back for a refund half an hour later. They're trying it on, and you've got to be quite tough.'

'I can imagine that,' she says, screwing up her face.

'Don't let me put you off, though.'

'No, you're not,' she says unconvincingly, 'but it's true I'm sure it's not the best place to work. And I can tell it can get a bit frantic over there.'

Within the same hour Molly from customer service pops over during her break.

'How's it going today?' I ask.

'I've been training people up for customer service, but I just don't think they've put the right kind forward. They're training them up all wrong. You really have to be the kind of person that can stand up for yourself. And to be honest, they're not.' Molly is a tough cookie, but I've seen her shed tears a number of times since I've been here.

It's heaving in the store today and the first two hours of my shift are chaos. Parents are pouring in with their kids and there is nothing but half-term stress and tension in the air; bickering, squabbling, snapping and much wrangling. Every transaction ends with a parent asking me to take something out of the basket because 'I've no idea how that ended up in there. I did say "No"', followed by an irritated glance at the child beside them. Other kids are luckier and there is some toy purchasing. One woman buys a toy fitness centre for her daughter and it costs just under a tenner.

'I'm buying it to keep her busy over the next few days. It'll keep her out of my hair and, let's face it, it's dirt cheap. In my day, toys like that cost a small fortune. I suppose that's why all our homes are bursting at the seams with cheap plastic toys.'

Hayley comes over with an assessment form for me to fill in with my feedback about working here. I bite the bullet. I complain about absent and broken chairs and having to stay extra minutes at the end of my shift. I also make sure I mention my colleagues' supportiveness and comment on my growing confidence in handling customers. Being as supremely paranoid as I have now become, I spend the rest of the afternoon convinced that the supervisors are discussing my notes. And I feel grossly unjust to Hayley, who always takes me off early and never needs reminding about my break.

Katherine starts her shift an hour after me and sits beside me at the checkouts. Her favourite uncle is sick so Richard has given her some time off so she can spend it with him. We have a little rave about Richard, but Katherine is herself a supermarket star. Of all the Cogs that work here – and most of them are pretty good with customers – she is one of the best. She treats every customer like her first, charms the grumbling ones, and is sparkling and animated company no matter how slowly time passes. Across from us on customer service is Liza. She's a twenty-year-old single mum to a lovely, articulate four-year-old boy. She's studying graphic design at college, working here a few days a week while raising her little boy. This supermarket is sitting on the shoulders of hundreds of mums, young and old alike. Today I watch her tackle every customer with tact, grace and confidence. It's hard to believe she's only twenty.

I serve a customer working at a car auction site around the corner. 'If you read the papers, everyone's going on and on about the car business being dead, but we are busier than ever. Fortunately for all of us, it hasn't got quiet at all.' Right behind her is an ex-Morgan Stanley employee. He lost his job a year ago. 'I've got really down about how much time and effort I've put into looking for work. But there are thousands, just thousands, applying for a single job. The most depressing thing is you often don't even hear back from them … You work all your life, pay your taxes, put in your hours, and for what? Nothing.' He tells me his wife is supporting them both, but it's a struggle. 'I've decided to stop stressing about it because it was starting to drive me crazy. Now I just keep an eagle eye on what I'm spending.'

His shopping costs him £28.89. The woman behind him is listening in and after he leaves she shares her story.

'I lost my job this time last year too. I tried to see it as a positive thing and started calling it early retirement. But you know, after a year of being out of work, it's really hard. I can't bear to call myself unemployed.'

We're interrupted by a loud smash behind her. A young man carrying too many groceries in his arms drops two bottles on the floor. There is cider and fabric conditioner all over his suit and a puddle is growing at his feet. The bittersweet smell quickly fills the air. He's mortified but runs back down the store, half-drenched, to pick up replacements.

While the mess is being cleaned up, Hayley tells me to go on my break. As I'm heading off, I bump into Lesley. I say a quick hello even though she wants to stop for a chat. I only have twenty minutes for my break and, if I stop to chat to her, I won't have time to eat my lunch. I walk into the locker room and am met by the sight of Betty sprawled on a chair talking to her husband on the phone. They are dissecting their relationship and she continues to do this loudly despite the fact that I can hear every word.

I wolf down my food – I'm famished because my shift starts just before lunch and I have to wait until the late afternoon to eat. I wonder what the others do on this shift pattern. Richard told me that he prefers to spread the twelve-hour shifts over three days rather than two, and I think it's because it's more cost-efficient for them. There are no breaks in a four-hour shift, while those who do it over two six-hour days take a twenty-minute break each day. That means the supermarket loses forty minutes if they spread the hours over only two days. It's all above board, but seems a little unethical.

When I return, it's gone very quiet. So I pick up the green folder with information about Sainsbury's various initiatives that sits by the basket tills and read about Active School vouchers. Samantha, the Queen-bee of the till captains, passes by and asks me what I'm reading. I show her and she says, 'OK, but don't read that if a customer wants serving.' She passes by again ten minutes later and there are still no customers around. She makes it clear that she's not impressed that I am still reading it, so I quietly put it back and return to twiddling my thumbs.

Dear Supervisor,

Idle hands make light work. That's why you crack the whip every time it's quiet at the tills. You don't want us to sit around on our half-wrecked chairs doing nothing in between serving customers. That's why you take us off and send us to pick up hangers, security tags, do some reverse shopping and stack a couple of shelves. But look – I've tidied the invisible mess around my till. I've put some more plastic bags out. I've got a cloth and spray and done some dutiful cleaning of the checkout. There is NOTHING left to do. So I'm reading about Sainsbury's so I don't look like a total twit next time a customer asks me 'What kind of equipment can a school buy with these vouchers' and 'How long do you run this scheme for?'

Yours,

A. Cog

One customer who is a friend to Cogs everywhere tells me she witnessed a woman shouting at a checkout girl in the store two weeks ago.

'Your colleague was asked to close the till and take a trolley upstairs to the staff room and then head off for a break. So she started to do that and this customer just started yelling at her. I couldn't believe it. The poor girl went red from her toes to her forehead and just caved in and served her. Disgusting behaviour – I can't believe people can come to a supermarket and talk to staff like that.'

'It's one of the perks of the job,' I tell her.

A man in a neon yellow jacket puts two packets of white Maltesers down on the conveyor belt. 'Why is maple syrup now £5 a bottle?' he demands.

'Is it?'

'Yes, and it definitely wasn't that much last time I bought it. What's going on?'

'I couldn't tell you,' I lie. *It's called inflation*, I say silently.

'We wanted it for pancakes for the kids tomorrow. Well, they're just going to have Nutella instead.'

Sonia is behind me and I try desperately to listen in but sadly can't hear her customer service spiel today. She complains frequently that time is dragging. Like all Cogs here, she places her pen in front of her on the till screen where the timer is. It's at the bottom of the screen, in line with a Cog's direct eye level, so if there is no pen there, you can't help but clock-watch. It's the most painful way to spend your shift.

Magda is also with us on the baskets.

'I've come up with a plan to make the shift go quicker – I'm aiming to serve two hundred customers today.'

'That's a tough one. You're going to have to be super quick with them all to get through that many.'

'Well, I've done a hundred and forty-eight so far, so let's see.'

She can probably meet this target on baskets because we serve so many customers with just a few bits of shopping. And, *besides*, she's given me a new game to play. At that very moment Louisa approaches to pick up the reverse shopping.

'Yuck! Someone's left some beef here and it's been half eaten!' she announces, bouncing around in mock horror. Customers stare at her stunned – the girl is out of control.

A couple in their fifties are in chatty mood and are only at my till for two minutes. It's enough for them to tell me, unprompted, what they think about bankers who have lost their fortunes. 'They expect us to feel sorry for them because they've lost billions, when so many of us are losing jobs that only pay us the smaller part of five figures. They're having a laugh. I'd be very happy with a million pounds, very happy indeed, thank you very much.'

The *New Scientist* guy is back. He picks up his magazine to show me and grins when I catch his eye.

'How are you doing?'

'Rubbish. Hate me job.'

'What do you do?'

'I drive a van, do a bit of manual work. Been doing it for a year. It's boring, the work is shit. I hate it.'

'But people say you should feel lucky if you have a job right now,' I say.

'Probably about as lucky as you. Do you feel lucky?'

'Best I don't answer that. Why don't you do something else?'

'I've done it all – had my own business, was in the army, and for now it's this. No matter how much I hate it.'

'It sounds awful, but, hey, whatever happens you've always got the *New Scientist*.'

He grins broadly.

The end of my shift draws near and Betty comes over to tell me relief is on its way. Five minutes pass. Then ten minutes. I'm still serving customers and I can see Betty and Ayesha standing at the till captains' post. I wave at them and eventually Ayesha walks over.

'Why haven't you closed your till?'

'Because Betty told me relief was on its way.'

'Oh, right … OK … just … er … close up straight away, darling, all right?'

I walk to the supervisors' post and give the key back. Ayesha is apologetic and tells me that relief was sent to a trolley till instead. I have again given the supermarket fifteen extra minutes of my time. Based on my experience, it feels like this supermarket alone could be getting several extra hours of unpaid labour from its Cogs every single day. As I leave, I hear a roll call for till-trained staff to head to checkouts. A number of names are called out including Adil. I see him scanning prices on the floor and go over to tease him.

'Are you pretending to be deaf, Adil?'

'Pardon? Can't hear you.' He grins.

'Skiving, huh?'

'Fortunately, I have to finish this, so I have a water-tight excuse.'

Checkout guys hate the tills. I hear that one colleague has just quit after finding himself repeatedly on checkout duty. It's just not a job for the boys.

Saturday, 21 February 2009

I walk through the double doors and all of my senses are immediately hijacked. Babies are screaming in trolleys that clank loudly as they are wheeled down the aisles. The children, ladies and men's clothes are a multi-coloured eyesore with huge signs hanging from the ceiling signalling 25 per cent off. There is a scrum of greedy shoppers pushing and shoving, in spite of the biggest economic crisis of our time. I walk past the vegetables and the scent of the spring onion bulbs being loaded on to the shelves fills the air. As I pass the dairy aisle, I'm offered a sample of cheese which I promptly pop into my mouth – it's so strong my lips start to tingle.

I watch a young couple gush over their baby in the shopping trolley; Dad teases her by taking the dummy out of her mouth and placing it back in again. Mum smiles but tries to draw proceedings to an end. A boy rolls a red nose by my feet and I step over it to avoid trapping his little fingers. A customer is standing right by the entrance to the back of the store engrossed in a newspaper headlining the wedding preparations for a cancer-suffering Jade Goody. I ask him to move aside and he gives me a hostile stare. It's a typical Saturday afternoon.

I have five minutes before my shift so I stop in the canteen and have a coffee. A group of managers sitting nearby are congratulating another on his newborn baby and exchanging tips on baby-rearing. When I walk across the shop floor to the checkouts, I'm stopped by a woman looking for our make-up range. A moment later I'm stopped again: a mother looking for size-5 Huggies nappies; there are none left on the shelf. 'Can you check at the back, please?' she asks. I look around frantically for another assistant and a man suddenly grabs my arm; he wants razors. I ask each one to wait where they are and tell them I'll be right back. I go to Hayley and tell her I'll be a few minutes. I then get the customer looking for make-up and lead her to the cosmetics aisle. Next it's on to razors before hunting down the nappies. It takes a good ten minutes and a lot of searching for products as well as errant customers. Eventually I'm free to get to the tills, and I feel quite stressed. I am someone else's relief today and I apologise profusely to the Cog on Till 7. She's now ending her shift an unpaid fifteen minutes late and I'm fuming on her behalf although she is nice enough about it. 'It's been a long morning. I'm desperate to get out of here. It's not your fault

– it just happens all the time, I never get off on time. And if you say anything, they'll just say, "It's the nature of the beast."'

I serve a shop-floor assistant I don't know too well. I've seen her around, but her shift pattern is different to mine. She's worked here nine years. And like others before her, she sighs when I ask her how things have changed. 'There's more pressure to perform. We never had observations and assessments before, and now we have them all the time. It's a bit much when all you want is to come in, do the job and go home.'

Two forty-something sisters with a teenage daughter are speaking fluent French and have a trolley full of clothes with them. Mum and daughter are here on a week-long trip from France. 'The euro is so strong and your supermarkets are great. Even if it wasn't for the weak pound, your supermarkets are still a bargain compared to ours.' A mum and her heavily pregnant daughter have bought out Sainsbury's entire baby range in bulk: cotton wool, nappies, wipes, anti-rash cream, baby oil bottles, baby wash, cradle cap cream, gripe water, maternity pads, breast pads, bottles, baby milk.

'You've got every eventuality covered here,' I tell them.

'I'm going to have a credit-crunched maternity leave. And the deals are on now, so why not?' She pauses. 'I'm not paying for this, though. My mum's buying this for me now because I'm preparing for not having any money over the next year. I hope my job will still be there in a year, but you never know.'

One woman tells me she's now started to find the whole shopping experience stressful.

'From the wandering around looking for products that have moved yet again to the amount I end up spending. I'm really considering shopping online – at least I'll be able to control how much I spend then and not have to deal with the endless painful searching. The thing is though, I don't want my daughters to think that food comes from the internet. They need to know that farmers make it and then we select it …'

'How old are your girls?'

'Seven and ten. The irony is that they hate shopping here so much they refuse to come with me any more.'

A Greek couple in their late fifties want to use their gift card to pay. I check and there is nothing left on the card.

'Sorry, you don't seem to have anything left on the card.'

'Are you sure? I have lots on there. Check again.'

My screen tells me there is nothing. But I go through the act of checking again out of politeness.

'No, there is nothing. Sorry.'

'How can that be? There is definitely something on there – it can't be nothing.'

I pretend to check again just for the sake of it and then shrug my shoulders.

'Are you sure you haven't taken it off just now?'

WHAT???

'No, I haven't. If I had, it would have shown on your bill and it hasn't. You don't have anything on there, I'm afraid.'

'Are you sure?' she asks, looking at me suspiciously.

'Yes, I'm quite sure,' I say through gritted teeth.

'I think you have.' And she folds her arms.

'Look – I definitely haven't. Now, what would you like to do?'

'Hmm. It was there before we came to your till and it's not there now.'

'Look, if you just pay then I'll be able to show you that you have nothing left.'

They grunt and pay. I print off the gift-card receipt to prove my case. The woman continues to argue but her husband puts his hand on her shoulder and stops her. Eventually they leave.

* * *

I've started to notice that customers are now buying a lot more fresh vegetables, tinned food and fresh chicken and fish. There are fewer ready meals being bought, although people are buying lots of comfort food like ice cream. Some are still sharing their favourite recipes and the Basics range is starting to really take off. One woman is buying Basic mozzarella in bulk.

'Wow, you've got a lot of this stuff here,' I say, scanning twenty little packets.

'Oh yes! I love it. It's usually so expensive, but the Basics version is half the normal price.'

'Well, will you come back and tell me if it tastes just as good as the normal one?'

'Oh, definitely! You've got to save every penny in this climate, haven't you? What with jobs going every day. My best friend works in HR and she has to make fifty people redundant tomorrow and she hasn't been able to sleep for weeks. There are only four hundred people in the company, so that's a huge number gone – just like that –' And she clicks her fingers.

Saturday is also family day at the store – and it's not just fractious kids piling in. Grandma, grandpa, uncles and aunts are here on an outing. Today I meet four generations of one family – an eighty-something who pays the bill, with her son and grandson-in-law and her great granddaughter aged two. There are also many middle-aged men in the store today so there are pin-pad jokes galore. While all the middle-aged women instinctively hide the pad as they punch in their codes.

Dear Male but for the Most Part Female Customers,
    I know banks tell you to protect your pin, so you should. But when you're in a well-known supermarket, save yourself the trouble. Firstly, I can't see what your pin number is from where

I'm sitting, whether you cover it or not. And even if I could, you do after all take your card away at the end. Your receipt has too little information on it for me to carry out bank fraud on a massive scale. And frankly it makes you look ever so slightly paranoid. Worst of all, it ruins the cosy chat we've just had.

And apart from anything else, due to the slump, and your frenzied reaction when I asked you to pay, you're obviously broke.

Yours,

A. Cog

Connor, a twenty-three-year-old Cog, is sitting three tills down. He's not allowed to serve his family so his mum and sister come to my till. There are screaming babies and bickering couples all around us. Connor's mum tells me that when he was a baby he would save his biggest tantrums for when he got to the till. 'He hated coming to the supermarket as a child and I just find it hysterical that he works here now.'

'And he still hates it – so that makes it even more hysterical,' I tell her.

'Yes. He's always desperate to get out of here.' And she whispers, 'I bet you are, too, today.'

Not as much as the Cog behind me. She's had a really bad day. Customer after customer has given her a tough time, and she has remained resolutely silent. Her shift finishes at 4.30 and I notice that by the time the sign goes up she still has three customers with mammoth trolleys to serve. She doesn't leave for another twenty minutes. I resolve not to let this happen today, and at the end of my shift I start telling shoppers I'm closing, even though there is no relief and not a supervisor to be seen. The customers get irate, but I'm in the driving seat and it feels great.

Friday, 27 February 2009

My mother is sick and so there's no one to look after my kids. I don't want to let Richard down, but penalty points or no penalty points I have no choice. I call the absentee hotline and end up speaking to him directly; to my great relief he is sympathetic.

Saturday, 28 February 2009

Baskets again and Hayley asks me if everything is OK at home. After Richard, I love her the most. There is generally so little to like here that I no longer feel in halves.

It's very quiet on baskets today. There are too many of us and too few customers, so I come off to help Rachel stash bulbs on the shelf. We spend a long time staring at tiny numbers on the shelf, reading out barcodes and scanning them with machines. Rachel's face is lined with the many years she has spent decoding barcodes.

'I tidied this up this morning, went to help a customer for five minutes and when I came back it'd been turned upside down by shoppers rummaging for a bulb.'

She's desperate to have a moan about the supervisors on shift today.

'They're like a couple of sergeant majors,' she says as two supervisors pass by.

'They're just trying to prove themselves all the time – they're after their bonuses those two, they are,' whispers Caroline, a Cog who has just joined us.

'This isn't Barings. It's just a bleeding supermarket.' Then the conversation, as it often does here, shifts to the time and how many more hours we have to kill before we can go home. Another colleague suddenly appears.

'Have you lot seen the bloke who filled his trolley to the top with all the 2-for-1 teabags!' She is *livid*. 'I wanted to get a couple of them for my husband, and now they're all gone.'

'He's probably got a restaurant,' says Caroline.

'But it's not on, is it? What about the rest of us? They aren't all for him. It shouldn't be allowed.'

'They should make it illegal or put a limit on how many you can buy,' Rachel chimes in. 'The other day someone did it with the Coke – when they were on 2-for-1. I was well annoyed.'

'Look! Look! There he is.'

I turn away from my bulbs to see a man with a heaving trolley so full he is struggling to push it and he does indeed have a lot of teabags.

'And look, he's got all the Ribena, too. Ooh … I'm fuming, I am. It just isn't on.' The assistant walks away, narrowing her eyes at Teabag Man. We turn our attention back to the bulbs and Caroline and Rachel return to grumbling about the bulbs again before Richard interrupts.

'Oh, Richard, I'm really sorry about yesterday,' I splutter straight away. 'I know that must have been a real pain, letting you know a couple of hours before you were expecting me.'

'Oh, don't worry – it's OK. These things happen. Look, can you do some extra shifts next week in exchange for the unpaid leave you wanted?'

'Er, well … no, I can't.'

'Of course you can't. If your mum is ill, who's going to look after your kids? Don't worry, I'll find someone else.' And he turns away. There is a little drawer somewhere with my name on it; inside are all the favours that I owe him.

When I'm back at the till, it's still quiet. There are four of us sitting quietly watching the time pass. So Jenny and I play the age-guessing game – it's a favourite pastime here. I guess she is twenty-seven and she guesses I am twenty-four. We're both wrong. I'm older and she is only twenty-two. She's got a degree in business management but only just passed her exams, so she's here until she figures out her next move. 'There's no work out there, so for now I'm just here.' Like so many of the other graduates here. We're both bored and plead silently that passing supervisors will take us off. After months on the tills I'd give my right arm for some reverse shopping. Jenny is asked to come off and she spends the next four hours restocking chocolates and sweets at the tills.

Nelly is on the tills with us and it's soon time for her to go home. After a decade here, she's spectacularly rude to the supervisors, the Cogs and often the customers too. She is so fearless she shuts her till down five minutes early without asking. I watch as she confidently tucks her chair in, doesn't waste time saying goodbye to the rest of us and charges towards the till captains to return her key, unbothered by the fact that she is in fact clocking off a couple of minutes early. She's my hero.

At the baskets today are a couple with significant marital issues.

'That's £19.67, please.' I say.

The man in his fifties replies: 'I wish it was.'

'That's a fallacy,' says the wife.

'Women knew their place then.'

'I didn't.'

'That was the problem.'

'Still is.'

People are tired and in a rush. One woman hands me her library card instead of her credit card. Someone else gives me her driving licence, and several times a day I'm given a Tesco club card instead of the Nectar one. But it is mostly quiet and Hayley and Clare struggle to keep us busy. They don't take us off the tills but keep asking us to clean them. After the second bout with a spray and cloth, I can't fake it again.

Back to the rest of the newsletter and Richard has dedicated a full page to drumming home the importance of customer service. He's now trying the stick-and-carrot approach; threats about more observations and pats on the back for those who've been named by the mystery customer. OK so he's not perfect – well, he *is* a manager.

A lot of the customers who come to the basket tills often have DVDs with them – and these are being bought in bulk today. 'Why don't you just rent a film rather than buy one?'

'Because they are so cheap to buy these days, it almost costs the same. And I do like to watch my films several times.'

'Oh really? How many times?'

'Well I've watched *Mamma Mia* four times this month.'

A customer I serve with several DVDs in her basket tells me she has no recession worries on her mind. Her company are suppliers to Sainsbury's, 'so, for as long as you are in business, we are in business'. Not such positive talk from a woman still perspiring after a netball game. She tells me she is a personal trainer.

'It's gone very quiet. It's common knowledge, people just don't pay for personal trainers during recessions because it's a luxury. But I can't worry about it yet – I just have to keep going until it has all ground to a halt.'

Before I go home today I serve a beautician whose hours have been cut so she now works four days a week. 'The annoying thing is that people are still getting themselves waxed, getting their nails done and the rest of it, but our boss is using the recession as an excuse to make some cuts. The hair salon section has had cutbacks because people are colouring their hair at home now.'

'Yes, I've seen that – lots of people are buying home dye kits here,' I tell her.

'Well, that's probably why lots of salons are closing down. And also my customers have been telling me that they've been made redundant and stuff, but the thing is, for women, getting themselves down to the beauty salon is not a luxury, it's a necessity. Women need to look like women, no matter what the cost.'

'Your boss is probably making cuts because he thinks it might get rockier further down the road. Maybe he's planning for the long haul?'

'That's true, I suppose. But I've had enough now, so my boyfriend and I are heading off to Cyprus to try our luck there.' She tells me that her boyfriend has found a job in a kids' club at a big hotel and she will tout around for work in a spa hotel. She doesn't seem concerned that she hasn't tied a job down yet, but is keen to get away from here because the rent on her flat has gone up. 'In Cyprus, the rent on the villa we're hiring is about a quarter of what I've been paying here, but the salaries are more or less the same.'

A highly strung customer from my first few weeks interrupts my thoughts and throws down her shopping.

'How are you today?' I ask, knowing the answer full well.

'Really annoyed – you never have any food.'

'Oh, that's surprising,' I say, looking pointedly around the store that makes a fortune from selling the stuff.

'Every time I come, the shelves are empty.'

'What was missing?'

'No organic eggs, no organic butter, no organic bread, no organic milk. And I really need my eggs.'

'Did you ask anyone?' I dare to enquire.

'NO! I can't be bothered.'

'I'm sure if you did, they'd be able to find something for you.'

'No need now. I've written a letter of complaint to your manager and asked him if I should take my custom elsewhere.'

Rebecca and I get the bus home together today.

'I'm a real mug with customers. I let them put their shopping down even after they've put my till sign down,' she tells me.

'Why would you do that?'

'Because I don't want an argument. They can be so nasty sometimes.'

'You're too nice, Rebecca. You should see what they're like at my local supermarket, they couldn't care less.'

'I KNOW! Mine too. Do you think it's just our store?'

'What do you mean? The fact that we spend most of our energy seducing vile customers? Sadly, no. But we're not bad at it, are we?'

'Well, apart from all the rubbish that comes out of our mouths, I'd say we're pretty damn good.'

And not for the first time since I've met her, we laugh like two old women.

Thursday, 5 March 2009

Another historic day when interest rates fall by another half a point. They are now an astonishing 0.5 per cent. Does anyone need reminding that less than six months ago they were 5 per cent? The Bank of England has also started the process of print-ing money in an effort to kick-start the economy. But it's another dark day as house prices continue to fall and car sales plunge.

Tuesday, 10 March 2009

I'm at my local Sainsbury's for what I intend to be a quick top-up, but somehow ends up taking two hours. I no longer retain the right to silently mock customers who tell me they've been in the store 'for ever'. In my defence, it's because everything has been moved again, so I hunt down my colleagues to help locate my favourite table biscuits. I soon discover that there is no fear of the mystery customer here. The first one shrugs his shoul-ders. The second barely smiles as she looks aimlessly for my biscuits and then gives up after a couple of minutes – without telling me. Third time lucky; he takes me to the item and politely asks if I need anything else before returning to his shelf-stacking. I'm then forced to stalk him for the next ten minutes, walking past again and again in an attempt to read his name badge. He deserves a shining star and I'll be damned if he misses out on my watch. After passing him a fourth time and pretending not to stare in the direction of his left nipple, he gets suspicious so I move on.

Next on my list, sugar snap peas; there are none in the crates. I ask and the lethargic assistant says he'll take a look inside. He spends fifteen minutes in the back while I loiter amongst the vegetables and he is as listless on his return as he was when he first went in. 'Might be some here in forty-eight hours or so,' he says. Customer service here is so bad I contemplate popping my uniform on and slipping into the back to check their MCM score.

Standing in the clothing aisle, I'm choosing a handbag for my mother when two shop-floor assistants start chatting in front of me. A third walks past and they try to get his attention. 'I'm too busy, don't disturb me, I'm off to serve the mystery customer,' he jokes. The two remaining colleagues stand in silence for a few minutes rearranging scarves and then one of them says with more pride than is fitting, 'I served the mystery customer once AND they mentioned my name.'

'OH, REALLY?' says the other, in awe. I hang around the synthetic handbags for a few more minutes, but they say no more. I pick up my £15 bargain and head for the tills.

Doreen is there to greet me when I arrive and we start chatting. She tells me she started her shift at 11 a.m. and finishes at 7 p.m. and will get a thirty-minute lunch break. I ask if she enjoys the job and she shrugs her shoulders. Stupid question. Her manager interrupts and tries to usher her to the kiosk where they are short-staffed. He hangs around while she nervously puts my shopping through as quickly as possible. I wink at her as I leave and notice that she has sneaked me some extra school vouchers. I stop at customer service on my way out and do my usual roll call of shining stars, although, truth be told, these guys wouldn't last five minutes in my store.

Friday, 13 March 2009

It's a gorgeous sunny day and after a week off I have a little spring in my step. As I walk to the big glassy entrance, the amber Sainsbury's sign seems more vibrant than normal. It actually sparkles against the blue of the sky, and the trolleys clank louder in the spring breeze. A manager and trolley minnow are standing close to the doors, listening intently to a customer complaining. I try to eavesdrop as I pass, but it's too windy. In through the double doors and a shrunken out-of-shape Superman in a red shaggy wig is carrying a bucket with loose change. He looks deflated. I'm so distracted by him I walk straight into Richard. He gives me a big grin and an affectionate squeeze of the arm. 'Let's have a catch-up later,' he says. Although he's the boss, he has this disarming way of making you believe he's your best friend.

At the back of the store I'm met with a pleasant smile from a colleague who works on the fruit-and-veg section. A few weeks ago she pointed me in the direction of the staff discounted vegetables after noting my basket of shop-floor groceries. 'You don't have to pay full price, darling, you just need to know where to look.' Another Cog is pushing a trolley full of hangers and she shouts out to no one in particular: 'I ate three burgers yesterday and feel sick today.'

I'm in good spirits, but my first few customers today talk on their mobile phones throughout the transaction, not responding to my bright Hellos. Some smile reservedly at all my attempts to engage them while others doggedly refuse to make eye contact. But there are managers hanging around nearby so I have no choice but to start babbling to myself. The first customer I talk to is trying to fit his weekly shopping into his lunch hour. 'I don't know what I was thinking – I need to book a morning or afternoon in for it. I'm getting quite fed-up with all the moving around of products here – I know they're just doing it to get me to buy other stuff.'

'Why don't you just shop online?' I ask.

'I tell you, I'm this close to doing just that – and I'd bet I'd save a whole load too.'

Thirty minutes of unnerving staring pass and the bosses leave so we finally relax.

A bunch of apples are dropped on my till by a crabby customer. There is no sticker to identify them so I scrutinise them vacantly. I have about eleven varieties to choose from on the screen alone and apples are not really my thing. I sneak a look at the customer in the hope of a clue while I flick aimlessly through the selection on my screen; Bramley, Cox, Golden Delicious, Gala, Granny Smith, Pink Lady ... The apples are reddish, so that eliminates the yellow and green ones. I did say apples were not my thing.

'I'm really sorry, but I don't suppose you know what kind of apples these are, do you?'

'NO, why would I?' she answers brashly. 'And I'm astonished that you don't! Surely you should know that kind of thing by now – sitting here scanning so many apples every day. I mean, how many different types of fruits are there in here? A hundred, two hundred tops ...' She's still at it as I call for the supervisor, who takes one look and says, 'Braeburn.'

Thick skin is a basic requirement in this business, and not just with apple-eaters. People who don't speak English are often unintentionally (although sometimes intentionally) the rudest. They may not have mastered the language but they certainly rule Cog-dom. 'BAG!' 'PACK!' and 'CHECK PRICE!' is shouted at me countless times a day, deeming me as dense and as deaf as wood. I don't need a translator of Polish/Turkish/Greek/ Russian to know that this is then followed by some debate about my various demerits right in front of me. I'm getting pretty good at selective hearing.

I am not so good at ignoring customers who stall at the end of the till dissecting their receipts before leaving with a sigh and a shake of the head at the size of the bill. Sometimes though, I have to admit that this is my own doing. On numerous occasions I've scanned a reduced item at its original higher price because a reduced sticker has not been placed over the original barcode by a shop-floor colleague too lazy, bored or badly trained to do the job properly. The Cog is the one who ends up paying the price. Here's what usually happens: Cog scans barcode. Original price is charged. Customer suspects wrongdoing. Customer locates longed-for blunder on the receipt. Customer turns on Cog with toxic combination of triumph and hostility. Cog's feeble opt-out is 'Customer service will sort it out for you.' Customer has tantrum before realising that there is nothing a Cog can do. Long live the customer service desk.

Trolley Boy struts past me a couple of times today. He's wearing a yellow sun hat, matching glasses and a red nose. I will him to approach an unsuspecting customer. Instead he approaches a grumpy Cog one till down from me.

'Do you know who won Greece's first ever gold medal in judo in Athens?

'Er, no?'

'Ilias Iliadis.'

'Right.'

'Ahmed Al-Maktoum won the first gold medal for the Arab Emirates that year,' he says, smiling enthusiastically.

'Uh-huh,' says Cog, looking around for a customer.

'British women got a gold in the sailing then,' he adds, trying to draw her in.

She starts looking at her nails.

'You probably know about Denise Lewis in Sydney?'

'Nope – I don't, as it happens,' says Cog, looking like she wants to strangle him.

'She won gold in the heptathlon.'

'I'm not interested. I don't care about the Olympics.'

'The Americans got thirty-six gold medals that year.'

'Which part of "I'm not interested" don't you get?' says Cog, now dropping her polite act.

'I loved Michael Phelps in 2004 – eight medals in swimming.' And just before Cog is about to erupt he picks up the baskets by her tills and casually strolls away.

A mum in a rush to do the school pick-up has nothing but cheap toys in her basket: rattles, teething toys and small teddies, all marked between 10 and 29p. 'I take them to my daughter's nursery and then they send them on to children in poor countries every Christmas. They're cheap now so I thought I'd just buy them while I can.'

Despite the recession, we raise a fair bit for Red Nose Day. Most of the Cogs are wearing their own clothes and, out of their neon-orange fleeces and blue-pleated trousers, they are all really very attractive. The ladies' man on BWS (beers, wines and spirits) passes by making borderline sexually inappropriate comments about how striking the till area looks today. Some are wearing such ridiculous fancy dress that I have a problem identifying who or what they are supposed to be. There is a jolly green giant – complete with green tights, pixie shoes and a little off-the-shoulder leafy number. He flounces around the supermarket oblivious to the bemused attention he is getting. There is a witch with long tangled grey hair and a hideous green mole hanging off her chin, flashing her nails. A supervisor walks from till to till telling us *all* to dress up tomorrow. I do my selective hearing thing again.

* * *

I get a recipe for Greek-Bulgarian meatballs handed down the generations from a customer who shares it on condition that I make it in the next few weeks and give her feedback. I agree.

Hang the yogurt in a muslin cloth overnight over a plate to catch the drips so all the excess water seeps through. Mix it up with cucumber, olive oil, garlic, dill and chopped walnuts. Mix the minced beef with breadcrumbs, beaten egg, cumin, onion, black pepper and salt – make into balls and fry. Add tinned tomato sauce simmered with oregano and chopped onions. Eat.

Martina comes to my till with her shopping and while we chat I discover she has worked here for eleven years. I've been wondering for weeks why so many people stay in a job like this for quite so long and ask her this as directly as I dare.

'Because I like it here! I like the money. I don't get any trouble. I've got good friends, so why wouldn't I stay here? Anyone who doesn't like it here just doesn't belong here.'

I get my pay-back in the form of two Chanel-bag toting ladies. Neither of them responds to any version of my charm offensive – they offer only two sets of superior smiles. I wonder what they would make of the woman in her forties who asks quietly if we have any vacancies for her seventeen-year-old son, who has been looking for work since before Christmas and has had zero luck. Student jobs are increasingly thin on the ground and there should be no shame in working here.

But it's not the only kind of work that's disappearing fast. A woman in her forties with shoulder-length strawberry-blonde hair runs a boiler business with her husband.

'We decided to turn it into a limited company because if you'd asked my husband before Christmas about the credit crunch he would have said, "What credit crunch?" But now it's a different story … It's definitely quieter than normal, although it does tend to be quiet during the spring-summer for us anyway. People used to pay their bills straight away and now they are taking much longer about it. Not because they're trying to avoid paying but for genuine reasons – they just can't afford it. That's why we've become a limited company, so it can swallow up any problems for us.' She owns two mortgage-free houses and earns an income on the rental from one.

'I'm still worried that the worst may come to the worst, though.' Despite her concerns, she's not price-watching and her total comes to over £170.

The Mauritian couple behind her split their shopping. He pays for the alcohol because his wife doesn't drink.

'Why should I pay for it?' she asks.

'Yes, all right darling,' he sighs – before turning to me. 'We men are born to suffer.'

'Yes, it's really difficult being a man in a man's world,' she retorts.

They tell me they've been shopping exclusively at Sainsbury's for over forty-five years. Habit and good food are the main draw.

A customer wearing a red cardigan from the TU range has been in the shop since 12 p.m. It's now 2.30. She's beaten my record last week. 'Are you kidding me? What on earth have you been doing here for two and a half hours?'

'I don't even know,' she says, blowing a stray strand of hair off her forehead. 'I feel quite hot and sweaty, now. Your stores are so big – it takes ages to get around. And ever since this bloody recession I've been paying more attention to prices, so looking at those takes for ever.'

Every single one of these customers leaves something behind at the till after paying for it because they are so distracted: egg lasagne, a recycling bag, some fresh chicken slices and a Nectar card. Today alongside the multi-packs of mixed peppers, carrots and root vegetables comes the inevitable lone garlic bulb. Why are you alone? I ask it silently. Where I come from, these are bought in multiples. But now four bulbs of garlic are making their way towards me on the belt. And I just know without looking up that the customers buying these are Asian.

'Those garlic bulbs are the ultimate litmus test – even if I were colour-blind I'd have known you were Asian.'

'Well, garlic maketh the Indian meal,' says the wife, laughing. They tell me they're on a 'forced holiday'.

'It's our end-of-year leave that we hadn't taken, so we've got to have it now.' Further digging reveals they're not enjoying it much.

'What about the being-together bit?' I ask, bewildered, looking from one to the other. He shrugs his shoulders.

'Yes, two weeks is a long time,' she says, packing the shopping. 'I guess that's why we are here.'

Instead of at a Relate session, perhaps, like you ought to be.

There are moments of quiet and so I contemplate the large poster running the full length of the wall by the tills – crisp green salads in sparkling white bowls gaze back at me. The words Tasty, Fresh and Healthy torment my taste-buds and I start to drool. It's almost 3.15 and I'm starving. Hayley is on shift so I know it won't be long. She puts up my closing sign at exactly 3.30. I rush into the locker room and Betty is sprawled on a chair on her mobile phone. She has her legs stretched out in front of her so I have to step over them to get past. I shovel my tea and biscuits in the manner that my digestive system has now become accustomed to while watching the Cheltenham races blast from the TV in the corner. Trolley Boy is slumped in front of it on the sofa, still wearing the yellow sun hat, glasses and red nose. I'm not sure if he's having a nap or engrossed in the race, but he doesn't move a limb for all twenty minutes of my break.

Back on the shop floor it's gone 4 p.m. and the school-run, post-work crowd are piling in – the Friday scrum intent on beating the Saturday rush. A cleaner who's done with her scouring for the week tells me she is extremely busy cleaning two houses a day. On Fridays she only does one house and so gets to start her weekend early.

'I don't know why people get cleaners,' she confides. 'I certainly wouldn't waste my money on one. People are so lazy nowadays. I've got one woman who's got a massive house and she doesn't work at all, and all she does is follow me around like a lost puppy. I think she's just lonely.'

'Is she elderly?' I ask.

'Oh no, she's only thirty-five, but she just doesn't want to clean her own house. So I go around the house, vacuuming, polishing, dusting and she moves from room to room watching me. I'd never get a cleaner – even if I could afford it. That intrusion in your house, the short-cuts they can take, poking around your personal stuff – not that I do any of that, mind you,' she adds hurriedly. 'But I tell you what – I know long before anyone else if the husband is having an affair. Or if the kids are smoking dope. Or if the teenager is having sex. Or if the wife is an alcoholic. All of it, I find out first.'

I serve a couple more customers then Hayley closes my till and tells me to go in to see Richard. I'm waiting outside his office when Barbara walks past. She does a double take and I can see she wants to ask why I'm away from my till, but I avoid eye contact and she skulks away.

Richard is carrying out my three-month review.

'So why should I keep you on?' he asks.

'Because I love working here and I was born to do this.'

'Oh, stop bullshitting me. Seriously?'

I don't have an authentic answer to this question, but I give it a shot. 'Because I'm good with customers, it's what you want. It's important to Sainsbury's that we know how to talk to them and I know I can do it well …' But he has stopped listening.

'Well,' he announces in an unexpectedly grandiose style, 'I'm pleased to tell you that we would like to confirm you.'

'Oh, that's great,' I say with as much conviction as I can feign.

'Did you ever doubt that you'd be confirmed?'

'Not for a second.'

He then shows me my pitiful items per minute: I'm averaging about thirteen. It's so dismal it makes us both laugh.

'Talk, but keep scanning,' he tells me gently.

He congratulates me on my various strengths – attendance, performance – and asks about my shift change and if things have settled at home. I then make a ridiculous mistake.

'If the others ask about my shift change, is it OK to tell them?'

'Who wants to know?'

'Never you mind, can you just tell me if I can tell them without ruffling feathers?'

'Tell me who's asking.'

'That doesn't matter.'

'I'd really like to know who wants to know.'

'Why?'

'Because it's important I know who isn't happy with their shifts.'

'I AM not going to tell you that.'

He asks persistently and I stand my ground. He starts guessing names, and I still don't cave. I soon realise thirty people joined at the same time as me and there are one hundred Cogs in total. He could guess all day and still not get there. No thanks to me and my big mouth. I change the subject. 'Have you taken note of my comment about chairs?' I say, pointing to some notes I had written on one of my assessments. 'The chairs here really suck.'

'New ones have been ordered, so yes we're across that.'

'And what about the delay in coming off your till at the end of a shift?'

'Well, look – I don't know it to be a problem. But if it is, you need to tell me who is doing it so I can talk to them directly.'

He adds, 'I won't tell them it was you – I'll handle it as confidential feedback.'

'Can't you just have a general word?'

'No, because they're not all doing it.'

'That's true, but then not all the checkout girls are making mistakes on coupons, yet you retrain all of us.'

'Tell me who the main culprits are and I'll handle it,' he says firmly.

'No way.'

Fortunately another supervisor comes in and then they both tell me to think about upgrading to the kiosk or customer service.

'No thanks.'

'It'll be good for you – then you can do different things,' says the supervisor.

'I'm very happy where I am, thank you.'

'But it'll help you move around and up.'

'Thanks but no thanks,' I say steadfastly.

I've exhausted a good thirty minutes in his office and so the rest of my shift ends quickly.

As I leave, a Cog is boasting about her shining star. She stood at the door with a bucket and was told that if she managed to raise in excess of a hundred pounds she'd get one. I hear her trumpeting her feat to anyone who will listen. But her success has left Sharon at customer service seething.

'I'm really surprised they gave her one. It takes a lot for them to offer anyone a shining star here.'

Saturday, 14 March 2009

I wake to news this morning that the *Sun* has launched a competition to find Britain's Best Checkout Worker. The paper calls them the unsung heroes of the supermarkets who cheerfully greet every customer as if they were their first. I make a mental list of the Cogs most deserving of winning. While flicking through the paper I turn to page 35 and read Captain Crunch's column and the 'Basket League'. Justin King has mentioned this in one of his newsletters, so I know it's important to the supermarkets. Today Sainsbury's is second at £9.32 for a basket full of food essentials. Morrisons is in the top position at £9. I wonder how many customers will think 32p is a small cost to pay for first-class customer service.

The customer service desk phone rings throughout the day and there are back-to-back tannoys promoting ranges, new deals and sales. Short-tempered parents are fighting off shrill demands from their children for the snacks sitting by the basket tills. One mother shouts 'NO' so loudly I jump out of my chair. I serve a man with a baby under the age of two. He's buying three children's films that I'm quite sure the child is not old enough to understand. Dad tells me the toddler refuses to play with any of his toys and will only watch DVDS. In the same breath he says, 'But then he doesn't really watch the DVDs either, he switches it off and then puts on another, then switches it off and switches on another – paying very little attention to one or the other.' A woman says 'my son is an animal' describing the six-year-old running from one end of the store to the other. Another accompanies her twelve-year-old niece, who is wearing a full black abaya and bright pink head-scarf while rolling around the supermarket on her trainer skates, tripping over one customer and then bumping into another. One customer has a baby (maximum age eighteen months) dressed in head-to-toe pink, sitting in a pink push-chair, cuddling a pink bunny. She is buying *Alice in Wonderland* on DVD.

Nelly is on with me. She seems to live at the basket tills. She's due a lunch break soon after I arrive and she stops Danielle, who is walking towards the supervisors.

'Tell them I'm going for my lunch.'

'Tell them or *ask* them?' enquires Danielle.

'Ask them, I suppose.' Say Nelly as she ties her long hair back in a ponytail.

'I thought that's what you meant,' says Danielle.

Nelly gets her break. When she's on tills I know I'll be getting off on time. Her mother pops in for a shop with Nelly's three grown up kids and they have a quick chat. As she walks off, Nelly says, 'Just look at her.' I turn to see Mum of Nelly pushing an over-full trolley. 'She says she won't, but she always does. She can't help herself,' says Nelly, referring to the trolley that is in danger collapsing under the weight of £200 worth of shopping.

* * *

From where I'm sitting today I've got a clear view of the customer service desk where the most attractive Cogs are placed. Today there are giggles galore, flirty banter and suggestive eyelash flutters all around. The girls do a lot of hair flicking and the boys lean in to steal a smile. That is where a love story or two has got on course, but also where hearts have been broken. Sarita, who sometimes works on customer service, attracted the attention of her trolley boy ex-boyfriend at this very desk. Fast forward a year, and he couldn't hold her attention for much longer. She moved on to a young man working on beers, wines and spirits.

'Where are my vouchers?' I get asked for the millionth time.

'In your bag or pocket,' I respond automatically.

'Did you give me my Nectar card back?'

'YES!' I reply through jaw-achingly gritted teeth.

This usually concludes with customer frantically checking purse/pocket and the bashful presentation of errant card.

Mother's Day cards start coming down the belt. 'When is it?' I ask in a blind panic.

'Tomorrow, of course.' But I'm sure it is next week.

Eventually a colleague passes by.

'Excuse me, when is Mother's Day?'

'Next Sunday, love.'

'And you're sure about that?'

'I've ordered the flowers, darling. If I'm not sure, we'll be in big trouble.'

I amuse myself by not correcting the next ten customers.

* * *

One young man with a mammoth smile and a handsome face is buying flowers, a 'Congratulations to my wife' card and a 'New baby' card.

'Oh, how lovely – congratulations!'

He laughs: 'No, no, it's not for me. I haven't had a baby, it's my best friend. He's too tired to nip out of the house so he's asked me to get it, secretly and all, you know, on his behalf.'

'How you men pull off half your stunts, I will never know.'

Trolley Boy rolls by with his yellow sun hat, bizarre spectacles and red nose.

'You look gorgeous. I love your hair,' he tells one of my customers.

'Thank you,' she says, flicking her hair back and smiling widely.

'I like it red, it really suits you.' He flashes her a flirty grin and she blushes.

Two minutes later, up rides a Little Red Jacket in the Hood. I quietly open bags for her and her mother and listen to them bicker in a foreign language. The discussion seems intense so I silently scan their goods willing them away. When she pays I give her the change and say in a friendly voice, 'There you go.' She takes it and I close the lid on my cash till, turning to serve the next customer. I suddenly notice she is still standing there and is staring at me. I look at her nonplussed and wonder if she has forgotten something. 'Isn't "thank you" part of your vocabulary?' she lashes out.

Did I say thank you? Didn't I? God, I can't remember. My mind was switched off during most of the transaction so the frantic helpless searching I do into the dark recesses of my memory is neither helpful nor fruitful.

'You could have just said "please" couldn't you? Or a "thank you" maybe?'

I stare at her blankly, trying to think of a clever riposte.

'In all this time you didn't say thank you or please even the once,' she states.

I shrug my shoulders.

She then turns on her heels and storms off.

I suddenly find myself shouting:

'WELL, NEITHER DID YOOOOOU!'

I am now, officially, tragic. And shouting at her doesn't even make me feel better because she doesn't seem to have heard. It's a double disgrace because customers, alas, have been watching. The bloke at the front of the queue pulls a sympathetic face. I'm still all caught up in the heat of my humiliation when he says, 'People think they can talk to shop staff like shit. It happens to me all the time.'

Wednesday, 18 March 2009

UK unemployment has risen above two million for the first time since 1997 and economists are predicting it will go above three million by next year. The TUC says there are now ten jobseekers for every vacancy advertised in UK jobcentres. The Bank of England has also warned that Britain is heading towards a 1930s-style recession. I know that it's not just media scaremongering; my experience at the tills is reflecting the same shift.

Friday, 20 March 2009

Molly is at the front door, handing out leaflets, and she gives me a glum smile as I pass. I can see Clare at the basket tills, not supervising but actually serving. It *must* be busy today.

The discounted shelf to my left is over-flowing and customers are crowding around it – a bent tin and a half-open cereal box are lying on the floor. I know I should pick them up, but my legs have already moved on. In the biscuit aisle, the sales assistant grins as I grab one of his chocolate samples and pop it into my mouth. I'm so tired from being up all night with sick children that I pray for till 27 where I can doze in peace. But I'm on till 18. Right. In. Front. Of. The. Supervisors.

My first customer has a loaf of white bread that falls apart as he tries to pack. Barbara comes over to replace it and quips 'Lost your loaf, love?' to me. My second customer is buying two different newspapers and the *Investor's Chronicle*. 'You're certainly reading this at the right time,' I say, scanning it.

'Well, if I'm not going to be making any money, I'd like to know how those who have it are doing so.' He smiles. His shopping comes to £21.69 and he only has a £20 note. 'It's that bloody magazine that did it,' he says, paying on his credit card.

It's the lunch hour so customers are throwing their shopping down, opening bags hastily and looking emphatically at their watches. I've fast learnt the only way to control their behaviour is to draw attention to it. 'You're in a rush, aren't you?' now always prompts an apology. 'It takes too long to get your shopping done these days,' I say next.

And 'I'll get you out of here as soon as possible,' has them eating out of my hand.

* * *

One of Tracey's customers has come in especially to see her. An elderly lady who has been ill but wanted to let her know she is now feeling better. Tracey responds with great concern, but as lovely as she is I know it's not totally genuine. Following close behind her is what I now call a 'professional customer' – a Type-A. This customer knows their rights and makes sure YOU know that too. They don't so much give instruction as bark it. They are the equivalent of a nineteenth-century schoolmaster. If you don't stand to attention even when their back is turned, expect some figurative cane-whipping.

'I've got six bags, I'm going to pack myself but you open the bags for me.'

And,

'Why isn't this belt working?'

And,

'There's my Nectar and a £2 voucher off the bakery stuff – you don't need to check, I'm not lying.'

And,

'More bags.'

And,

'DON'T you dare put the fish next to the bread.'

And,

'Pass the detergents to the right, please.'

Needless to say, there is also strategic laying of shopping on the belt and strategic packing into bags. The little conversation we do have she tells me she's been coming here for twelve years. She is greeted warmly by various shop-floor staff and in between her chats with passing supervisors she instructs: 'You can keep opening bags for me in case you feel guilty for not doing anything.'

* * *

A six-foot-tall man with a stomach that jiggles when he giggles has an intriguing theory about plastic bags and supermarkets' pledges to cut down their usage. 'It's bloody supermarket hypocrisy. Pretending to care about the environment when they provide strawberries and raspberries all year round imported from all over the world. What about their carbon footprint, eh? You know why they don't want to give them bags out? It's because it costs so much to make them. M&S couldn't wait to charge, and now they love it! It's another way to make money. You lot are pretending to be environmentally conscious, but you're not – it's all about the money. Why do you think' – he picks up a bag and ruffles it – 'these are so thin and flimsy now? It's because they're made out of nothing. So, thanks, I'll have your free bags and won't be bringing any of my own. And no, I certainly won't be *buying* any of yours.' And with that he changes my entire world view.

Turnips have been troubling me for four months, so today I see if I can unlock their mystery. 'Tracey, what kind of turnips are these?' I say, holding the small white root vegetable with green and pink stains. 'Scottish or Loose White?'

'Darling, I have absolutely no idea. Do what a man in a brothel would do – pick whichever is cheapest.'

Colleagues are running around sporting egg-yolk yellow T-shirts promoting Sainsbury's Finance, and there is frenetic activity about our name badges. Supervisors are darting about like headless chickens checking that all our tills are tidy and asking Cogs to tie their hair back.

Tracey's been waiting for a tea break for some time and she's now told she can go in a minute. Ten seconds later, Hayley comes over.

'Sorry, Tracey, you can't go yet. I'll let you know in a bit.' And Hayley scuttles off.

'Go to tea, don't go to tea, wear your shirt, don't wear your shirt. I don't know what's going on today.' Tracey's annoyed, but shrugs it off with good humour.

'What's happening today – why the big panic?' I whisper to her.

'I'll tell you later,' she whispers back.

A young couple have some computer games in their trolley and it brings the total up to just over a hundred pounds. She chastises him for his £35 games. 'Bloody hell, we haven't even got the food shopping in yet.' And she shoots him a you're-in-big-trouble-the-minute-we-get-out-of-here look.

Customers ask one after the other to check their Nectar reward points. 'Do I have anything to take off?'

'I'll just check.' I check. 'You have £5.'

Points are disappearing fast – everyone is spending them. She thinks about the fiver she has on in points and says, 'I'll have it off.'

'Ooo errr …' grins her one-track-minded husband.

It's another beautiful spring day but the dramatic change in season has left many under the weather. Alongside all the medication that comes down the conveyor belt, there's the stuff that makes me grin wickedly to myself. Haemorrhoid cream, thrush ointment, HRT vitamins, personal-hygiene wipes, extra-strong deodorant, condoms and whipped cream (last two are often bought together). Usually I scan, slide and pass the items as if they were just another can of baked beans, but in an unguarded moment I once lifted a bottle of intimate feminine wash to read the label, uncertain, as I was, of its function. It took a good few seconds before I realised the customer before me was looking intensely disconcerted. Today I struggle with a box of extra-sensitive condoms. They sit in a security container and I can't get the thing open. If that isn't bad enough, I have to call a supervisor. The customers behind are ogling, and the supervisor and I pretend we are not trying to facilitate a successful night-in for the customer. I never see him again.

A housewife who asks after my health has her own freight to off-load. 'Oh yes, I'm tired too. I've been busy doing the house-work all morning and I've got to do the school run later.' She's in her late forties with a neatly cut blonde bob and blue-rimmed glasses. She's well spoken and well educated and has chosen to stay at home, but it's clear that it's a decision that sits uncomfortably with her. 'I mean, I enjoy the freedom but it's boring at times. There's always something to do, but are they things that *really* need to be done? I don't know. Cleaning, shopping, gardening, picking the kids up, going to the dry-cleaners – I feel like a robot fulfilling my function on earth – but could a machine do what I do? Yes, I think so. And does anyone value what I do? Not a soul …'

It's coming up to three hours into my shift and I'm about to keel over with fatigue. The customer I'm serving has Pro-Plus, several cans of Bolt (Sainsbury's version of Red Bull) and ten packets of two-minute meals. 'Who needs an extra couple of hours' kip or a freshly cooked meal – when all the answers are on this till?' I say. He's jumps out of his semi-dazed state and looks at me with gaping eyes. 'It's OK, I know exactly how you feel.' I add.

Trolley Boy arrives and stands by a supervisor who is scruti-nising some paperwork. He strokes her fringe repeatedly and they are both standing in silence. She has beautiful shiny black hair and he obviously thinks so too. She keeps looking down. He keeps stroking. It's not exactly an act of intimacy and I feel like I'm watching a Tracey Emin installation – oddly fascinating, a little disturbing and totally incomprehensible. This continues for a whole minute and then it's suddenly over. He approaches a customer I'm serving. 'Your hair is beautiful that colour. Have you just coloured it?' Hair is a thing with him.

'Oh yes, yes. I have. Thank you for noticing.'

'It really suits you. You look lovely.'

And he leans down, picks up the empty baskets by my tills and wanders off. 'Isn't he charming?' I say to the blushing customer by my till.

'He REALLY is,' she gushes. 'I've been coming here for ten years and he always comes over and has a little chat – usually about something off the wall, but I think he's a very unique person. I gave him my phone number once and since then every year on my birthday, he texts me. I just can't believe that he remembers it every single year. His ability to recall dates is remarkable. He should be working for the government, saving the world or something. They should devise a comic-book hero after him.'

'I know! He could be Super-RAM,' I say, surprising myself with my brilliant unexpected wit.

A woman struggles to open a plastic bag. 'Do you get training in how to open bags?' she asks earnestly.

'Yup. Two whole days of it. In that time we're taught how to lick our fingers, flick the bag and slip it open. It's a real skill. Takes time to master.' She looks slightly wounded. I've evolved into one of the over-tired toddlers that venture in on weekends – so exhausted that only a spectacular tantrum will make me feel better. Failing that, extreme petulance will suffice.

Still no break in sight. My next customer is a girl after my own heart: a former Tesco Cog with lots of tales about life at the till. 'I worked there for ten years and the only thing I learnt is that customers talk to checkout girls like the dog crap stuck to their shoe. They don't realise how nasty they can be or how upsetting it is. I used to cry in the toilets in the beginning, but after a while I started to stand up for myself.'

'Well, I'm not there quite yet, but I do get traumatised straight after something happens and then can't concentrate for the next hour.'

She laughs. 'It's like post-traumatic stress disorder. I went through the same thing. It's all that shouting, telling you off and throwing their cards and cash at you – and just never, EVER, being able to say anything back.' She sighs. 'It's depressing just thinking about it again – it used to happen at least once a shift.'

'That sounds about right.'

'I'm a sales assistant in clothing and it's so much better.' She smiles brightly. 'Don't worry, darling, you'll escape too.'

It's after school time and teenagers are piling in for a fix of sugary drinks and salty crisps. Three school girls come to the till with chocolate brownies, cheese-and-onion crisps and fairy cakes. Behind them is a customer who spends £8.24 and then goes to the toilet. Samantha finally emerges and tells me to go on my break. As I'm closing my till the customer emerges.

'Did you give me my school vouchers?'

'Um … er … I don't know now – how much did you spend?'

'Over £8.'

'I'm sorry no – you get one voucher for every £10 you spend. It doesn't look like you spent enough.'

'I don't understand. One … voucher … for?'

Samantha butts in.

'Listen, love, you've got to spend £10. You didn't. So you get nothing. Now, excuse this young lady. She needs to go on her break.' And with that she ushers me on my way.

I'm standing in the canteen gloomily contemplating the soggy tuna sandwich and dried-out Cornish pasty in the sandwich dispenser when Barbara appears at the coffee machine.

'You all right, love?' she asks me chirpily.

I·manage to choke out a reply.

'Yes, fine thanks. I'm starving, but these don't look good.'

'Yeah, it's really unhealthy here – this canteen is rubbish.'

I turn towards the chocolate and crisp machine.

'I've got a sausage roll in the fridge, if you'd like it,' she offers. 'But it's pork – you probably don't eat pork,' she continues sweetly.

'No, I don't, but that is really very nice of you.' I'm genuinely touched. 'Thanks anyway.'

'Well, I've got a packet of nuts if you want that instead?'

'Thanks, Barbara, but I'll get some crisps from here. You save it for yourself. Thank you though.'

As far as Barbara is concerned, it seems I may have finally earned my stripes.

Twenty minutes later I'm back on the shop floor orbiting the soup aisle trying to locate Cup-a-Soup. Susie appears out of nowhere – except she doesn't look much like Susie. Gone is her over-sized orange fleece jacket and the neatly tied back hair. In its place are a tight black top with a large belt tucking her ample bosom in, tight black jeans and a little blue cropped jacket. Her hair falls in soft curls around her shoulders – she has make-up on and is glowing. She beams when I tell her how exquisite her downtime guise is. She looks like a cover girl – albeit for *Women's Weekly*. When I get back to my till, Barbara walks past and gives me a wink. There is too much love in the room and I feel distinctly unsettled.

Connor has been snared and is now sitting at the checkout behind me. He, like most of the other checkout guys, loathes being on till duty. It takes him away from his main goal while here, which is to score with as many of the fairer Cogs as possible. Sitting at a checkout, forced into small talk with grannies, housewives and middle-aged men, just cramps his style on the shop floor.

'They got you eventually, then?'

'Yeah, well, at least I got to skive all afternoon.'

'Not now, though – there'll be no escape.'

'And probably for the rest of my shift too, because of "the visit".'

Before I can ask him what he means, we're interrupted by customers. One of these customers tells me what the frenzy has been about today. She has a friend who works at the store, who told her that a bigwig from head office has been paying a visit. That explains the wide-scale panic about fully occupied tills, name tags, T-shirts and tidy checkouts. I turn to share this with Connor but he seems to have shrunk a foot.

'Connor, why are you sitting so low? You look ridiculous.' His head is only just above the till belt.

'My chair's just got stuck – it's the lowest level and I can't get it to move.' He tugs and jostles the chair.

'You look like a mole peeping out the top of his hole,' I giggle. 'Customers are going to die laughing.'

He doesn't find it quite so funny – but every time I turn to look at him I crack up.

* * *

I take my trolleyload of shopping to Jane's till and we compile a list we call 'Ten Things I Hate about You – Dear Customer':

1. Reaction to the cost of shopping. Some variety would be good.
2. Saying 'Oh I'm sorry, I forgot my bags!' Followed by guilty blabbing.
3. Asking 'Why are the shelves empty?' And then holding Cog accountable.
4. Responding to a disingenuous 'How are you today?' with a genuine 'I don't feel good today.'
5. Trying to use more than one voucher per transaction and/or out-of-date vouchers. Forcefully.
6. Insisting you have more Nectar reward points than you do. Forcefully.
7. Urging us to speed up (using hostile body language rather than words).
8. Asking us to slow down (using hostile body language *and* words).
9. Assuming Cog is guilty before proved innocent – applies to a variety of problems.
10. Pin-pad innuendo. It's like going from 0–60 – good for cars, bad for Cogs. 'Not even if you're rich and handsome,' we agree.

And because Jane is drop dead gorgeous she adds another – 'Always trying to pull us. Even the old ones.'

Saturday, 21 March 2009

I'm rebelling today by wearing my own black trousers because my Sainsbury's pleats are in the wash. I am also held up in horrendous traffic. I call the absentee line and cross my fingers because the response is entirely luck of the draw. 'It's no problem,' I get told today.

Once I get in, I see that there are swarms of us running late. In the end I'm only delayed by three minutes – which wouldn't raise an eyebrow in most jobs. Here, though, it's often a cardinal sin.

Martina is handing out leaflets at the front. I make sympathetic sounds. She tells me she's been there for an hour already and is stuck there until two. She'll have been on her feet for two and a half hours in total. 'It could be worse,' she tells me. How? I don't say aloud. I walk to the tills with a cluster of Cogs.

'I'm really not in the mood for tills today.'

'Yeah, all that "Hi! Have a nice day." Can't be bothered with it.'

'Have a nice day! I don't give a shit if they've had a nice day.'

When we get to the till captain, Barbara is barking orders at record speed.

'YOU take till 10. YOU'RE on 5. Here's another for baskets – take 2. YOU'RE relieving 24 …'

Elderly couples who missed their chance to come in during the week are rushing through the tills like the plague is at their heels. One couple are so daunted by the queues building up behind them, they fumble nervously for their change, decide not to look for their Nectar card and muddle up their pin number. Another old lady types and re-types her pin incorrectly and is close to both tears and abandoning her shopping. 'Take your time,' I whisper to her about the crowd behind. 'Don't worry, I'll deal with them.'

A couple try to get me to give them more points because they have really large bags. 'It doesn't matter if your bag is the size of this supermarket, it's still just the one bag,' I tell them. They smile awkwardly and I wonder why I'm reverting to type again; I immediately grant them three points.

It's Mother's Day tomorrow, so those who didn't make a gargantuan cock-up last week are buying their cards and flowers today. One man buys a huge pink Hydrangea planter – a British garden bloom. 'Get you and your great big impressive flowers,' I say, making a note to myself about my own mother. Another customer is planning her 'Mother's Day strike' tomorrow. I talk flowers, cards and mums until I've covered every conceivable angle on mothering. Women buying gifts for both Mum and Mum-in-law ensure the former gets the better pick. I consider pointing this out and decide it will probably not go down well, no matter how I put it, so I savour the amusement from this privately.

One woman tells me she'll pay for her Mother's Day cards after all the groceries have gone through. She hangs on to them at the end of the till. I put her shopping through and she packs, pays and leaves. A minute or so after she's gone, I realise she didn't pay for her cards. And try as I might to shrug it off, it continues to irk me for the rest of the day.

A housewife who comes in every Saturday is at my till again. She has a mouth with an inbuilt megaphone and her voice echoes around the store the minute she enters. Today Megaphone Mum decides to pick a fight with another customer. The lady in front of her has left her trolley and gone to fetch a forgotten item. When she returns, Megaphone Mum has started loading her groceries on the belt.

'Oh, I'm sorry, but I was next in the queue,' says customer who-dared-to-leave-trolley-in-queue.

'BUT YOU LEFT YOUR STUFF AND WENT AWAY, SO HOW WAS I TO KNOW?'

Everyone in a ten-mile radius stops to look.

'YOU CAN'T JUST DUMP YOUR SHOPPING AND GO AWAY.'

The lady who connived to keep her place in the queue looks more shell-shocked than a trauma victim.

'I HATE IT WHEN PEOPLE DO THAT – IT'S SO SELFISH.'

Customer stares at floor, willing it to open and swallow her whole.

'AND THEN THE REST OF US WHO ARE QUEUING UP THE RIGHT WAY HAVE TO WAIT UNTIL YOU COME BACK.'

This is by far the worst form of humiliation I've witnessed in four months here.

Another one of my regulars stops by. Last time we talked, work had been troubling him. He works for a company that supplies jackets to a high street store that now owe his company £700,000 which they can't repay. 'They've just been taken over, but we're not going to get anything from that deal. We'll be lucky if we get a few thousand back.'

'So what does that mean for you?'

'Well, redundancies, of course. There are eighty of us and a handful have already been released. In the short term there'll be another ten to go.'

'And are you likely to be one of them?'

'Maybe, I don't know,' he says, shrugging his shoulders. 'I've got three kids, and I've still got to put one of them through law college. Fortunately, I don't have a mortgage any more, but paying college fees is like having a mortgage.' He talks incessantly and nervously. Of the many customers who shared their recession woes with me, he seems the most perturbed of all. 'It's so quiet at work you could cut the atmosphere with a knife – we're all just putting our heads down now.' His shopping costs £105.

'Oh dear,' he says, looking at the total screen anxiously. 'It's a bigger shop than normal because of Mother's Day. The kids wanted to spoil their mum, so I've bought extra bits. Can you check my Nectar points, please?' He has £125. 'Just take £7.50 off. I'm saving the rest for the rainy days ahead.' And he leaves, his despair visibly dragging him down.

Magda's mum is at my till with her weekly shopping. I know she is her mum because throughout her time at my till Magda bombards her with one annoying question after another. When she proceeds to ask her mother for some tissues, Mum cracks. 'I only came in for my frigging shopping, not to have you bothering me. Get your own tissues!'

'Oh, come on, Mum, my nose is dripping.'

Mum obliges, but not before saying: 'Next you'll be asking me to wipe it for you.'

A pretty curly-haired woman in her twenties walks past me on her own. She has learning difficulties and usually comes in with her prickly, short-tempered mother. Despite this, the young woman normally has a sunny smile on her face. Today, though, she looks quite lost. I look around for her mum and she is nowhere to be seen. The young woman leaves the store alone, still looking disorientated. I want to do something but am approached by a customer gesticulating wildly and ranting at the top of his voice as he piles his shopping at my till. He's tall, stocky and rather fierce looking – to top it all, his tirade is in a foreign language so sounds even more threatening. And he's shouting to himself. I lift the divider, while my stomach cartwheels, look up at him and meekly say hello. He turns to me, gives me a big smile and I catch a glimpse of the tiny Bluetooth headset in his right ear. 'Oh, thank goodness!' I splutter out. 'I thought you were a nutter.' There is a moment of incredulous silence as we both ingest my words. He then says: 'Don't be

fooled by the earpiece, darling, I AM a nutter.' And he roars
with laughter. He relays my blunder to the friend on the phone.

Rebecca pops by at 3 p.m. to say hello. She's having her break
only a couple of hours into her shift. 'I hate it when they do
that. I don't need a break now – I've only been here a little
while.'

'Which till are you on? I can't see you from here.'

'Naughty corner – Till 26. I've been loafing all afternoon.'

'You lucky thing. Can you believe where they've stuck me?'

'They need to keep an eye on you – I've told them you're
trouble.'

Two Cogs behind me are also teasing each other – about
leaflet distribution. It's the job everyone's trying to avoid today.
'The first ten minutes are OK – it's a bit like a honeymoon
period. You know, you're really keen and putting yourself out
there – and then after the tenth time of being blanked, you just
want to chuck them all in the bin and run back to the tills.'

I set myself a target to beat my personal best on items
scanned per minute. I'm speeding through them when the
Italian grandmother I'm serving shouts, 'NO, TOO QUICK.'
The couple behind her stare at her with such ill will, I'm
surprised she doesn't come out in smallpox. Instead she stops
to comment on the price, then the food, then the store. All the
while she chatters away with her daughter, who's being served
at a neighbouring till. I stupidly forget to give her the cash-back
she requested, close the till, and start serving the next customer.

'Oh no, *cara mia*,' she says, returning seconds later, 'you
forgotuh to geeve me my taen poundsuh.'

'I'm so sorry, let me just serve this customer and I'll give it to
you straight away.'

'No problemo, let me go to the kiosky, get my lotto ticket and
I come backa. OK?'

Ten minutes pass and she's still not back. Samantha closes my till and tells me to go for my break. I spiral into a cycle of panic-hysteria-panic. No one knows what she looks like apart from me and I don't want her coming back, finding I've gone and thinking I'm a lying, thieving checkout girl. Samantha tells me I can wait for a minute or two longer, but the Italian mama still doesn't show up. 'Sorry, love, you've got to go now – I need to send the others on their break after you.' I start dithering under my till, trying to find any excuse to give her a little longer to get back. Just as I'm about to throw in the towel, she strolls back casually to my till. I literally fling the money at her.

After my break, just as I sit myself back down, Hayley comes over and plops some papers down on the belt. 'Oh no, have I just had an observation?' I say, panic-stricken.

'You have, my dear.'

'I knew it. Is that why I've been sitting here for two days?'

'Well, I did it yesterday, not today.' I think back to yesterday and my black mood, slumped lethargically in my chair, not caring who might be watching.

'Oh well, give it to me – how did I do?'

'You were absolutely fine. You did great, actually.' They obviously caught me at a good moment.

'You were polite, tailor-made your service and maintained a generally high standard of customer care.' I'm so relieved I write exactly that in the comments box and sign it.

Back at the tills, there are bag ladies flaunting their wares. There might be a recession on, but fashionistas need not despair; the designer bag with its thousand-pound price tag should move aside, the new IT bag on the block will cost only a hundredth of the price. Supermarket bags are the new way for customers to show off their latest arm candy and so now they bring in fewer of the jute and recycled bags sold by the stores themselves and more of their own cloth, canvas and vinyl bags. Bags with pink polka dots, bags with blue and purple flowers, bags that look like over-sized handbags, and even cute cheap bags imported from abroad. A customer has a très chic French shopping bag to pack her groceries in and tells me proudly that she picked it up in Calais. 'I love using it and all the checkout girls comment on it.' Other customers have popped in with classical ones. Today I see a lovely large blue bag with the vintage Sainsbury's logo on it. The customer tells me she's had it since the seventies.

'You better hang on to that – I bet it'll be worth something one day.'

She laughs. 'You're having me on, aren't you?'

Michelle is sat at the till opposite and is asked to come off. She's standing by Richard's door and hisses to get my attention. 'Have you been confirmed yet?' she whispers.

'Yes,' I whisper back.

'Wish me luck.' And in she goes. Ten minutes later she emerges grim-faced and a little brow-beaten. As she makes her way back to the till she says, 'Guess what? Another probationary period.'

A customer has a small radio in her shopping.

'Do you do the Basics radio any more?'

Here we go again. I'll cut to the chase: millions of items in the store. Cog only knows what Cog has to know – scanning, sliding and passing. A bit of aimless chat. No more. I tell her this – although with a more delicate choice of words. I then scan the Kenwood Smoothie-making machine she has picked up. It's £31.99. 'Oh, I think I've picked up the wrong one. I thought it was £7.50.' Sighs at the back of the queue. Supervisor to the rescue. Clare goes on the hunt. The customer behind is just one gas emission short of eruption. The woman then says, 'Oh, I forgot my eggs. I'll just get some.' And off she trots. The customer behind her picks up a magazine in a pointed manner. The returning customer is completely unfazed. 'I can't WAIT to make some smoothies – what a bargain!' she tells her boyfriend excitedly.

Another of my regulars tells me she's decided to cut back on her shopping. 'I'm spending too much and I've got to make some cuts. I've got to work out where to make the cuts, though.'

'Do you want to guess how much your shopping is today?' I ask, playing the latest game I've invented.

'Hmm, I could live with £100.'

'Prepare yourself,' I grimace: '£194.86.'

'WHAT??? Oh my goodness. I feel quite faint.'

'Do you want me to check your nectar points?'

'God, yes!' She takes all £5 off and when I give her the shopping bill it's almost a metre long.

I've got an hour left until I am out of here and the chatty customer at my till has £74.60 worth of shopping. He hands me a voucher which gives him £6 off a £60 shop. The voucher isn't valid until the following day. 'I'm sorry, you can't use this until tomorrow,' I tell him, handing it back.

'You can put it through. I've done my shopping for the week now,' he says firmly.

'No … I'm afraid I really can't do that.'

'They did it last time.' He pushes the voucher back on the till towards me. 'Go on, just put it through.' I decide against my default position (calling a supervisor) and try to hold my ground.

'I'm sorry, but I just can't.'

'Look, I'm telling you that one of your colleagues at the other end did it, and you can do it too.' He is gritting his teeth, suddenly no more Mr Nice Guy. I've died and slipped into a bad Guy Ritchie film.

'If I do it, I could lose my job. It starts tomorrow, so that's the best time for you to use it.'

'Just do it. I'm not coming back again this week. That's my shopping done now.'

'I can't, I'm sorry.'

'Call your supervisor,' he finally says. Phew.

Helen comes along and tells him the same thing. He then silently tucks the voucher back into his wallet, abandons the shopping trolley, complete with packed shopping and storms off. Helen shrugs her shoulders, cancels the transaction and takes the trolley full of his groceries back to the shelves.

It goes very quiet in the last few minutes before I leave. An Irish lady wants to talk. She was a pub landlady for fifteen years and she likens her job to mine. 'I bet you, people tell you incredible things here,' she says, her eyes twinkling knowingly. 'You're full of the secrets of the world, aren't you, darling?' I smile.

'You're not just some silly little checkout girl. You're their therapist, mother, daughter, sister, friend, financial adviser and doctor too. Am I right or what?' I smile some more.

'You've got a face that makes people want to tell you things. It's what one of my punters used to call a Nice-Cup-of-Tea face. I'd pour them a drink and they'd pour out their life story.' There's a fine line between a Nice-Cup-of-Tea face and my Ask-a-Stupid-Question mug, but I take her point, and put one such foolish question to my final customer.

'Look, can I ask you something that's been bothering me for weeks?' I pick up his one lone courgette. 'Why is it that every

177

single customer, without exception, always has one of these in their shopping?'

He's bemused. 'Because … they're going to eat it?'

'No, no, you don't get it. I'm a good cook. I cook for my kids. I cook for my friends. But courgettes … they're kind of a non-food. It sort of doesn't matter what you do to them, they just don't taste like food. The texture is non-existent. The taste is forgettable. But everyone's buying them. Am I missing some-thing?'

He rises to the challenge almost immediately.

'Yes, you definitely are. You just don't know what to do with them. Stop thinking too hard. Keep it simple. Cook them on their own with garlic. Cook them in a tomato sauce with chicken. Throw them in a risotto. They're not a nondescript, part-of-the-furniture kind of vegetable. Once you know how to cook them, you won't look back.' I'm not convinced, but I love the fact that he tries to advocate the virtues of the not-so-cool cousin of the cucumber.

Rebecca and I drive home together. She's exhausted from her seven-day weeks but doesn't want to rock the boat. 'You've got to say something – you're burnt out.' I tell her.

'I know, I know, I should – I'm starting to lose the plot,' she says, rubbing her forehead. And then she pinpoints the exact moment at which the screw well and truly came loose. 'This customer was in his thirties and really very good-looking. So I just told him straight up, 'You're actually a very handsome man.' And he blushed a little but, you know, looked quite pleased with himself. And so I continued scanning his shopping and telling him what a lovely face he had – and THEN … I don't know what came over me, but I said, "But by the look of these sanitary towels I can tell that you're not single"'.

I splutter the sip of water I've just taken all over my driving wheel. Ignoring my half-choke, half-guffaw, she continues.

'He just went really quiet. And I'm thinking, "Oh dear, Rebecca, you've gone too far this time." And there was this awful, deafening silence and then he said, "You've missed your vocation in life, haven't you? You were meant to be a comedienne." But by that point I was just chucking his stuff down the till – just DESPERATE to get him out of there.' I'm laughing so hard I have to pull over.

Monday, 23 March 2009

I go to my local supermarket with the children today and buy three doughnuts on a 3-for-2 offer at a reduced price of 15p each. The Cog was too busy talking to the kids to notice that not only did she charge me full price for each doughnut, I didn't get one free either. I don't waste my time with her and go straight to the customer service desk. She gives me back the overcharged money but still charges me fifteen pence for each one – I'm still not getting one for free. It's only 15p, but I'm not going down without a fight. I try to get her attention but she turns away. She serves another customer, and takes a phone call despite knowing that I'm still there. She wants me to go away but, as we've long established, I'm going nowhere fast. 'I'm sorry, but you charged me for all three – the offer says 3-for-2.'

She doesn't take my word for it and calls a colleague and asks them to go check the price. This whole process takes fifteen minutes. She hands me back my overcharged 15p and doesn't apologise. I leave, angry. I allow myself to think self-righteously that Cogs like her give us all a bad name.

Wednesday, 25 March 2009

Turn on the radio today and Justin King is talking about how Sainsbury's is defying the economic downturn. True. He says the store is helping people manage their household budgets with their 'Feed your family for a fiver' recipes. Also true. And that there has been a 60 per cent rise in sales of the Basics range. Definitely true. He also says more money is being spent in supermarkets and less on takeaways and restaurants. Absolutely true. He adds that people are cooking more and the family meal is becoming more of an occasion. Nothing but the truth. He says that their profit increase is because they are selling more items to customers and not just due to inflation, which doesn't ring entirely true.

Friday, 27 March 2009

Near the clocking-in machine are the words 'WE DID IT' cut out of gold paper. It names everyone who helped the store meet its MCM target. Just for a laugh, I look for my name. It's not there. I laugh. The Cogs are all talking about it downstairs and I hear some say that you only get the bonus if you've been here a year – 'so don't get too excited.'

My first customer is showing off her quaint Sainsbury's totes from the seventies. 'My mum and I bought them together back then. They're faded, but they are still going. I love them. They're a whole lot less dowdy than the recycled bags they sell today.'

A woman in her sixties asks me how to persuade her kids to have a family. 'They're thirty-two and thirty-eight and I keep telling them they need to marry and settle down because I want grandchildren. But they've always got excuses lined up. The latest one is it's not a good time to have a family because of the recession.'

'And by the time the recession passes – they'll be infertile,' I jest. She looks up, alarmed. 'I mean, probably not infertile as such,' I back-track. 'You know, there's always IVF and, er, sperm donation and … erm … surrogacy and …'

She leaves in silence.

One man buys nothing but eight packets of multi-pack powdered soup. 'Convenience food is just too convenient – and I don't have the time to cook.' But there are so few nutrients in there, I tell him. 'Unless you're prepared to come round and cook for me, I'll be walking out with these.'

A customer buying three separate newspapers grabs my attention but her onions take my breath away. 'I think there might be something wrong these onions,' I tell her. 'They smell too strong.' We check and they ARE off. She's blown over by my first-class olfactory sense. 'I can tell what someone's had for breakfast even if they're standing five feet from me. It's been a life curse – exacerbated like you would not believe during pregnancy.'

'You're like Grenouille in *Perfume*,' she tells me.

'Except without the serial-killer instinct,' I add.

'Well, I'd guess that would depend on who you're serving.' I laugh.

'So why are you reading so many newspapers? Only journalists or people with no life do that kind of thing?' I ask, scanning the *Indy*, *Times* and *Guardian*.

'I'm in the latter category – I used to work in government and am now so depressed by how this recession is turning out that I pore over the papers every morning. It drives my husband crazy. But that's what retired people do – long for the life they used to have.'

I'd love to know more about her, but there are other customers to serve. Behind her is a bubbly woman with tumbling dark curls. As we chat about schools, our young kids and family life, she puts back a couple of items. Three-quarters of the way through scanning her stuff, she asks me for a sub-total.

'Um … it's £65.36,' I tell her casually.

She freezes on the spot and exclaims, 'You're joking!'

'Um, no …'

'No way …' she utters in a half-whisper, half-gasp. She seems to be going into an anaphylactic shock. The customers behind her have stopped loading their shopping and are watching intently. Her reaction is a little distressing and she needs to come to her senses.

'How much did you want to spend?' I say quietly, leaning towards her.

'Sixty pounds, maximum,' she manages to reply.

'What do you want to do?' I ask. She stares back at me, blank.

'Do you want to leave the rest of the shop?' I whisper.

'Yes, yes please,' she whispers back. 'I'm so embarrassed; I just can't believe it's that much.'

'Don't worry about it,' I say, taking stuff off the belt. 'Do you want to put some other things back, you know, from the stuff I've already scanned?' I say, indicating her packed shopping. She hesitates. She wants to, but the ogling crowd by the till are making her feel like a freak show.

'Yes,' she finally braves. She gives me the fresh chicken and her window-cleaner spray and it takes it down to just over £60. She also has a £6-off-a-£60-shop voucher and I put it through. She apologises fervently. I pass her change over quickly.

* * *

I get another sixty-second recipe from a customer today.

Roasted chicken pieces marinated in Mediterranean cuisine herbs (i.e. Italian herbs, mixed spice and garlic). Pop in the oven for thirty minutes. Et voilá.

A group of grown-up girls arrives up at my till and argues loudly about how the bill should be split. They ask me to check if the Persil tablets are £7 for fifty-six tablets. With the help of a supervisor we establish that there are fifty-six tablets in each pack and, no, it's not two packets for that price. They put those back. They shout 'you charged that twice' just as I realise this myself. Their vouchers are out of date. They run around the till looking for something small to buy to bring the total over £20. They present yet another voucher. They argue again over who pays and who should take the change. By the time they leave, I feel worn out.

I serve a middle-aged man with his wife in tow who thinks he's the first person ever to allude to pin-pad innuendo. 'Ha ha ha, that's so funny,' I say. 'And do you know your wife's giant white baps cost 65 pence?' I add, startling both myself and him.

Today there are posters hanging from the ceiling that have big baskets full of Sainsbury's own-brand goods. *Switch and Save* it tells the recession-struck shoppers who walk past semi-comatose, too busy splurging to notice any proposition that may help them save money.

Dear Customer,

Hard times call for hard choices. Will it be the Basics pizza bases or the frozen ready-made ones? Will it be the six bottles of wine or a basket of necessities? Because you can't keep buying both. If you don't want to be paying the equivalent of your mortgage every month – and, let's face it, many of you are – you need to stop. Right now. A family of four, by my reckoning, are spending between £400 and £600 a month. Does that hurt? It hurts me to say it. Calm down when you're shopping. Take a deep breath. You're not playing Supermarket Sweep.

Here is your sixty-second master-class in how to shop. Check the prices. And if they're not there, ask someone to check for you. Walk into the store and walk towards the food. You are here to buy food, not DVDs/toys/clothes/random household paraphernalia. Give the goods stocked at the entrance a wide berth. Forgo luxuries, stick to the basics. Make a list and stick to it. Take your trolley to the till and ask the Cog to tell you when it gets close to your upper limit. She's on your side, trust me.

Yours,

A. Cog

PS. If you're brave enough, take a calculator. You might get stared at, but it'll be mostly appreciative glances.

A man who doesn't know how to cook buys chicken with the skin on. He asks me what he should do with it.

'What do you normally do?'

'I just boil it, grill it and salt it.'

'That sounds dull. Do the boiling bit. Then try marinating it with some herbs and spices – pick anything you like, but you could try paprika, garlic, turmeric, salt and pepper, and maybe some thyme and a little bit of rosemary and sage. And then put it under the grill.'

'Sounds yum. Thanks, Nigella.'

I serve an ex-Cog who worked in this store nine years ago for about three years. She's shopping with her mum and I'm fishing for some stories. 'The worst part of the job back then was the supervisors and the manager. If I was even a minute late, I'd get into deep trouble – and then I'd always finish late, which always infuriated me. And then, of course, there were the customers,' she says, looking at me meaningfully.

'I hear you.'

'So they haven't changed then? Why doesn't that surprise me?' She picks up her scanned packet of croissants and pauses. 'It was always tiny things would set them off, like if I asked them for their Nectar card twice, you know, by mistake. Or if an item came up higher than they thought. By the time I left, I was desperate to get out of here.'

One customer's bill comes to £99.66.

'Oh, isn't that a funny number?' she starts to tell me. 'I went to this party once at 9.19 p.m. on the 19th of the 9th 1999. We all had to wear black and white clothes and eat red and green food. It was one of the strangest nights of my life.'

One of my regular customers is a teacher in a secondary school and she complains about how unruly secondary school children are becoming. 'When they get to senior school, single-sex environments are best for both sexes. Although, if you ask me, I much prefer teaching teenage boys to teenage girls. You wouldn't believe what girls are like these days.'

I meet such a girl not long after. She's no more than eleven and wearing her hair high in a ponytail, a lot of clunky jewellery and a white hoodie with 'star-maker' in gold letters emblazoned on the back. Her teeny little skirt stops just above the level of acceptability.

'Oh, come on, Mum.'

'NO.'

'Please, Mum, everyone else is shaving them now.'

'I don't care – you're too young. And anyway, you don't have anything there.'

'OK then, can I wax them?'

'NO!' says Mum, rolling her eyes.

'Thanks a lot, Mum, I'll just go to school with my Hairy Biker legs then, shall I?' And she turns her back to the till, folds her arms and actually curls her lower lip. She remains frozen in this monumental strop until I finish up with Mum five minutes later.

More normal-sized toddlers are being toddlers and having tantrums in every corner. Old people are being old people and grumbling about it at every till. An elderly couple have a full-on tiff about their packing. They argue about the biscuits, the bottles and the bread. 'You'll squash it all, you don't think logically when you pack.'

My hands get bloody from a joint of meat I scan and I ask Ayesha if I can wash my hands. She's none too pleased. 'I'm not supposed to take over if you are in the middle of a transaction.' My hands have a distinct and rather disgusting browny-red smudge on them. She sees that I may retch and so reluctantly takes over. I run to the toilets, scrub them down and race back to the till. The usual end-of-transaction queries about missing Nectar cards continue. Even in polite society it appears more fitting to interrogate the Cog before checking own belongings.

I get taken off the tills for my last hour and refill the 'Try something new today' recipe booklets. They have been disappearing fast so I open several new boxes to replace them. I refill the booklets at a freshly captured Connor's till.

'I haven't found a good enough hiding place yet,' he tells me.

'Try diving into the freezers under the frozen fish – they won't think to look there,' I advise wisely.

'Been there, done that.'

'You need to hide where the others do – where do Phillipe, Jeremy and David hide?'

'They don't hide, they vanish into the thin air that is their other jobs. My main thing here is checkouts.'

We're interrupted by a customer who shouts 'FREE?' at Connor. It's more a command than a question, so I leave.

I walk past Nelly on baskets. 'You're on baskets again – are you ALWAYS there?'

'You noticed then?' she says testily.

I pass Magda and she jibes: 'Taken off because you're not up to the standard of customer service required, huh?'

A Cog nearby has finished her shift but no one has closed her till. She continues to quietly serve customers but it doesn't sit well with me. I march straight up to the supervisors and remind them it's the end of her shift.

At the end of my shift I take my shopping to Jeremy, who has a lot of theories. After almost a decade here he's seen the full gamut of changes in retail and he talks about deflation and how 'people will start buying their food shopping on credit soon'. He also tells me male colleagues only make it to checkout if they excelled in their previous role. He rocked in the freezer sections, so here he is.

Saturday, 28 March 2009

I decide to count the exact number of customers I serve today – I've just been making rough estimates for weeks and it will help pass the time. I'm serving one of my first customers when Susie comes over with a price enquiry. The customer I'm serving is struggling with the pin-pad so I've swiped her card on my till. 'Can you take your card out?' I ask absentmindedly.

'No, because you have it,' says the customer. And then Susie and the customer laugh at me. Not with me – AT me. That's important.

One customer has left his ailing wife in the car. 'And because of that not only have I saved my ears from all her moaning, I've saved money and time. Twenty minutes flat, it took me.'

Anya Hindmarch's 'I'm Not a Plastic Bag' is yesterday's news. Today a customer is showing off her large Missoni-style bags imported from a Mauritian supermarket for 25p apiece. 'I'm the envy of all my friends. I keep getting asked why I didn't buy dozens. But I did – just not for anyone else.' She giggles.

'Mother, how did we manage to spend that?' asks her eldest daughter breathlessly as her mum hands over a cool £251. 'Mother' blames the youngest for buying a few pencil cases and T-shirts. Taking a quick look at the bill, I can see most of it is actually 'Mother's' doing.

The scanner is playing up again and does this just as a woman who definitely does not need to add to the extra inches on her hips tries purchasing a particularly creamy carrot cake. The barcode is at the bottom of the pack and I have to turn it on its side to scan it.

'Just leave it.'

'I have to scan it, I'm afraid, and it's not scanning from this angle.'

'You'll spoil it.'

'I'm trying to make sure I don't.'

'Leave it.'

'I'll try typing in the barcode, but I still need to turn it on its side to read it.'

'No! Leave it.'

'If I don't scan it, you *do* know you can't have it?'

'Just leave it.'

'You want to leave it then? Are you sure?'

It suddenly scans.

'Well, now you've spoilt it.'

I *haven't* spoilt it.

'It's only the tiniest bit of cream at the top of the pack,' I plead. And there is just a bare smidgen of cream pecking the inside of the plastic lid. I leave it on the belt for her to stare at for a while.

'Give me another bag!' she snaps, just to have something to snap at. She takes the cake and neither of us says goodbye.

One of my regular customers is suffering another one of her migraines. She seems to get them every time she comes to the store. She's been asking my advice (it's that medical student thing again) so I suggest yoga, stretches, fresh air and massages. 'It happens as many as three times a week now and I've got to be careful about which painkillers I take because of my epilepsy.'

'You've got to get it checked out properly,' I insist.

You don't need to be a doctor to know her lifestyle is also a contributing factor. She teaches at a school where she deals with autistic children. She has three kids aged sixteen, thirteen and eleven, of whom the two girls are driving her around the bend. She tells me about the latest drama involving her teenage daughters and I try to reassure her that, once they get out the other side, they'll be OK. She was frazzled and tense on arrival and is smiling broadly by the time she's paid up. My work with her is done.

One man puts all the scanned shopping back into his trolley – despite having two large bags with him.

'Sorry, can I ask– why aren't you packing it all in the bags?' I enquire.

'It's quicker. I know what it's like to be waiting in a queue. I get fed up if someone is spending their time packing. I'll just do it when I get to the car.' He's probably pulling his hair out when he's stuck behind a customer being chatted up by a Cog.

I have my tea break and as I head back to the floor I see a tearful supervisor saying, 'I just don't want to do it.' A distraught-looking manager follows close behind. It's unnerving watching her cry because she's always so together and in control. I learn later that he wants her to start taking on an extra task she's not keen on – observing the customer service of the Cogs on duty. I don't blame her, it's not a job that makes any of the supervisors popular.

I serve a customer based at head office who tells me she's witnessed Sainsbury's emphasis on customer service for as long as she's been with the company – at least five years. Her husband joins in. 'It's well worth it because the whole supermarket experience at Sainsbury's is head and shoulders above Tesco.' She adds, 'They're going to hire lots more shop-floor staff now too, because they've just got rid of a raft of middle-management jobs.'

'So they've got rid of expensive employees so they can hire cheaper ones?'

'NO. NO. It was just taking too much red tape to get the littlest thing done. Now things will be a lot better, simpler.'

A woman with dyed orange hair, blood-red lippie and thick kohl lining her eyes is buying an expensive anti-wrinkle cream. I tell her gently that I don't believe they really work. 'Oh, I know that. It just makes me feel better and it feels nice – and when you see the gorgeous skin that Hollywood stars have, it does make you reach for the creams.'

'But you DO know that it's not the cream that's done that – it's probably the round-the-clock nutritionists, expensive facials and cosmetic surgery on tap.' I say.

'Oh yes – some of them do look dreadful though, don't they?'

We list the names of the worst faces in Hollywood and I suddenly notice that husband looks quite left out – so I draw him in playfully.

'So what do you think, should a woman age gracefully or get work done?'

'Oh, get work done, definitely.' He grins and I laugh. But his wife does neither. 'You can talk – you need work,' she says, glowering at him. My grin gets uncomfortable. He says nothing. 'I could make a really long list of what you should get done.' She's really scowling now. He distracts himself with rearranging the shopping and I scan more quickly. 'In fact, you should get yourself down to the plastic surgeon, right now,' she finishes.

More trouble onboard the love boat when another couple arrive at my till. The wife asks me to do a sub-total of the first ten items. They include merlot wine, chocolate mousse, apple-and-blackberry pie and three doughnut rings. It comes to £13.28. She whispers to me: 'Don't say anything, just continue.' Husband is at the other end of the till loading on the rest of the shopping. When he finishes he comes over. 'Well, how much was your stuff?' She smiles guiltily but pretends not to hear him. 'She spends a fortune when she comes shopping. When I come alone it takes forty minutes to shop, but when SHE comes alone she spends two hours! So now she gets her bits separately and I pay for the stuff that's actually ON the shopping list.' He tells me he's been compiling a shopping list ever since the credit crunch kicked in and following it religiously. 'We only replace what we eat now and don't buy anything extra unless we've run out – but if I let her shop we throw lots away. She really needs to eat before she comes out too.' Their shopping comes to £52.70. 'If I hadn't bought the extra stuff it would have been thirty something, wouldn't it?' the wife says pensively.

Rebecca and I drive home together. 'This customer actually asked me for a discount today. And she was one 100 per cent serious. I was like, "Um, madam, I'm not quite sure how you expect me to do that?" And do you know what she said? "Well, what about your discount card – can't you use that?" Can you believe the gall?' Rebecca then tells me about her soap-opera moment. 'This family had a massive argument RIGHT IN FRONT OF ME. After which the daughter and her boyfriend just stormed off, leaving Mum to pay.'

'How embarrassing …'

'Especially as Mum then started going on and on about the dodgy boyfriend and how he sponges off them both. And all I was thinking is, this isn't the *Jeremy Kyle Show*, love – it's a supermarket – have some dignity.'

Friday, 3 April 2009

I say a quick hello to Lesley and head down. The cleaner is at the bottom of the stairs wiping up a big oil spillage by the discounted goods. OK, so there's a job I'm glad I'm not doing. Hayley is on duty and gives me a big hello.

'Your hair looks different – what have you done?' she asks chirpily. Cog hair has to be tied up or tied back. 'Oh, it's just in a ponytail – I usually clip it back. Aren't you observant, Hayley?'

'Yes, I notice things like that – it changes your face. Right – you, my dear, are on till 6.'

It's lunchtime on the baskets and that means trouble. Ten customers are queuing impatiently. I'm relieving a checkout guy and his printer has frozen, the supervisor bell isn't working and his frantic waving has come to nothing. So I go to fetch a supervisor. The crowd starts to rumble. Clare strolls casually over – just the person for the job – and in a calm and leisurely fashion sorts the mess out. It takes four minutes. I'm quite sure we're about to be pelted by tomatoes when Maya races across and takes over a till.

Two curly-haired blonde women with two sets of icy blue eyes and matching furry gilets try to push in. Not on this Cog's watch. I tell them to go to the back of the queue. They comply. Cog – One. Basket customer – Nil.

Every customer I serve for the next ten minutes is seething. They refuse to say hello and ignore my apologies for the delay, but eventually I serve a customer who wants to talk. She has forty Pink Lady apples. 'I've got to admit it is a bit of an addiction. I eat about five a day.'

'Do you eat anything else?' I say, looking at her stick-thin figure.

'Well, they are quite filling. And at least I'm getting my "five a day".'

'You need some vegetables in there, too. You'll get ill if you just survive on these.' She gives me a fixed smile and goes.

There's a green sticker on the till with more mystery customer propaganda. 'We did it. New Year, New beginnings. MCM – only twenty-six left. Be a grinner, make us a winner.'

A dark-haired customer in her forties tells me she works at Budgens and travels a staggering fifty miles a day for the job. 'We only get £5.73 an hour – it's just the minimum wage.'

'And you must spend at least half of it on petrol.'

'That's why I'm desperate to leave – it's not worth it.' She then says quietly, 'Do you know if there are any vacancies here?'

'Try in three weeks – they might start looking then.' It's roughly when I hand in my notice and if anyone deserves this job, it's her.

The mum of one of the Cogs comes to the till looking shattered. 'How's your car-rental business now?'

'Oh, it's doing a lot better than before Christmas, but now everything else has got so expensive that we just can't keep up.'

As per usual on Friday there are more Cogs on baskets than there are customers. We all try to avoid clock-watching, except for Nelly, who insists on providing half-hourly count-downs.

A checkout newsletter is sitting nearby so I grab it for a quick read. It's full of Richard's usual upbeat assessment of our customer service. He congratulates us all for passing after two consecutive years of failure. And he names the Cogs who made it happen. Then he announces the new rules of engagement. Shop-floor assistance on customer stock enquiries now has to involve offering an alternative, checking to see when the product will be back in, or looking in the warehouse at the back of the store. He talks about grabbing overtime while it's available as there are likely to be reductions in this 'on the horizon' and says the last couple of checkout chairs are on their way. To which we all reply – 'Last couple? Where are all the rest?'

Tracey is having a bad day with *her* chair. Every time she gets off it, it shoots up in the air. 'I'll be headed to the moon in a minute.' She decides to spend her shift standing instead. Michaela is also on baskets. A twenty-year-old femme fatale with thick caramel-brown hair she wears slung over her right shoulder, she draws pubescent males in their dozens. Today a Lynx deodorant-carrying teenager arrives at her till. 'Oh, could

I smell it?' she says, offering him her open wrist. He sprays it on, hands shaking nervously and watches her inhale deeply. 'Oooo, it smells of chocolate,' she coos. Michaela is wasted here – she should put on her own erotic show.

Maya is also sitting with Tracey, Michaela and I. She offers us all a Murray Mint. 'I got into trouble last time I took a chewing gum,' I say.

'Chewing is different – your face is constantly moving. But with a sweet you have a suck then you tuck it into a corner of your mouth. And then have another suck and then tuck it in,' says Tracey, demonstrating the technique.

'And if a manager walks by and sees the lump tucked into your cheek?' I ask.

'There is a knack to it. Maya and I have been here long enough to do it – I'd say it takes a good fifteen years. But girls, practice makes perfect.'

'And what happens when you're talking to a customer?' Michaela pipes up.

'Just nestle it in the side of your mouth. And even if they see it, customers don't care.'

'Yes, but with all the talking we have to do – it could just suddenly pop out,' says Michaela solemnly.

'Well then you can just offer it to the watching customer instead.'

Katherine is sitting opposite me, and has been off spending time with her uncle. She mouths to me that he is still unwell. She's worried, but being the true professional she is, every time I glance over she is chatting wholeheartedly with her customers.

A construction man comes to my till. 'Business is booming. I work on £30–£40 million houses. At that end of the scale there's always work.'

'So why are you shopping here? You should be in Harrods 102.'

'I'm just here for the dog. The chicken and rice is for him.'

Trolley Boy wanders over to customers at my till intermittently. 'I bet Barack Obama eats bananas,' he tells one bewildered customer. And to another: 'I bet Barack Obama eats jerk chicken.' And then, 'I bet Barack Obama drinks OJ.' Every single customer is stupefied. And because his exceptional rhetoric cannot be matched, they don't even try.

Today I dish out advice to a set of parents-to-be on childbirth, good hospitals and sleepless nights. I console a mum whose only son hasn't got into any of their local primary schools, and give tips to the grandmother babysitting two out-of-control toddlers. A woman purchasing one bottle of wine is tense: 'I've got to pack for my holiday and I've only got an hour. I'm not an alcoholic, I swear, but if I don't down this bottle when I get in, I'll cry like a baby.'

A mum with a three-month-old baby is buying jar food. 'I'm exhausted and she's not drinking any milk, so I'm going to give her puréed food. I've been told I shouldn't, but I think she's starving.' I watch anxiously as she sits down in the café opposite my till and feeds the baby which doesn't yet have the digestive system to cope with solids.

A dapper customer in his fifties arrives at my till with flowers. 'Oh, three bunches of beautiful flowers for one lovely lady. Or is it – three bunches of beautiful flowers for three lovely ladies?' And I throw in a wink for extra tacky measure. 'Um, er … no … actually … they're for my mother's grave.'

Later, to a customer with a large stomach and a baby in a pram: 'And how wonderful – you're expecting another?' I ask.

'No, I'm not, actually. This is just my baby fat – I haven't lost it yet.'

Two regular customers in neon-yellow jackets and filthy hands. 'How come you guys are always so mucky?' It's that absent folly filter again. 'We spend a lot of time on forklift trucks and they are filthy, the things we have to move around are filthy. You think it LOOKS bad? Well, it FEELS vile. We hate it, but after a while there's no point trying to stay clean so we just wait until the end of the day and then have a good scrub.'

Samantha is in an obstreperous mood. She is called over to a till where a credit card isn't working. When she arrives she says at the top of her voice, 'It's a man; what do you expect? They just can't do things properly, can they?' A boy at my till listening in asks his mother what she means. She squeezes his hand and smiles.

And Samantha gets away with it because this is perhaps the only corner of the earth in which women rule.

'Feed your family for a fiver' is as big a hit with the customers as the Basics range. A fan of the salmon recipe seems to have stepped straight out of a Sainsbury's marketing meeting. 'The best bit is that you've got all the ingredients in your larder or fridge – stock cubes, rice, oil – so it doesn't cost any more than the price of the salmon. I love it.'

And then in comes *New Scientist* bloke. I give him a warm smile. 'Hello, *New Scientist* guy, how you keeping?'

'Busy, too busy. How about you?' He smiles back.

'Good. How's the van-driving business?'

'Yeah, it's good, but I'm working too hard …' he pauses for effect, '… to meet anyone.' And he looks at me in a way that can only be described as meaningful.

'I've got two teenagers and I get some time with them, but most of the time I'm just working and, well, just can't … meet anyone …' Deep look in the eyes again. There's a moment of toe-curling awkwardness and I keep looking down and scanning. For once I am totally lost for words. 'So, how about you?' he asks.

'Married with kids,' I reply, more quickly than is necessary.

'Oh yeah,' he says, looking at my left hand. 'I should've seen the ring, I guess.' And then we both say nothing. I scan. He packs. And off he goes. I barely know the guy, but I feel like it's the end of a beautiful friendship.

I'm pondering our little 'When-Harry-Met-Sally' moment when I'm interrupted by a customer laying into Maya.

'I'm sorry, I just can't give you any change. We're not allowed to do it,' she is saying to a customer at her till.

'That's ridiculous. I just want a couple of fivers and some coins,' he's yelling.

'I'm sorry. I can't do it.' Maya is going red in the face and has pushed herself and her chair away from him. The customer gesticulates wildly. 'It's just a little transaction. I don't understand why you can't do it.'

'Please go to customer service and see if they will help you,' she says, now standing up. He grabs his shopping, sending the other plastic bags at her till flying, and goes over to the customer service desk. He doesn't queue and stands at the side of the desk trying to get Sharon's attention – still shouting and thrusting a £20 note at her.

The customer I'm serving tuts. 'I know what it's like – I've been working in Tesco's for twelve years. The public can be so rude and unreasonable.'

'Has it got worse, then?' I ask her, still a little distracted by the yelling at customer service.

'Oh, definitely, and the things they get annoyed about are so ridiculous. If you haven't opened your till, or because you're doing something else, or you've forgotten to put their points on their cards – or anything. Sometimes I think I should just stop and say, "I'm sorry, I'm not perfect, I have so much to remember I can't always get it right." But then I think, what's the point? It's not like they're going to feel sorry for you. You've just got to keep your mouth shut and grit your teeth, don't you?'

'Did you get any training there to deal with it?'

She laughs. 'You got to be kidding! Managers don't care about that. It's awful, just awful how people can be.'

As I walk over to hand my keys in, I see a customer trying to bully a Cog who is cashing up into serving him. He only has two items. But she's done for the day and it's too late. He talks loudly, stands at the belt with his items and keeps going at her. She stands her ground but is red from her neck up.

Saturday, 4 April 2009

I bump into Rebecca in the locker room and we've both got back pain and wonder if sitting at the tills is doing it. As we make our way down, she gives every Cog we pass a warm hello. We get to the checkouts and I'm sat right in front of the till captains – again. Am I having yet another observation? I decide not: it's only been a week since my last one. And it gets so busy I can't worry about it until later. My first two customers speak no English and one of them struggles to open a plastic bag. I show him my finger-lickin' trick. He can barely contain his excitement and grins broadly. The crowd behind him is heaving and impatient so I gently usher him on his way. A couple with two trolleys' worth of shopping spend ten minutes loading and then make their way over to the top end of the till. I ask how many bags she has and start scanning her food. 'You've got so much fresh food here – I bet you're a good cook.'

'I am, actually. I'm a chef – I work in a school.'

'Aha! You know, I could tell – you've got lots of different kinds of food here and it all needs cooking from fresh.' I ask her how she's managing rising food prices.

'Oh, there's definitely an increase in prices, but I have to buy organic.' She has six large bottles of organic milk. 'It's expensive but worth it, I think, for the health benefits.' She also has organic meat, organic chocolates and organic bread. I ask her husband how he competes with such high standards in the kitchen. 'I don't even bother,' he says, laughing. Her shop costs her £221.59 and she doesn't flinch.

Behind her is a lady with a large trolley full of shopping. Her mood matches the black dress she's wearing. She has her back to me as she loads her shopping. I wait. She eventually comes over to my end of the till and throws her bags down. 'I've got four bags,' she tells me brusquely. I ask about her day as she packs. She gives me brief responses. A Cog passes by and asks if she wants help loading the rest of her shopping on the belt. 'No,' she snaps.

'Are you having a difficult day today?' I ask with not-entirely-sincere concern.

'Yes, I'm tired and I've got to look after my grandkids this afternoon,' she says curtly.

'You look too young to be a grandmother. How old are they?'

'Four and six – a boy and a girl. The boy is the one that's a handful – he's too active.' She's still making very little eye contact. 'But they're good kids.'

'Yes, I'm sure they are. It must be tiring – you've already done it once and now you have to do it all over again,' I say sympathetically, even though I feel sorrier for the poor kids lumbered with grumpy granny this afternoon. 'Hmm yes.' She's barely listening. I decide silence may be the best approach and so slide, scan and pass quietly – she's obviously in no mood to talk.

'Why aren't you helping me pack?' she suddenly barks.

'B-b-because you didn't ask me. Do you *want* me to help you?'

'Yes please,' she says sarcastically.

'It's just not one of those things we ask automatically any more.'

'Well how come the others always ask me? They see my shopping and offer straight away.' I acquiesce and silently pack. After a couple of minutes, Susie comes over and asks me to close my till. It's only been about thirty minutes into my shift. I lock my till and a manager I don't know too well takes me into Richard's office.

'Right,' she says as she sits down, 'I wasn't impressed with your customer service so you are getting a red. You were not interested, you didn't make any effort and you showed very poor customer service,' she bulldozes on while I try to compute events.

'Look, can I just say something?' I interrupt eventually. 'I've been here less than thirty minutes and have only served a couple of customers so far – so I really don't know what you mean.'

'Right, well, you weren't trying to engage your customers. You didn't do what you were supposed to …'

'I'm sorry, but which customer did you observe me not talking too? My first two customers didn't speak any English and the one after that I could probably tell you her life story.'

'Right, let me get the till captain.' She gets up to go to the door and calls the supervisor on duty in.

'This young lady,' says Manager in highly condescending tone, 'disagrees with what I'm telling her.'

'Look,' says the till captain, 'I saw you sitting like this –' and she puts her hand to her cheek and leans on it, hamming up a bored face.

I actually had my hand curled up under my chin while waiting for customers to turn around and don't know a Cog alive who would have the audacity to sit as she is suggesting. Not even in *my* local supermarket. No matter, though – I know that the supervisor has to kowtow to the manager, so I let it ride. 'And when I saw you,' she continues, 'I said, "That's not like her. She's always so ready to chat."' I smile even though I feel like throttling them both.

'I really think you misread the situation. I was just waiting for the customers to turn around. And I WAS serving ones who don't speak English; it's very difficult to engage with them, so you just do the basics as politely as you can.'

'No,' says the till captain, 'that's where you've got it wrong. You've still got to do the same with them and treat them like the mystery customer.'

'Well, I don't know how you do that beyond doing what I did. And certainly in terms of the other two—'

The manager dives back in the game. 'Well, I saw the Italian lady put her bags down and you just asked her how many bags she had. I didn't see you give her a big smile or a big hello or anything.' This is so preposterous, I suddenly want to laugh.

'But you don't always have to say hello to be friendly. You can sometimes just have a different interaction and it can still be good customer service, can't it?' I ask, looking from one face to the other.

'Look, I don't mark someone down if they are ignoring the customer just because the customer is difficult. It would have been easy for me to mark you down, but I—'

I barge back in. 'My customer was actually really difficult, but obviously you couldn't see that from where you were standing.' The manager then starts to talk over me and I suddenly find myself doing the same.

'It's not natural to always say hello – I've got to see how each customer behaves before I decide how to deal with them.'

'No, it's up to you to give them a fantastic greeting …' she responds.

'If you stopped those customers and asked them if they were happy with the customer service they got—'

'It's not about that, it's about the customer service we see you giving.'

'Look, all I can tell you is that I had just started my shift and it does usually take a few minutes to get into the swing of things – and despite all of that, each customer needs something different. And my scanner was playing up and so I had to ask a supervisor to come over—'

The manager leaps in again. 'If your scanner isn't working, you can't let it show. Look, I've done observations so many times – I'm really good at them. I know what I'm doing and that what I'm seeing is right.' I suddenly allow my reasons to run dry. It's time to lay down the sword.

'OK, I accept your observation for what it was. I still maintain that you don't know how that conversation really went – what you saw and what actually went on were two different things. But either way, I accept it.' I know I've stepped outside the norms of Cog etiquette and the impasse has to end.

'It would have been very easy for me to say you hadn't done anything, but I didn't. It would have been easy for me to say you had failed … but I didn't. I've assessed you before and you were very good – so … I'm actually going to give you a green.' She passes me the paperwork and I've passed on everything except for my greeting. She asks me to add my comments. I resist the urge to write 'Stick it where the sun don't shine.' Instead I scribble something faintly professional: 'I treat every customer differently, depending on how they behave. It's not always natural to give them a big "hello". But I do accept Sainsbury's policies!' I try to lighten the dark mood that has descended between us, but she's having none of it. Managers here aren't used to being challenged – and I'm not quite sure what came over me. I struggle to get it out of my head and my interaction with every customer over the next hour feels even more artificial than normal. Fortunately one of my customers is a loquacious chap who lets me do all the listening.

'I don't let me wife come shopping any more. She ends up spending £50 more than me every time. She goes absolutely crazy, so I let her come once every three months. But then we spend the entire time arguing and when the kids are with her, they all spend even more.'

'How old are the kids?'

'Eight, ten and twelve. I had the snip, otherwise I'd have ended up having more. She's so greedy she has no limits when it comes to food and when it comes to kids.'

A granddad spending the weekend with his two grandkids fails to recall their ages accurately, to the utter chagrin of the six-year-old and nine-year-old. 'GRANDPA – how can you not know how old we are?' says the six-year-old.

'Give him a break,' I say, 'he's already done time with your parents – you're lucky he still wants to hang out with you.'

One of my regular customers pops in today – Harry the electrician – I call him the Electrical Philosopher. Like most of my regular customers he doesn't immediately remember me – until I give him a little prompt. Customers will reveal extremely private details to me but forget me, my name and my face the moment they walk away. In any case, this personal curse has been a professional gain – helping me to sneak in and out of tricky situations unnoticed.

Harry's having another one of his full-blown rants about modern life. Last week it was how family life has been reduced to nothing 'because of time in front of the box'. Today he complains about the disappearance of good manners from public life. 'I was coming into the car park just now. And a lady let me pass – so I thanked her. Then I let one car pull out. Did I get a thank you? – You bet I didn't. Then I pulled over to the left for three minutes to let a woman slot in and park her car – did I get a thank you, then? Nope – nothing. What are these people teaching their kids? What kind of message are they sending to me? You do something for me – and in return I won't even have the decency to give you a little wave. A little flick of my hazard lights, a smile – nothing. What kind of way is that to behave?' He's a twenty-first-century moral compass – part crusader, part spoilsport, part moan master. I love him – if he was prime minister he'd put the world to rights within twenty-four hours.

I decide to practise greetings the management way and one of my customers gets the Full Monty: a big smile and a 'fantastic' greeting. It fails miserably with the customer, who is in no mood for a chat. I'm in the middle of babbling inanely about the weather when Rebecca stops by. 'Excuse me, madam, I'm a member of management here, can you tell me what you think of this lady's customer service?'

Customer looks up alarmed and says hurriedly, 'Oh yes, it's very good.'

'Don't worry, she's not really management,' I say, laughing.

'No, I insist I am,' says Rebecca. 'Did you find her genuine?'
The lady relaxes. 'Hmm, I'd say so-so.'

After my break I'm taken off the tills so I tidy up, do some reverse shopping and pack away hangers and security tags. I'm stopped repeatedly and have to remind myself to offer alternatives. I make them up. We've run out of maple syrup so I suggest honey.

'No, it's maple syrup I want. If I wanted honey – I'd just buy honey, wouldn't I?' says the customer, not entirely unreasonably.

One lady asks me if we have soya milk originals in the back.
'I'll need to just go and look.'
'OK, come looking for me,' she says and wanders off. My ferreting in the back proves to be unsuccessful and I come back to find the customer. I search in aisle after aisle, looking for a large mass of blonde hair. After fifteen minutes and walking up and down the full length of the shop twice, I give up and go back to my reverse shopping. She comes looking for me some five minutes later and accepts the substitute I picked out randomly. I then watch her at the till buying my big fat bluff.

I'm putting some nappies back when I pass a Japanese woman with her English husband bickering by the baby milk. 'No can come tomorrow, too busy for the shop,' she says.

'No can come tomorrow?' he mocks rather unkindly. 'If it's important enough, you CAN come tomorrow.'

'But she says no guarantee.'

'Well, why don't you just try to see what happens? Is that too much to ask?' he asks caustically.

An eight-year-old boy standing on the side of the trolley his mother is pushing nearly collides with me. 'Be careful, James,' says Mum.

'YOU'RE THE ONE DRIVING, YOU BE CAREFUL,' he shouts at her.

I can't locate where Instant Apple Tea should go back on the shelf and bump into Jane, who makes an admirable effort to find it for me. 'Just dump it there,' she says, pointing to the Yorkshire Tea. 'See, look, gravy granules have been dumped on the coffee shelf.' We *all* do it.

Ayesha asks me to close David's till and send him over. Supermarket code for he's just had an observation. He comes back looking downtrodden and tells me he got a red. 'Customers don't want to talk – what am I supposed to do?' He's right. They only talk to me because I corner them into it.

I get stopped by a woman who mumbles something to me about our flower section. 'I'm sorry, do you mean flower or flour?'

'FLOUUUUUWERRRRRR,' she growls, lacing the first half with arsenic and rolling the r at the end somewhat unhelpfully. I'm scared, I'm not ashamed to say, so don't ask for more clarification. I lead her to the flour aisle, praying silently. She walks a step or two ahead even though I'm supposed to be leading her.

'I'm sorry, I just wasn't sure if you were saying flour or flowers.' Adding the plural in a bid to see if that helps elucidate further.

'Well, at least you answered me. One of your colleagues seemed like he had a hearing problem.'

I'm really proud of myself today. I manage to stay off the tills for a solid 150 minutes – almost half my shift, and spend a lot of time talking to Rebecca. I cash-up seven minutes early for the first time ever.

'It's not fair, why don't I ever get taken off?' she asks me.

'Because you are too good at the customer service malarkey.'

On the way home I tell her about my fisticuffs with the manager. 'It sounds to me like the two of you should have taken it outside for a full-on catfight. I'd have paid good money to watch that show.'

I know I have to share some big news with her.

'Look, I've got something to tell you and I don't want you to be too upset.'

'Why ... what is it?' she asks, looking at me concerned.

'I'm leaving.'

'What do you mean, *leaving*?'

'Going, quitting, clocking off, *hasta la vista* ...'

'NOOOOO.'

'Yes.'

'You can't do that to me, you can't.'

'I'm sorry.'

'NO. I won't let you. How can you desert me? What am I going to do without you? How can you do this? NOOOO!' She says laughing and shaking me by the arm at the same time.

'Pull yourself together, woman,' I say, giggling. 'We can't turn into those people who will only stay somewhere because their mates work there. You'll be fine – you already have so many other friends there.'

'Not like you – they're not like you. They're not sensible like you.' And she throws in some mock-sobs for humorous effect. Her full-blown act of simulated fury is followed by her grabbing her shopping bags, slamming the door and saying archly through the window, 'You've let the side down!' before 'storming' off. Still laughing, I watch her go. Then a sombre thought flicks through my mind: I wonder if she'll feel I betrayed her when the truth comes out.

Friday, 10 April 2009

I spend the morning devising and revising reasons to give Richard for resigning. I hope he'll just shrug it off. I keep going over the different permutations of every excuse I may make. I arrive and walk straight into his office. He's on the phone but invites me to sit down while he listens to what seem like endless messages. Meanwhile my heart is thumping so loud, I'm convinced it's echoing in the room. Eventually he puts the phone down and smiles at me.

'How are you? Everything good with you?'

'Yes, everything is just fine, I …'

'Good, good, I'm glad to hear it.'

'I've got some bad news, well, it's not bad news for me, but … but I'm … I'm leaving.'

'Oh.' He looks at me fixedly, his green eyes not blinking. All my rehearsals go out the window.

'It's, it's just time for me, you know, to … um … move on – and you know it's not you … you've been fantastic, but I … I … I guess I just want to do other things.'

'Yes, of course, course …' It feels like a teenage break-up.

'And I know you've done so much to accommodate me,' I race on unsteadily, 'but you know I'm keen to just do something else … I'm so sorry.' He's been sitting very still staring straight at me, absorbing my words in eerie silence. He's a fireball of energy so it's the longest I've ever seen him not move a muscle and I wonder for a second if he's fallen asleep with his eyes open. 'Well …' he suddenly bursts out, 'obviously I'm really disappointed. I can't pretend I'm not. But you seem very convinced …'

'Yes, I've definitely made up my mind,' I say as definitively as I can. If he starts to persuade me to stay, I might just end up staying.

'Is there any point me trying to ...'

'No, definitely not.'

Suddenly the store manager walks in. 'There are customers pouring in and there are no trolleys at all, Richard.'

'OK,' says Richard firmly, 'Just give me five minutes.'

'Well, it's pretty bad out there. So really you need to ...'

'OK, just GIVE me a minute,' says Richard sternly and the manager walks back out. Richard rolls his eyes and turns back to me. 'Well, you know there were ways I wanted to develop you, but if this is what you want to do, then of course I understand. Are you going on to something else?' he asks tentatively.

'Er ... no.'

'OK. Well, I hope you feel your time here has gone well. You got out of the house and away from the kids and hopefully it gave you the confidence to get work and get out and about, didn't it?' He is so obliging – it's quite unbearable.

'Yes, of course – and I just want you to know ...' I start to feel a little stream of emotion open up '... that you are such a great guy ... a brilliant manager, and that I don't have a bad word to say about you ...'

I can't stop. '... You know, you hear about places like this and how awful they can be, but really you've been great – with the kids and everything so ... so ... thank you.' And thus my mushy, unseemly resignation speech ends.

'Thank you. You're sweet. I DO try to do my best. Oh, give me a hug,' he says, opening his arms. So I do. It should be one of those truly awkward moments, like watching a boss burst into tears in a meeting or walking in on your boyfriend's dad on the loo. But actually, it's rather comfortable: just a Cog and her manager locked in platonic embrace.

Within minutes Hayley has heard I'm leaving and pops over to my till to wish me luck. If my colleagues are being wonderful, customers are typically letting themselves down. A thirty-something woman and her friend arrive with full trolleys. And start unloading. 'Get me a packer,' she shouts from her end of the checkout. A packer? I'm the only packer around here. She turns back to her shopping and will be unable to hear me unless I shout. Which I. Will. Not. Do. When she eventually turns around again I ask her:

'Do you mean you want ME to pack?'

'NO … I WANT a packer.' She's not old, infirm or with kids. She only has one trolley of shopping and a friend with her. It's an unspoken rule at the tills – customers that come in twos help each other pack.

'Well … we don't. We don't usually have packers. But if you want help, I can pack for you,' I say to mollify her.

'Huh! All right then,' she says, clearly put out. I start packing and she stands nearby opening bags. When I scan and pack it takes three times longer than normal. After a few seconds, her friend shouts down to her. 'Didn't they get you a packer?'

'NOO! Disgusting, isn't it?'

I look at her in disbelief.

'Can't believe there's no one here to help the disabled.' I almost choke.

'Sorry, I didn't realise … are you OK?'

'I've got a back problem,' she says, leaning her hand into her lower back and scowling for effect.

'Well, look, if you want me to get you someone, then I can try – it's just very busy today.' I look around and can't see any available staff.

'I think everyone might be busy,' I tell her.

'Well, get me a manager to pack then,' she demands. Ho, ho, ho – this WILL be fun. I summon Hayley over.

'This lady would like some help packing,' I say, stifling a wicked smile. Hayley's eyes dart from the customer to me and back to the customer. She's puzzled but a true professional. 'Yes, of course,' she says, and starts to pack. The customer then leans against the till opposite mine, folds her arms and stares into mid-air, still scowling. Hayley, with her back now to the customer, pulls a face and starts opening bags. We chat as she packs. Once she's piled all the bags into the trolley she turns back to the customer. 'Are you all right then, love? Not feeling well?'

'It's my knees.' What happened to her back? 'Can you get me someone to push my trolley out?'

It's less a request and more a decree. David is summoned. He has to stand to attention for ten further minutes until her friend has also finished her shopping and he then pushes the trolley out. I find out later that he emptied her shopping into the car too. She doesn't say thank you once – not to me, not to Hayley and not to David.

While some packing is left to Cogs like me, others wouldn't trust their own mother to do it. One such man is at my till with his wife and daughter behind. He shouts orders at them: 'Put heavy things at the bottom!' And they mock him behind his back. He actually empties the bags they've packed and repacks them.

One of my customers has a pregnancy kit. I struggle to get it out of its security container. A little scandal lasts me a long time, so I'm desperate to get the story. The couple's faces give nothing away. But there are two kits in the box, which by my calculations equates to please-let-there-be-a-little-blue-line. I try to pull it apart and it's decidedly stuck. The Cog next to me has to help. Once it's out I apologise and they exchange a private smile. Always the opportunist, I leap in: 'Would it be good news if you're pregnant?'

'Oh yes, definitely,' she says.

'I thought so – your double kit gave you away.'

'We've been trying for months – and I'm now a few days late, so I really hope so ...' she says, looking at me eagerly.

'I'm sure the fertility gods are smiling down at you.'

'Well, as long as they're not having yet another laugh.'

'Good luck,' I say.

'Thank you,' they reply, both grinning broadly.

'Please come back and tell me,' I add pathetically to their backs. They don't hear me. It's the most agonising part of this job – the endless cliff-hangers and tantalising unfinished stories. She's not the only customer with pregnancy news. A customer buying the magazine *I'm Pregnant* unwittingly shares early bun-in-the-oven news with me. A gentle grilling reveals she is only five weeks gone. As is often the case, I know before most of her family and any of her friends.

A customer with a fresh tan, smart suit and a swagger thinks it's fun to mock Cogs. 'Do you need some bags?' I ask as he piles his trolley-load on.

'And how do you expect me to carry all that back – with my bare hands?' he scoffs, flashing his freshly whitened teeth in a cheesy smirk.

'You could try, but I wouldn't want it to ruin your manicure,' I suddenly find myself saying. He's taken aback. I'm taken aback. I've crossed a line, but he deserved it. I smooth things over and learn that he's just 'jetted in from the States'. He delights in sharing endless tales of his 'remarkable life in Manhattan'. A photographer by trade, he's working in advertising, which he says has been untouched by the recession: 'I'm still rolling in it,' he tells me shamelessly.

Magda is on the till opposite me. Her mum is being served at the till behind me. Magda's customers are arguing furiously.

They throw their shopping down on the belt, thrust bags at each other, and at one point the husband yells at the wife, 'Just get on with it, will you?' They are causing such a scene I can barely concentrate on my own customer. Magda is so busy pestering her mother that she doesn't even notice.

People are buying clothes by the dozen and worried that they'll get marked by the black conveyor belt. They hand them over to me carefully, asking to keep it on the hanger. I scan and then hold the item in mid-air. One lady wearing a baby blue Barbie T-shirt leaves me with my arm dangling in mid-air for a whole minute, simply ignoring me.

Another shouts 'STOP!' when I pass her food on to the belt after scanning it. I freeze and look up. 'DON'T PUT THE MEAT ON THE VEG,' she roars.

However big her mouth may be, it's not big enough for the super-sized Easter eggs stacked on the supermarket shelves. I scan several giant-sized eggs costing in the region of £10. Who's going to eat an Easter egg that big? No wonder children's teeth are such a mess. And half the customers that come in here are overweight. One woman buying several of these Easter eggs gets to £72.91 and starts to put her shopping back. Instead of the human-sized eggs, I put back slug & snail killer, an anti-bug spray and a white blouse.

People are doing big shops today and cash flows heavily into the till. I have to tuck the notes in because they are literally spilling out – and many are choosing to pay in cash. Most people's shopping is costing in the region of £130–£170. And, as usual, they're all getting their fair share of nasty shocks. But who can resist the pull of cheap-chic clothes? One woman buys some pretty floral dresses for her three-year-old and six-year-old granddaughters. With the 25 per cent sale discount they only cost her £14 and £11. 'I just bought two dresses from

Monsoon that look almost the same and that cost me £58. I'll be taking those back, straight away.' She's so pleased with her bargain shop, she shares this information with the customer behind her, who is suitably impressed. I then see *that* customer lingering in the clothing section, moments after leaving my till.

A couple in their fifties are going away for a short break and are in to stock up for their seventeen- and twenty-year-old sons. They buy a lot of easy-cook rice, ready meals and Basics curry sauce for 10p as, you guessed it, the boys don't cook. They spend £194.05.

'OH MY DAYS!' cries Mum.

'We usually spend £150 on proper fresh food. This is awful,' says Dad. He turns to Mum and says, 'You know what will happen, as well? They'll run out of food and order pizza.'

One couple are so embroiled in a row they don't notice me tuning in to their grumblings. First it's the peas, then the choice of mayonnaise and then the £19.99 music system the wife tries to justify purchasing for their teenage daughter. 'Why does she need a new one? She's only had it a couple of weeks,' asks Dad.

'Because she's broken it.'

'Well, that should be it. We can't keep buying her one a month.'

Somehow the stereo stays. They argue next about the custard they may or may not already have at home. Then the value of canned potatoes versus fresh potatoes, canned carrots versus fresh carrots. In the end, the cans win. Every item is dissected by Dad and then defended by Mum.

On my way up to my break, two Cogs are walking speedily through the aisles. 'Quick, quick,' they mutter to each other, racing ahead, 'don't look sideways, don't look ahead, just look down. They may grab us.'

In the canteen, Barbara walks past me, flashing a smile and a big wink, and for the first time I don't jump out of my skin.

When I get back down after my break, I go to see Rebecca. 'So was Richard devastated?'

'Devastation would be a slight exaggeration. Disappointed is better. But, you know, he was good about it.'

'What do you think he'll say when I tell him I'm out of here next?'

'He won't say anything, because you're not going anywhere. This is your calling, lady. Accept it.'

Adam walks past and I call him over for a quick chat. As usual, he's floating from department to department. 'It's so busy on the floor today I haven't been able to do anything on my tick list. Just been running back and forth trying to find something customers want that is invariably out of stock or doesn't exist.'

Connor passes Magda's till and stops for a quick chat. 'Was that your mum in earlier?' he asks.

'Yes.'

'I thought so – we had a little chat. She looks and sounds just like you.'

'Everyone says that,' says Magda, and then they are interrupted by Ayesha.

'Move away, Connor, stop talking to her,' Ayesha says through gritted teeth.

Connor is used to being reprimanded, so shrugs it off. 'Slap, slap,' he jokes to Magda as he walks down towards the pet-food aisle. I'm tempted to ask customers if they really do mind a quick exchange between two Cogs.

I see Connor later, wandering around, arms laden with abandoned items set to return to the shelves. As he passes by, I psst him. 'Connor, what's the trick? How do you manage to get off the tills so often?'

'It's simple. Just stare at the supervisors, directly in the eyes, don't look away and don't blink. Oh, and look really bored, like you're not doing anything. Throw in a yawn if you're brave enough, and then watch the magic happen.'

It's clocking-off time and the *Closed Checkout* sign is on my belt, so I cash up. I check my till roll and see I've served exactly 100 customers today. A woman arrives and starts piling her shopping on the belt. 'I'm sorry I'm closed now,' I tell her with the cash notes in my hand, mid-count. She picks her shopping up, shoots me an evil stare and says into the phone pressed to her ear: 'The F****** B**** won't serve me.'

I have to pop into Richard's office on my way out. 'Everyone's very upset that you are leaving!' he exclaims. I look at Ayesha draped on the chair next to him half-asleep and she nods lamely. Barbara, busy scribbling something with her back to me, asks, 'Who's leaving?'

'SHE is,' says Richard. Barbara looks over her shoulder and, without a word, turns back to her paperwork. I don't think *everyone* cares, but I appreciate the sentiment.

Saturday, 11 April 2009

Rebecca's lost her locker key but I have no space in my locker for her bag today. Another Cog we don't know too well offers to store her things at the customer service desk in the store. 'Thanks, that's really very nice of you,' says Rebecca.

'No worries,' says the Cog, flicking back her hair and preening herself while we watch gormlessly.

'What's your name?' asks Rebecca.

'Ai-li.'

'That's a gorgeous name, what does it mean?'

'Lovely,' she says with slow deliberate intent.

'Oh, how appropriate,' says Rebecca, taking the bait, almost entirely for her own amusement.

'I KNOW …' Ai-li says excitedly. 'People really think I'm making it up, but that's just what it means. They keep saying that's so right for me, but I'm like, honestly – yeah – I didn't make it up.' Another flick of the hair.

'How lucky for you that your parents named you so well. I think *my* name just means hairy armpits,' says Rebecca as I chortle quietly.

We walk down the stairs on our way to the shop floor and a warehouse assistant on his way up sees Rebecca and immediately his face lights up. She teases him and he glows. 'You don't need me,' I say. 'You've got admirers, fans and friends in every nook and cranny of this store.' She smiles and puts her arm through mine. It's heaving as we walk through the double doors and into the store.

'I'm not in the mood for this today,' we chime, looking at each other and laughing. 'Let's just turn around. We could go to the cinema and watch back-to-back movies.'

'Oh, what a great idea. Do you think they'd notice we weren't here?'

By the tills, my brain can't process the chaos. Even the aisles are now filling with customers queuing. The Cog I relieve is so annoyed she's had to stay on for two further minutes that my greetings are met with a stony silence. I ask her where the school vouchers are and she blanks me. I don't blame her one bit. Working one extra unpaid minute in this place feels like a gross breach of human rights.

It's the holidays and that has to explain the craziness. I look to the door and there is a steady flow – no, not a flow, a veritable *flood* of customers pouring into the store. 'Why aren't people on holiday?' I ask one of my customers.

'I imagine people can't afford to go abroad so they're just staying here, aren't they? I'm having a – what did the papers call it again? Oh yes, a "staycation" with my family – it's the new recession-friendly holiday.'

One customer has a basket full of groceries entirely from the Basics range: curry noodles, crème caramel, salmon, trifle, mashed potato, meatballs – she has several meals for the next few days all for less than £20. But then she has to go and spend £11.99 on a bottle of Teacher's whisky.

There is such an endless swarm of customers. I try to get through them quickly. But one customer, to misquote the Pointer Sisters, wants a Cog with a slow hand. 'I know all about your items per minute, but you need to slow down.'

'Oh, how do you know about that?' I say, going into slack motion.

'My friend works in a supermarket. You lot need to tell your managers that we don't want to be rushed – and I certainly like to pack properly.' But by trying to please them all, you fail to please anyone. Sainsbury's customer service policy empowers the customer but disembowels the Cog. It stands to reason that customers paying a premium for their food now see it as their right to insist on a tailor-made service – and that's what the store expects Cogs to deliver. In this climate, Cogs are being expected to work ever harder for their money. The problem is perpetually second-guessing and constantly custom-making the service is much easier to demand than it is to actually do.

I serve a chatty, friendly customer but things turn when I give him his change. 'I gave you £20.'

'No you didn't, you gave me £10.'

'No, I only had a £20 note on me – and it was a new crisp one. Have a look in your till.'

I look in my till, which is bursting with both new and old £20 notes. I think he gave me a tenner but now I'm not sure, and by the looks of him I can tell he isn't either. If I give him the extra £10 back, I could be in trouble. If I insist and I'm wrong, he'll be out of pocket. Deadlock. Supervisor is buzzed.

Ayesha comes over and tells him that at the end of the day the contents of the till will be totalled and if it is £10 over he'll get his money back on Tuesday. He seems happy enough with this, but if it had been me I'd have kicked up a fuss.

A customer close behind doesn't have any bags.

'I'll carry my tins home and won't use one of your bags, but could you put a point on my Oyster card?'

'You mean Nectar card, but yes, sure.' I give her a point, hand her the receipt and then watch her pick up a bag and put her tins in. She's forfeiting her integrity for a point that is not even worth a penny.

A Nigerian mum and dad are in, minus their three kids aged seventeen, fourteen and seven.

'The fourteen-year-old is the human vacuum cleaner. He eats everything in sight.' The kids send Mum and Dad into the store with their huge shopping lists.

'That defies the laws of nature. You guys should make them come with you,' I tell them.

'It's far better than bringing them with us – otherwise we end up spending more.' They tell me they usually spend about £250 every week, or a minimum of £800 a month. For a change I'm the one that's shocked. 'That's how much my mortgage costs me every month,' I tell them.

'I know … I know … but we can't figure out how to make savings. In the last six months our shopping has started costing up to an extra £150 per month – it's the prices that are going up.' They spend a staggering £320. I find myself giving them a quick master-class in my till-side 'Cog Clinic'. 'Make a list and stick to it. Pay in cash and buy cheap versions of everything – usually kids can't tell the difference. Give your kids a budget and tell them to come with you next time and insist they shop within that budget.' They listen closely and leave, clutching their hefty bill and over-sized trolley.

People are still buying the giant Easter eggs. And another customer blows hard into a bag to open it. 'That's the second time I've seen that strange behaviour,' I blurt out. 'Why don't you just lick your fingers and open it?' 'Because this is the best way,' comes the odd reply.

Easter eggs aside, everyone is buying compost. One customer says they want to start growing their own little vegetable plot in the garden to save on their grocery shop, another tells me it's because they're on offer at £2.49 a pop.

BOGOF shoppers are annoying me with their repeated questions mid-scan about every single offer. 'It will come off at the end or you'll see it on this little screen up here,' I say, pointing to the screen in her eye-line. She bought her two ice creams for £3 and two stock-cube packs for £1.50 and she doesn't want to pay a penny more. She continues hounding me about every deal.

In a quiet moment I catch the eye of the Cog opposite me. 'I'm so bored.'

'*I'm* so tired.'

'*I* want to get out of here.'

'If you run now, I promise I'll follow.'

* * *

Here is what the list of someone who came in to buy Easter eggs looks like:

Jute bag x 2
Quavers crisps
Wotsits crisps
Skittles x 2
White bread
Mini doughnuts
Ferrero Rocher chocs
Tropicana juice
Heinz mayonnaise x 2
Cosmetic creams gift bag
Tampons
Salsa dip
Heat magazine
Greetings cards x 3
Bunch of roses
Chocolate fudge pudding
Gift wrap

Grand total: £53.76. She is so appalled she stands there enraged with herself. 'I'm so disgusted I can't even be bothered to get my Nectar card out.' I can tell she wants to dump it all and if Ayesha wasn't standing so close I'd tell her to abandon it and run. She pays up and hates herself for it. I tell her she'll find the Easter eggs at the front of the store.

When I get back down after my break, fed and watered, a man is at the till with his daughters – all five of them. They tell me they are eighteen, sixteen, fourteen, twelve and six. They have a very natural, loving relationship and playfully tease each other. I assume the two female customers at the bottom end of the till are the mother and grandmother. 'Look at you with your tribe,' I say to Dad. 'Your beautiful daughters and wife and mum – aren't you a lucky man? Although you are, of course, seriously outnumbered.' He looks at me, confused, and then his eighteen-year-old daughter says, 'Oh no, they're not with us,' looking at the two older women at the other end of the till. 'But, yes, there are a lot of females in our family.' We talk about their family life and she tells me what it's like to grow up in a home full of women; how Dad is outnumbered, the divvying up of bedrooms, the time spent in bathrooms, the borrowing of clothes and shoes that clutter up the hallway. It's also easy to see that they are all the very best of friends. They are a delightful, colourful bunch with smiles that stretch from ear to ear.

'I'm surrounded by boys upwards, sideways and downwards, so can't imagine what it'd be like in a house full of girls,' I tell them.

'Oh, it's great. We're thinking of starting our own pop group – Only Girls Allowed,' quips the fourteen-year-old.

'The constant talk of boys, celebs and menstrual cycles does do my head in a bit,' says the straight-talking sixteen-year-old.

'And don't forget our nasty cat-fights,' adds the twelve-year-old.

Dad is listening and smiling quietly to himself. He turns away for a minute and the eldest of the girls leans in and whispers, 'The thing is, we're just trying to do our best at the moment because our mum just passed away in January. So we're kind of still coping with that …' My heart breaks into two big chunks and falls into my stomach.

She continues, 'It's hard, but we're just trying to keep it together for him,' indicating Dad, 'and her,' glancing at the youngest being teased by a sister at the end of the till.

'Do you have any other family?'

'No.'

'No aunts, grandmothers?'

'No. We're just happy that we've got each other.'

The two older girls tell me they want to go into dentistry and graphic design. I get a lump in my throat as I watch this motherless family courageously walk away with their heads held high despite the giant heart-shaped piece that is missing.

My thoughts are still dwelling on them thirty minutes later and I think I serve the mystery customer without realising. I suspect this because she doesn't offer her Nectar card until I ask for it. She doesn't tell me about her bags, which I see in her trolley as she leaves. I barely made any conversation and hardly any eye contact. And she tries to look discreetly at my name badge at the end.

The last fifteen minutes are really quiet but the two Cogs sitting by me are dreading the unwelcome last customer with their over-flowing trolley. The three of us make a unanimous decision at 6.25 to only serve basket customers. At 6.27 we see two large trolleys heading our way and immediately decide to close our tills and suffer the consequences. Fortunately, Hayley is of the same mind and shouts over to us to cash-up.

I pick up my own Easter eggs on the way home and take them to Michelle's till. She's banging on about her favourite subject – probation. The fact that someone so obsessed with our trial period is still *on* a trial period is an unbearable twist of fate. 'I just hate the uncertainty. The hours are better, but I just want to know if I'm staying on. I got a green recently, so I hope so. But I just find it stressful.'

I hope she gets to stay on – it clearly means a lot to her.

On the way home Rebecca and I swap horror stories about the amounts people are spending. I've become obsessed with the recession myself – working behind the checkout, hearing other people's financial woes, watching their horrendous spending habits is doing me no good at all.

Friday, 17 April 2009

It's chock-a-block and chaos reigns. Screaming babies, yelling toddlers, mums on the edge of a breakdown shouting orders at their offspring:

'NOOO, NO CHOCOLATE!' 'GET OVER HERE.' 'WHERE ARE YOU???' Child-free customers can barely hide their disdain. The queues are heaving. To add insult to injury, it's the lunch hour and I'm on baskets. I serve a woman who works at a distributor's around the corner – they specialise in ethnic foods. 'Business is good. But you know, food always does well in a recession – a bit like here. People have to eat and they are more likely to eat in and cook right now.'

A customer who was made redundant a few months ago passes by. Last time I spoke to him he was getting a little work from an agency. I will him to come to my till. About ten minutes later he goes to another checkout – leaving me dangling in mid-air like one of the blousons I've just scanned. Every story needs a beginning and an end – but the endings here often vanish into thin air, like an unfinished book left behind on a train.

People are presenting their bonus point vouchers and prepared to put up a fight for every last point. A customer who wants to use a voucher so she can get 100 Nectar points (the equivalent of 50p) needs to spend another 30p on either bread, bakery or cake. She only has toffee pudding and bagels. Off she goes towards the bakery, leaving her husband behind at my check-out. I send the customers behind them to other tills. He kills time by discussing a front-page story about Gordon Ramsay with me. She's gone for a good ten minutes and comes back clutching two crusty white rolls. I put them through and then say mischievously, 'I'm afraid you've not got enough yet.'

'You are kidding!' she shrieks. Because my courage has a limit, I quit while I'm ahead. Her husband thinks it's hilarious.

An Italian woman asks me to check her Nectar points. I tell her she has £5 worth.

'Do you want me to take it off?'

'I have more. Check again,' she orders.

I check again. 'You have £5, I'm afraid.'

'That's not right. I have more.'

'You probably do have more, but for reasons I can't explain it's telling me you only have £5 worth. Do you want me to take it off?'

She's angry. I wait a few beats.

'Would you like me to take it off?'

'I have more points than that,' she frowns. 'Something is wrong.'

'Yes, the thing is, we aren't Nectar. And I don't have the experience to tell you why that may be the case.' I haven't had any training on Nectar points so can't tell her what is going on. Sometimes people can't redeem points if they don't normally shop in that store, sometimes the points are all there but the card is blocked. Usually, though, I just don't know. And anyway, she is holding up the queue.

'Would you like me to take it off or leave it?' More silence and a frown.

'Should I just leave it on then?'

Nothing again and now I'm out of patience.

'Do you want to go around to customer service and see if they can find out why? It's just there.' I point to the desk behind me.

'Hmm. Something is wrong. I have about £20. You've got it wrong.'

Enough is enough.

'Well, I can't do anything else here. I can either take it off or leave it on – please tell me what you'd like me to do?'

There's more hostile staring, some steely contemplation and then ... 'Leave it, please.' I print off the receipt and it indicates that she definitely has more – about £20 – but my till only tells me what my till chooses to tell me and so my hands are tied. I start to point this out gently but she grabs the receipt and storms off. As I serve the next customer I can hear her at customer service.

'SOMETHING IS WRONG – WHERE ARE ALL MY BLOODY POINTS?'

Diana is with us on the baskets and fiddles with her hair a lot today. 'I'm bored,' she says repeatedly. Barbara walks by.

'I'm really bored,' says Diana. 'Can I come off for a bit?'

'Yes, you can,' says Barbara. 'But those two are going soon, so you'll have to go back on again after a while.' And Diana locks her till and walks away to shop-floor freedom. The two older Cogs left behind mutter to each other. 'If we said we were bored, we wouldn't just get to come off ...'

'No, we'd get our knuckles rapped and then get given a spray and a cloth to get scrubbing.'

* * *

Granddad is in the queue with two teenagers. The woman in front of him offers to drop back in the queue. She has her reasons. She leaves her basket to hold her place for her while she wanders off to fetch a forgotten item. He's not impressed and tells the other customers, 'We're not going to wait for her.' His basket is full of reduced items. One item refuses to scan and the barcode misbehaves when I type it in. I suggest getting a supervisor. 'If they can't mark it up properly then leave it for someone else to buy.' He's ready to detonate by the time we're done, so when I give him his change back he's looking for a scrap.

'You've only given me £3.53.'

'Yes, that's right.'

'Well, how much is it?' I show him his receipt – his shopping came to £6.47.

'So the right change from £10 would be £3.53,' I tell him. He stares at his change for a bit longer and then stands to the side (to unnerve me more than anything else). He double-checks the receipt and counts the change slowly. Twice. He wants trouble but he won't find it on my shift.

One bloke is buying three packets of barbecue crisps for his lunch. 'Come on, you can do better than that,' I joke.

'It'll fill me up and it only costs a couple of quid.'

'But keep that up and you'll pay a higher price with your health,' I tell him.

Foreigners frequent the tills doing their getting-by-without-speaking-the-language thing. By my estimation, one in five customers at the basket tills doesn't speak English. My questions about bags, Nectar cards and school vouchers are met with baffled expressions. A man with two white bloomer loaves responds with the same ambiguous grunt to every single question I ask him.

My collection of customer recipes is rapidly growing. A Jamaican woman gives me her favourite beans-and-rice combo:

Boil a tin of kidney beans and rice. Add salt, pepper and Thai spice. Leave until cooked. 'You'll never look back.'

A cordon-bleu chef recommends Jane Asher's chocolate fudge cake mix as the best chocolate cake on the market. 'Even better than what I could put together myself.'

As the afternoon passes, dads start piling in with their Indian meals for one, which can only mean that lots of the mums in this part of London are on a girls' night out. And for the ladies staying in, their menfolk have Friday-night romance in mind. I scan many bunches of flowers, chocolate trays, easy-listening CD sets and, of course, condoms. The girls, though, are obsessing over domestic matters. 'I only came in for some kitchen scales/pasta sauce/rice/loaf of bread. How did I end up with this lot?' asks one female customer after another. This is what the shopping list of a woman who came in to buy cleaning cloths that would have cost her 34p looks like:

Linguine x 2
Tagliatelle
Lurpak spread
Napoletana sauce x 2
Yoplait Frubes
Tropical juice
Green dessert pears
Fruitella

It costs her £9.83. Her expression tells me everything I need to know about how appalled she is with herself.

Another customer who came in to exchange a toy got distracted by the clothes. She spends £40 on deodorant and clothes. Her six-year-old is out of his mind with boredom and she has in twenty minutes flat bought a pair of jeans, two sets of bikinis (despite the rain today), a black top, a jersey cardigan and two toothbrushes. She is also, predictably, standing at the till doing a little emotional self-harm.

Michaela only has an hour until she leaves, so as Barbara passes she asks, 'Do I have relief tonight?' This is the only sure-fire way of knowing if you will be staying beyond your shift. 'I don't know,' says Barbara in a sing-song voice. 'You're just going to have to wait until 5.30 to find out.' And with that she charges back to her till captain high horse.

I don't know if it's Michaela and her sexual allure, but men are flocking to the baskets in even larger droves than normal. Most of them, due to what I have now concluded is an inherent dysfunctional dexterity, struggle to open the plastic bags. Proof, if we're to buy into supermarket biologi-cal determinism, that blokes are, without doubt, the dumber sex.

One of my last customers tonight is a pregnant woman with a stomach so large, her tummy arrives first and her face ninety seconds later. With my usual diplomacy and delicacy I blurt out the first thing that comes to mind.

'Oh, my goodness – are you about to give birth now?'

'No,' she laughs, 'three more months left. I've got twins in there.'

Like an overexcited seal, I start flapping my hands together. 'Do you know what you're having?'

'One of each.'

I'm so excited I'm ready to go into labour on her behalf. But she just looks exhausted. 'Can you come back to me again in a few weeks?' I plead. 'I really want to see how you're getting on.'

'Yes, of course. And I'll bring them in to meet you when they're born too,' she says kindly. I nod fervently. But I know that I'll be long gone before they arrive.

Rebecca is doing some overtime and ends up sitting on baskets with me for the last two hours of my shift and insists on telling our customers that they should be served by me rather than her 'due to the excellent customer service that she provides'. And so they come to me, while she kicks back and relaxes.

When I finish my shift I head to Grace's till. She finishes at 7 p.m. I look at my watch and it is 7 p.m. She has three other customers behind me and there is no closed sign on her check-out. 'You are a lunatic, Grace. Do you WANT to be here till 10 p.m.?' I whisper to her.

'I know, I know, you're right.'

'Look, Betty is over there – tell her you've finished.' Betty sends someone to get a sign for the till. A customer joins the queue anyway – and Grace says nothing. I know she'll be here until 7.30 p.m.

'You're too polite, Grace.' She gives me a feeble smile. As I grab my bags I notice the man behind me has two packets of condoms, two bottles of white wine, strawberries and some melting chocolate. Grace scans his things with the discretion of a secret service agent. As I walk out of the store I promise to muster up the courage to walk into a store (that I have no intention of returning to) and strut to the checkout with a full-on X-rated shop – condoms, pregnancy tests, sexy knickers. Just to prove to myself what I've long known: it takes a lot to shock a Cog.

Friday, 24 April 2009

The sun is shining and it is without a doubt the most exquisite day we've had all year. As a misguided press officer once said – a good day for bad news. This recession is worse than predicted and more severe than anyone expected. The Chancellor, Alistair Darling, has now said this is the deepest recession since the Second World War and the number of people out of work has risen to 2.1 million.

There seems to be a determined gear change amongst those who are intent on making cuts. One customer buys only the Basics range and it costs him £40.77. His basket includes chopped tomatoes, tins of sweetcorn, corned beef, vodka and eggs. Others are buying honey, carrots, herbs, peppers, mushrooms and mozzarella – all from the cheaper range – and vouchers and points are being used more frequently than ever before. A Polish couple seem to have emptied the shelves of the entire range. Everything in their basket is in the tell-tale white packaging with orange writing: cola, tomato ketchup, Swiss roll, chicken noodles, carrots, beans, apples, pasta, chicken kiev, pizza, sausage rolls, salmon trimmings, coleslaw, pork luncheon meat and yogurt. The grand total is £24.35, probably half of what the more expensive ranges would have cost them.

One woman tells me, 'I'm an impulse buyer and a place like this is quite dangerous for me, especially since you now do all these clothes, DVDs, books and videos – I'm going to end up broke coming in here.' She'd save a fortune if she shopped online like one of my regular customers, a mum to three boys:

'It only cost me £100, but it was a complete disaster – I couldn't remember everything we have and the boys just whinged because of what I had missed.'

So today her shopping costs £154. 'I don't mind. It's a small price to pay for not having them all moan at me.'

A customer arrives at the till and does what many customers do. 'Can you tell me how many points I've got on my card?'

'Yes, if you give me your card, I can tell you at the end.'

'Can't you tell me now?'

'Um, no, because I haven't swiped your card yet, for one. And two, I need to put something on your bill to be able to take something off your card.' She looks totally confused and affronted. I don't expect her to understand the entire transaction process, but this is not complex physics. 'It's the same logic as at the bank: give me your card and I'll tell you what you've got. Until you give it to me to scan, how can I tell you?' It takes another minute before it clicks.

Heat does a funny thing to our heads. We experience it so infrequently that, when it arrives, we rip our clothes off, throw back more drinks and go on shopping binges. The Barbecue Bunch are buying meat, BBQ utensils, coal, salad, strawberries and wine by the gallon. One couple who haven't done their weekly food shop yet spend £121.26 on this stuff. They contemplate for a few moments putting back the extra £12 they've spent on DVDs for their eighteen-month-old before deciding, 'At least it'll keep him busy while we do the barbecue.'

After my break I serve an old lady with severely twisted fingers and chronic arthritis. It's so bad she can't pack, can't take her cash out and can't put her change back. I help her pack, take the money out and put the change back in her purse for her. I wonder how she will get her shopping into her house – and how she copes generally. 'I know what you're thinking, love,' she suddenly says. 'Don't worry about me, I get by, I rely on the kindness of strangers.'

I've lost count of the number of times a Mr or Mrs Elderly has been 'holding up' the queue while packing their shopping slowly with arthritic hands. Meanwhile customers sigh deeply and loudly behind them. Shopping is a tense affair – this much I've learnt in my time here. And the dumping ground for all the tension acquired while traipsing around the store is the till. Sometimes I'm the garbage can and sometimes, sadly, it's the customer causing the delay. I feel another letter coming on.

Dear Supermarket Giant,

Far be it from me to tell you how to do your job, but are you aware that one of your key customer groups are the golden-agers?

I know you probably do a lot to make lives easier for them – I've seen the trolley boys who help them with their shopping to the car and we Cogs are always ready to pack for them when they want it. But these OAPs come in during the week to avoid the weekend scrum. Their jowls wobble, they are almost deaf, but somehow they still hear the crowd of unsympathetic customers exhaling noisily behind them. They punch their pin numbers in over and over again and it brings them to their rheumatism-ridden knees every time. Often it's not because they can't remember their numbers but because the pin-pads are not as responsive to their hands. It's painful to watch and crushing to tell them it's still not registered. Those wretched pin-pads are not made for eyes that have to squint hard to read instructions.

Don't mistake me for a Help the Aged campaigner; truth be told, I find many of them ill-tempered and cantankerous, but my mum is seventy-plus and I can't bear the thought of her going through this kind of ritual humiliation once a week. So here's what I suggest.

Give your staff some training so they know how to handle
and help them, and more importantly, how to deal with the
insensitive customers queuing up behind. And make an
exception on the receipt-signing issue – if they can't remember
their pin or get it right and they look old enough, just let them
sign, will you? I've had to turn away an elderly lady who
couldn't get her pin right and didn't have another card with her.
She had spent a good hour in your store and almost two hours
of her day on the shopping trip. She was happy to give you a
good £40 from her pension, so why turn away her business?

Yours,

A. Cog

A woman stops off post-gym session. I can smell her from five
yards away. The sixty-four-year-old man in front of her doesn't
need his school vouchers.

'Why don't you give my school vouchers to this … er … man
…' He turns to look at her properly. 'Um … sorry … er … lady
… um … man …' He trails off, grabs his bags and races out of
the store.

A customer arrives with a full trolley. She throws her bag
down, doesn't look at me and doesn't respond to my hello.

'I've got six bags.' She's still loading and I can see she's in a
hurry.

'Should I pack for you?' I ask. She nods. I put two sets of
toilet roll packs, a bar of soap, a hand cream and cotton pads in
one bag. When she has finished loading she comes back to my
end of the till. She takes the bag I've just packed, looks at it and
tuts loudly. She then empties it and starts again.

One woman gives me her coupons. 'I've spent the amount it
says I need to in order to get that money off,' she tells me
assertively.

'I'm quite sure you have, but I have to check anyway. Just bear with me.'

Painstakingly I go through all £89.34 of her shopping to see if she really does have £6 worth of meat and £4 worth of fruit. It requires a lot of mental arithmetic, which I haven't done since aged ten, and so it takes a while. She turns to the customer behind her in exasperation. 'Can you believe that they have to check everything before they can give me my money off?'

'They don't in Tesco,' says the co-customer, 'it just comes off.'

'I know! I won't be doing this again. It's so humiliating. Never again … this is really quite embarrassing.'

'You should check the receipt too, because they always get things wrong.'

My least favourite part of this job is being ignored by customers. Second to that is when they talk about me like I'm not there. The stress makes me do my sums wrong so I give up and just put the coupons through. By the time I get to customer number 2 she's ready to throw a grenade at me. I say hello. She ignores me. I ask her how she is. She mutters a barely audible reply. When I wind up the transaction she stands at the end and methodically checks her bill. I pretend not to notice. She leaves.

Today we have the results of our first MCM in the new financial year, and we have failed. The mystery customer did their rounds in the store, trying to get products located, observing the helpfulness of the shop-floor staff, assessing our dress code and name badges and so on. We fail because the colleague who was approached to find a product did not smile or give a warm greeting, their customer service was minimal and they didn't offer 'an individualised, tailored service'. The Cog at the tills apparently did the same thing – no points for the bag, distracted, and offered a basic minimal service – and I can't help thinking that it was me. There are hand-scribbled management notes all over the report:

'What happened here? Not a good start!'

'Any colleagues not carrying out the right behaviours will now be named to the store manager.' And where that would lead, nobody knows.

When I get back from my break there's a little sign on my till saying:

> 'Make consistency matter.'
> Always remember the three service principles.
> *Great start ... smile!!!!
> *Happy to serve ... focused friendly tailored service
> *Perfect finish ... smile!!!
> And never forget eye contact.

This is interspersed with lots of smiley faces.

At 5.30, it's time for Michaela to leave. Betty tells her she has relief but Samantha is ready to send her on her way now. 'Don't worry, I'll deal with Betty,' she tells a confused-looking Michaela. Samantha stands at the end of her till like a human *Closed Checkout* sign, frightening the customers away. When it's my turn Betty closes my till early and I'm out of there on the dot. She also throws in a 'Bye, darling.' On my way up the stairs I read the maxims on the wall again: *Say goodbye. Say hello – they hardly ever bite. Be friendly. Talk to the customer. Take them to the product not the aisle. Do they want anything else? They pay our wages. Suggest an alternative. Wear your badge.*

Saturday, 25 April 2009

Six months ago there were days I couldn't quite believe that supermarkets were doing as well as reported. Now things are even better – they are bustling round the clock. Customers have also changed in that time. Back then, everyone was feeling flush, now the Basics range is flying off the shelves, people are paying in cash more frequently, they're taking items off their lists and some are shopping more cautiously.

One customer nips at me constantly. 'These are all reduced,' she says, picking up three meat pies I've already scanned.

'I know – that's how I've scanned them.'

She throws her Nectar card down, demanding I check her points. Most annoyingly, she stops at the end of the till to check her bill. As they walk off, I see her turn to look at me repeatedly and whisper to her husband.

Even those not tightening the purse strings are on edge. 'Would you let me know how many bags you use?' I ask my next customer.

'I'll let you know once I know how many we use,' he answers acerbically.

'Well, that's what I meant,' I snap right back. No more Ms Nice Cog, I decide.

One customer has caught on to how supermarkets manipulate shoppers into spending more than they intend. 'I know all about their frequent floor-plan changes and moving products from one shelf to the other and putting the most expensive ones at eye level. I prepare myself for these tricks the minute I walk in here.' Nonetheless, she ends up spending £30 more than she planned.

A couple with three kids aged seven, five and four tell me they haven't been to Sainsbury's for years because they find it cheaper to shop at Tesco and Asda where they spend around £200 a week. They guesstimate their shopping cost at £350 and are pleasantly surprised when I tell them the total is £209. 'Hmm, we might just come back here again,' they say.

Others are not so lucky:

WOMAN A. Normal weekly expenditure: £130–£150. Estimate: £165. Actual spend: £181.60. Reaction: Stumped.

WOMAN B. Normal expenditure: £120. Estimate: £135. Actual spend: £170.26. Reaction: Mortified. And then embarrassed bizarre justifying to couple behind.

WOMAN C. Normal expenditure: £130. Estimate: £130. Actual spend: £151.96. Reaction: Self-hate. Followed by shopping thrown into bag angrily.

WOMAN D. Normal expenditure: £90. Estimate: £110. Actual spend: £140. Reaction: Blame. 'If it weren't for the clothes placed at the entrance on the way in, I'd save £30 each time. It's very hard to walk by.'

WOMAN E. Normal expenditure: £125. Estimate: £140. Actual spend: £173.21. Reaction: Grit. She gives me her gift card, from which I redeem £30, her coin star voucher worth £18 and Nectar points totalling £7.50. This brings it all down to a more reasonable £117.71.

WOMAN F. Normal expenditure: £100–£115 Estimate: She tells me to get to £100 and then stop selling her anything. Actual spend: £82.82. Reaction: Relief. 'It's still painful, but at least it's not more than a hundred quid.'

A customer tells me that twenty years ago her mother was able to fill a trolley bursting to full capacity for £50 – now the same trolley costs her four times that.

Richard's old school teacher comes to my till and tells me that he was as lovely a child as he is an adult today. Her own child is torturing her. 'They need to make supermarkets more child-friendly – I pull my hair out when I bring him in shopping.'

Rebecca is on her usual charm-offensive and as she passes she throws some of her fairy dust over my checkout. 'You look wonderful,' she tells the lady I'm serving. 'That scarf looks stunning. I bet you're going out tonight,' she oozes.

'Oh, thank you. I am, as it happens.'

'Well, you'll knock him dead,' says Rebecca, flashing her a charming smile.

A number of customers tell me today that they haven't been affected by the recession themselves but they're making plans for what may lie ahead.

'We've all been talked into it, so I've started to make savings where I can.' This customer uses £10 worth of Nectar points, £50 in cash and the remainder on her credit card to pay the bill of £126. This sort of split payment is typical of a shopper struggling to make ends meet.

I finally meet the customer Sainsbury's has spent months trying to seduce. 'I was a devotee of M&S and now I only come here. That's what the recession has reduced me to. It's not the same, you know – all that over-priced fair-trade stuff in their classic packaging, the extortionate mixed fruit packs, the biscuits and bread brought in directly from the finest bakeries in the land – all that tosh. Oh, how I will miss it!' he jokes. He gives me £20 for his £12.70 shop. I give him £7.30 in change.

'But I gave you £20.'

'Yes, you did,' I tell him.

'I thought it cost £7.30.'

'No …' I take the receipt and show him. 'Your shopping cost £12.70. Your *change* is £7.30.'

'Aha,' he laughs, 'And if it wasn't for the recession I wouldn't even have bothered querying that – I'd just have silently walked away. Now every penny makes me tetchy.'

One customer is truly going back to basics and has started making her own cream liqueur. 'Is this tiny bottle of rum for a cake you're making?'

'No, no.'

'And I'm presuming it's not because you're planning to swig it back on the way home?'

'No,' she laughs. 'We've started making our own Baileys. My husband does it with a bit of whisky, rum, condensed milk and cream. It's as delicious as the real thing and a tenth of the price.'

A blonde with a slim band holding her curly hair back tells me she's making ruthless cuts. 'I usually spend at least £400 a month on my shopping, sometimes even up to £600. So now what I do is go around the store with a list and put everything on the list in order of the layout in the shop. Look –' She shows me her list and she's grouped all like items together in a number of different sub-lists. 'Although, it still doesn't stop the impulse buys.' Today her shopping costs her £114.45.

I've spent the last six months watching the death of the local greengrocer. *This* seems to be the first pit-stop for consumers after their fruit and veg.

'Why don't you just get this fresh from your greengrocer's?' I ask one customer who has virtually every variety of fruit and vegetable in the store on the belt.

'Because I'm lazy and I don't want to have to stop somewhere else. This is my one-stop shop. It's a lot easier if you can just get it all in one place, isn't it?'

A number of my customers want to give me huge packs of bottled water to lift over the till and then scan. And someone tries to give me several heavy boxes of extra-large ready meals. 'Sorry, could you just put it down at the end of the till and let it come down the belt? If I lift that from this position I'm going to damage my back.' And when the customer grumbles I actually put the words 'health' and 'safety' together.

I get my break at 5.20 today, almost five hours after I started and just over an hour before I finish. When I get back I only have half an hour of my shift left.

One of my last customers today is wearing bright blue eye shadow to match her aqua blue top. She works at UBS. 'They've cut 15,000 people there, then another 8000 and now it'll be another 8500 still to go. So 30 per cent of the workforce is gone.' She then laughs. 'It's so crazy that it's actually quite funny. So I try not to worry about it because it just drags you down. And if I laugh about it – it doesn't seem so bad.'

I see Jeremy, one of the Cogs, before I go home and he says: 'I hear that you're leaving. Have you had enough?' He's caught me off guard and so I mumble something about moving on to other things.

I give Rebecca a lift home for what will be the last time.

'You know that Katherine's sad that you're leaving?'

'Oh, is she? That's sweet,' I say, genuinely touched.

'She was going on and on about it, and all I could think was – *you've* got friends here other than *me*? I thought you were supposed to be a Billy-no-mates,' she teases. As she gets out of my car she leans in through the window. 'Goodbye, Judas,' she says with mock-disgust. 'You betrayed me.' And then she laughs.

Friday, 1 May 2009

News of the swine flu outbreak is all over the television and Lesley catches me buying antibacterial gel. 'Not you as well! Customers have been buying loads of that stuff today.'

'I can see that, look there's hardly any left on the shelf.' The entire section has been raided. Hayley offers me my 140th anniversary badge to wear and tells me that the store is intending to celebrate with gusto.

An elderly customer is in early, keen to beat the crowds. She needs help with her packing and is in the mood for a chat. 'I'd like to shop around but am too old to do it. My sister does it, though. She gets on the bus and goes to Iceland, and then Tesco and Morrisons and then her local grocer's. I find it exhausting just listening to her. She says she saves a fortune, mind you. I come here because it's where my daughter shops. She gives me a lift – but it is very expensive to shop here.'

Molly from customer service comes over with the MCM report from last week and tells me she's going to be spending some of her time on checkouts from next week.

'Do you like it on checkouts?'

'No, I absolutely hate it.' She says, her blue eyes shining angrily.

'So how come you're back? Don't you like customer service?'

She shifts uncomfortably. 'It's just the way things have turned out.'

'It's hard there, isn't it?'

'Yes, but I've always loved the customer service desk. And not *all* customers are horrid, it's just a small percentage. Look …

See that lady in pink behind you?' I turn to look at the customer Grace is serving. 'She comes in almost every day. She bought a toaster that wasn't working last month but she didn't have the receipt and so I had to make a decision about whether to say, "Sorry, can't do anything – how do I know you haven't had it for a while and didn't just take it home and break it?" or decide if it was worth keeping her custom and give her the refund. It took me two seconds to decide. And she left happy and satisfied. So now every time she comes in, she comes over for a chat. She's like a friend for life.'

'You sound like you're really good at customer service.'

A dark cloud passes over her face and she looks upset. 'Yes … I … love it.' She won't tell me why she's coming back to checkouts except to say that she's 'not allowed to talk about it'. I can only conclude that eventually someone upstairs decided she wasn't cut out for it – even though, it seems to me, she was born to do it. I notice the Cog she was training up a few weeks ago seems to have taken Molly's place at the desk.

A couple who like cooking Indian food ask for my tips about where to shop for Indian spices.

'Should we get them in here?' they whisper.

'Not unless you want to pay double the price,' I whisper back.

'Where do you get yours from?' And even though it's extremely unprofessional, I give them the address of my local Indian food store.

A customer spending £85 tells me she ends up throwing away 15 per cent of her shopping every week. 'I like to have a full larder. And so when I'm down on just a couple of things I pop back in here. And spend more than I need to just to fill the fridge and cupboard up. You'd think my generation would know better, wouldn't you? What a waste, eh?'

A woman only has £40 on her, she needs another £3.71. She digs around in her pocket for loose change and pulls out a few pennies. She empties her purse on the till in a panic. She then empties her entire bag on the till. It's so painful to watch that if I was allowed to carry any cash on me I'd have happily paid the difference. She's about to abandon the entire shop when I suggest she takes something off the list. Red in the face, she leaves her cupcakes, chicken slices and juices. 'I'll have to come back in tomorrow for those,' she says regretfully.

An elderly lady tells me that before Christmas her shopping used to cost her £33 a time and now it is £40.90 for exactly the same food. One man's shop comes to £68.03. 'Argh. How did that happen?' And then, 'If the wife had come, we would probably have doubled it!'

Samantha catches me yawning and indicates to me to cover my mouth. 'Are we keeping you up, love?'

Lesley is sitting behind me and teases me about my swine flu panic. Grace, on the other hand, has the same concerns and leans over for a squirt of my gel every four customers she serves.

Katherine's on her way home with her shopping and comes to my checkout. She looks tired from fretting about her sick uncle. 'You need to stop and rest, woman.' I say, noticing that she is not wearing her trademark crimson lipstick and blue mascara.

'No, no rest for the wicked. I'm doing some painting and gardening tomorrow.'

Two minutes before the end of my shift and I grab the bull by its horns. I tell an approaching customer than I'm closing after the one I'm currently serving. He takes his trolley to another Cog. She says the same. He bellows at the top of his voice, 'YOU'RE ALL BLOODY CLOSING! WHO THE F***'S

GOING TO STAY OPEN TO SERVE US?' He does this right in front of the till captains. Then, one of my regular customers comes to my till, two minutes after my shift has ended and I'm still serving the previous shopper.

'I'm really sorry, but I'm closing after this customer,' I tell her. The customer I'm serving is still emptying her trolley.

'But … but … I have my son with me,' she says. Ai-li passes by and I ask her to get me a closing sign. 'I'll get you one, but you've got to serve this customer anyway.' I'm not sure she has the authority to tell me this, but the regular starts to load her shopping on. A junior supervisor comes to my till.

'Ayesha says you've got relief tonight. She also says you can't close your till until she SAYS so.'

After my relief arrives, I cash up and get ready to leave, but one of Grace's customers wants something from me. 'Can you get me something to wrap this mirror in?' We don't sell extra wrapping here so what she wants I cannot provide. In any case, I. Have. Finished.

'I'm on my way home now, I'm afraid,' I dare to say for the first time since I've worked here.

'Well, I can't take it like this – it's ridiculous. Can't you get me something?' I look at her with my most convincing customer service face. 'If you pop to the desk at the front of the store I'm sure they will find you something.' I wink at a grinning Grace and whisper, 'Watch and learn,' in her ear as I walk away.

Saturday, 2 May 2009

Adam's in the canteen, swearing at his paperwork. I nip over for a quick chat while devouring my lunch at breakneck speed. He was after the job going in the pharmacy, but the hours didn't add up. So for now he splits his time between the newspapers and the car park trolleys. He's at the end of his tether with customers. 'I mean, seriously, did you pick up *Twinky* magazine from over there? No? I didn't think so. So why put it there? Why, I ask you?' he grumbles. 'I'm sure I do it too, but why do they insist on picking up the fourth newspaper from the top? Today I actually said to a customer: "You know the one at the top, the one at the bottom, they're all the same."'

In the canteen Justin King's newsletters are piled high on a table. The only thing that grabs my attention is the delay of the new uniforms. They won't be introduced until next year now – I wonder if they'll forgo the polyester.

The Talkback 2008 results are on the wall with feedback from staff. The results look good for management – with more than three-quarters of staff claiming to be happy working at the supermarket, believing the pay is good compared to other places and intending to be here beyond a year. A Cog I've recently befriended walks down with me. 'I can't remember filling out the questionnaire, you know.'

'Maybe they made it up,' I say, naughtily.

'They were a bit high, weren't they?' We giggle.

It's a gorgeous day and according to meteorologists we're headed for our hottest summer in years – fitting, I think, just as we are going into financial meltdown. Customers are rolling in with summer purchases: sun loungers, summery clothes, sun cream, ice cream, Halloumi cheese, BBQ equipment and lots and lots of booze. A man who works in IT tells me there were big redundancies in his company just before Christmas.

'There are still more ahead. But it looks like *you* are doing all right in here.'

'We are. And because of the sunshine, people are queuing up for all the summer stuff too.'

He scans the store. 'You wouldn't think there was a recession on by the looks of things in here. And actually, now I come to think of it … I went to the Lakes last week and it was really busy. Busier than ever, in fact. Although that could be because people are staying here rather than going abroad.'

Yesterday it was compost, today people are buying seeds for their garden – carrots, onions, radishes, beans and tomatoes. Brits are now turning to burying their hands in the soil in order to save some cash. During my break, Danielle and I sit together and she shares her customer service tales, all of which inevitably end with customers threatening to take their trade to Tesco. 'And I'm thinking – do you *really* think I care?' she says scornfully.

When I get back a couple with a toddler spend £42.91. Dad pays a visit to the toilet and is appalled by the amount he has to hand over when he returns. 'We only came in for a magazine for her and bottle of whisky for me … how did that happen?' He starts digging around in his wallet. 'It's basically a quid an item and ten pounds a bag isn't it?'

'Well, it's probably those gourmet burgers that did it,' says his wife.

'But I fancied something special. It IS expensive, but it's cheaper than eating out,' he says as he hands over his credit card.

A woman has spent £95.39 on a lot of cakes and an awful lot of biscuits. 'The most frustrating bit of spending so much on my food is the fact that it doesn't last long and there is nothing to show for it. Well, except for the extra inches around your middle.'

Adam walks by at a moment when I'm daydreaming and tuned into the satisfying ping of my scanner. He draws a grin on his face with his fingers to tell me to smile. Ayesha tells a Cog to push her hair off her face. Samantha tells another Cog to quieten down. It's like convent school in here. Next someone will be telling me to pull my socks up.

The cleaner I served two months ago is back.

'How are things with you?' I ask.

'Oh, I'm still very busy – more than ever, actually. I'm getting a lot of work.'

'But aren't people cutting back on cleaners to save money?'

'Not my clients. They're all really rich so they can easily afford their cleaners. I'm turning down work at the moment, to be honest.'

I don't close my till today and wait for a prompt from Ayesha. She closes my till four minutes early.

Friday, 8 May 2009

It's my final day and I'm determined to savour every single moment. Down at the tills, Hayley gives me a big hello and says brightly, 'Last day, girl.' And she gives me the keys to a basket till.

I arrive at my checkout and sit down on the notorious sinking chair. 'No, no, no!' I yelp, jumping off and laughing – much to the irritation of the waiting customer. Today she can wait.

Tracey is on baskets shelling out good will, smiles and her Saturday Special: first-class customer service. And so is a Cog who I've never sat with before – Yanis. She tells me she has been here almost fourteen years.

'I bet customers have changed a lot in that time,' I remark.

'Oh yes. They've always been rude, but they've now started to get more aggressive.'

'How do you mean?'

'Well, before they'd just be brash and abrupt. But now they shout and physically throw their weight about. They grab things, they get in your face.' I ask her about the mystery customer.

'That started about four years ago. And now we're just obsessed with it.'

Tracey tells us there is a new MCM report to read. 'We failed on checkouts apparently,' she says.

'I don't care,' says Yanis defiantly.

'I know you don't care, because it's not you, is it? Nor me. It's the others – them slackers,' Tracey says, pointing at all the other Cogs. We all laugh. I have a quick look at the report – the person on checkouts did everything right but was too busy talking to the Cog standing by the side of the till to engage with the customer. From where I'm sitting today I have a direct view of all my colleagues at the tills. Katherine is busy serving and smiling at shoppers. Connor is staring into mid-air totally oblivious to his customer, and Sonia is sharing another one of her horror stories. There are brand-new signs dangling from the ceiling the full length of the store carrying a number of different messages: *Celebrating 140 years of great products at fair prices. £42 million raised for comic relief since 1999. All our fresh sausages are made from British meat.*

A Cog who works on clothing comes to my till and, as we're chatting, asks why I no longer work at the store pharmacy.

'Pharmacy? I've never worked at the pharmacy,' I tell her, bewildered.

'Why do I think that, then?'

'Was there someone there who looked like me?'

'No. I thought it was you. I always thought that.'

'I've always been on checkouts.'

'Funny – I was really sure you did. I don't know why I thought you were pharmacy. Strange that.'

It's my doctorly face playing mind games again.

Lesley comes to my till and the customer in front of her has just put apples down on my till. He doesn't know what kind they are and neither do I. 'Come on, Lesley, prove your worth.'

'They're Gala. Don't you eat apples, girl?'

'I do – just not the one million varieties that we sell.'

'I recognise each one by sight, don't even need the barcode,' she tells us proudly.

Yanis and I get customer after customer today pushing trolleys but wanting to be served at the baskets. I bow to Yanis' superior knowledge and take her lead. She serves them so I do too. Even the couple with three multi-packs of Coca Cola bottles, large bottles of oil and several crates of beer. And that's despite the grunts from the crowd behind.

Today is just another day in the soap opera life of a checkout girl.

1. I serve some customers not having a good day and telling me as much. One is ill and should be in bed – another is caught off guard and says 'I'm not good at all,' with a slightly sad look in her eyes.
2. Couples argue at the till. One man storms off. Wife is left to pack shame-faced.
3. I sell thirty-eight hair-dye kits. One customer says she's swapped home dye for a session with her hairdresser: 'What's £6.74 compared to £60?'
4. Bag shame continues. Although one man is cheeky enough to say, 'Yes, I do have my own bag. *This* bag is now mine,' picking up the one at the till.
5. People leave their wallets at home and squirm. Happens twice today. They leave with their heads hung low.
6. I struggle with another pregnancy kit. Nelly opens it for me, but not before drawing the attention of everyone in the queue.

'Reckon you might be pregnant, then?' she asks outright. Her indiscretion is my gain. The customer tells us she has an eighteen-year-old and a nine-year-old and this is her last chance to conceive. I wonder why she only tries once every nine years.

7. Mums, mums-to-be and acting mums want my advice. A young aunt looking after her baby nephew is buying baby milk and butternut squash. It transpires that she doesn't really know what to do with it.

8. Customers try to hide their pin. One does it so his friend feels compelled to say: 'Even you can't see what you're typing, mate.' I jump in with: 'Don't worry, I couldn't commit fraud if I wanted to.' 'Oh, it's not you – I don't want him to see it.' 'Thanks, mate,' says his friend.

9. People bring baskets over with just one item in. This happened three times today. One pack of sanitary towels. One Bounty bar. And (of course) one Lynx deodorant.

I take two last shots at playing Numerology for Idiots.

First up, £19.65.

'The year that Malcolm X died.'

'Oh was it?'

'Yes, I think so – I thought Martin Luther King for a second, but he died later didn't he?'

'Hmm, late sixties I think.'

'Was it a good year for you?'

'It certainly was. The year I got married.'

He's retired and has been enjoying the sunshine by playing golf.

'Are you worried about the recession?'

'Not a bit.'

'But for your kids?'

'Oh yes – I've been bailing them out with deposits, mort-gages and rent – it's not good for them. But I guess that's what dads are for.'

Shame everyone doesn't have a dad like him.

And then: £10.01.

'Like *One Thousand and One Arabian Nights*,' I say to the chap before me.

'That was quite a sexy book, wasn't it?' He responds a little too quickly. Not quite how I was hoping this would go down.

'Um … well … it's kind of a kids' book – but yes there was the whole nervous tension between the king and Scheherazade.'

'Arabian princesses – they're well up for it, I bet,' he says, giving me a rather creepy grin.

'Uh-huh, you reckon?' I try to say distractedly.

'All that sitting around in harems, wearing those silky face scarves – definitely …' I think he actually starts to visualise this now.

'Your name looks Arabic – where are you from then?' And it's time to send him on his way.

Hayley tells me my break is next, straight after Yanis. Half an hour later, Yanis is still sitting at the till. It becomes evident that Hayley forgot to tell her to go. I tell her, but Yanis likes to toe the line.

'Unless I hear it from Hayley, I ain't going. Otherwise they'll say I just went off.'

'Well, you can just tell them it was me – she definitely told me that you should go.'

Yanis waits an extra thirty minutes even though she is desperate for a break. Another supervisor eventually sanctions her break. During my own break, I spot a new plasma screen hanging in the canteen carrying messages: 'Let's celebrate our

140th birthday.' It gives the dates, talks about cakes, dressing up in Victorian style to celebrate and bangs on about the MCM again.

'Please continue to smile and greet all customers and show them to the product and finally end with a goodbye and a smile. Continue this and we will get our bonus.' Nobody is paying any attention to this but me. I also spot a notice hanging next to it that dates from June last year saying that by April 2009 Sainsbury's expect to have cut bag usage by 50 per cent. If my experience at the till is anything to go by they are far from meeting this target.

When I return I serve two chaps wearing BMW T-shirts.

'How's it going down there?'

'Good, thanks.'

'Don't lie,' says the other suddenly. 'It's crap.'

'OK, scrap that. It's not looking good at all.'

'No one knows how long we've got a job for.'

I talk to a man who works in insurance and he tells me things have never been busier. 'People are making claims galore – usually employment-, or lack of it, related, of course.' He smiles like a man in insurance would.

A customer tells me she's making her speciality tonight for her friends:

Two large butternut squash, prawns, fine green beans, chilli, coconut milk and a small jar of Thai spices. Stir fry, pour in the coconut milk. Simmer until cooked.

A large Russian customer with his English wife walks to the checkout. Both Yanis and I are free. And he roars in a loud Russian way:

'WHO LIKES TO WORK?'

Yanis says, 'Both of us.'

And I say, 'Neither of us.' At the same time. He puts his basket down on my till with a 'WELL, THERE YOU ARE THEN, WOMAN.' I don't pick up my forfeit because the woman behind him has already placed her basket at my till. Poor Yanis has to listen to him bellow instead.

Sarita arrives at the end of her shift and flashes her blinking ring finger at Yanis.

'Wow, that's gorgeous, when did that happen?' asks Yanis, holding Sarita's hand and staring at the flashing diamond solitaire.

'Last weekend,' says Sarita, showing off her ring proudly.

I do some quick maths – she's only been with the new boyfriend since after I started working here – a matter of months. I wonder how this will go down with the ex and his mum. Sarita has no such concerns on her mind.

'We're getting married in India so that we can have a big, traditional Asian wedding,' she says happily, and for the first time since I met her, she smiles brightly.

One of my last customers is a PE teacher. He has a deep tan and when I ask him about it he tells me it's because he spends most of his time outdoors. Nelly is with me and standing at her till, she turns to inspect him from head to toe. He looks slightly uneasy. 'So what do you do then?' she asks.

'I'm a PE teacher,' he repeats.

'Ooh, physical, then?' Nelly is close to fifty, and this man is unfortunately half her age.

I smother a giggle and he looks distinctly uncomfortable. She takes a good look at his shorts – he is, by now, actually squirming. As he scarpers out the store she watches him (and his butt):

'Should have known he was a PE teacher. Look at them legs in them shorts … nice.'

Betty comes over and stops at my till for … a … chat.

'I was thinking about you today and wondering why I hadn't seen you. Have you been in all day?'

'Yes,' I say, trying to keep myself together. 'I think it's because you started halfway through my shift and I've been down at this end most of the day.'

'Hmm, that's strange. I'd been wondering why I hadn't seen you for a while. Anyway, just close your till when you finish, OK?'

My last customer is my 230th of the day.

'Congratulations you are my last customer in this job. Ever.'

'Oh wow. I feel so honoured,' says the pretty blonde twenty-something.

'Tell me something about yourself that I will always remember – no pressure.'

'Oh well, that's easy enough – I'm absolutely shaking with nerves because I'm going on a date tonight with a guy I met several weeks ago who I thought I'd never see again. He's coming down from Newcastle and just phoned me a couple of hours ago. And I really like him! We spent all night talking the first time we met and he's probably Mr Right, but I thought nothing would ever come of it … and then out of the blue he phoned!'

'How very *Before Sunrise*,' I say, grinning broadly. She gets the reference and laughs.

'I know! I really want to knock him out, but nothing is open now so I nipped in here to buy this top for tonight. What do you think?' She holds up the delicate white blouse with a £15 price-tag. It'll look really pretty against her tanned skin, green eyes and blonde hair. I tell her this and she beams. Behind her are a mass of customers. 'I'm sorry, but I really have to close,' I say, not once, not twice but eight times. Everyone grunts. Everyone rolls their eyes.

'You must get so fed up, having to tell people that over and over again.'

'I used to. But today, I just don't care,' I say, grinning widely. I close my till for the last time. I do my last cash-up. I log off, send the pod up to the office and take my key towards the till captains. Betty, Ayesha, Louisa, and the Cogs starting the next shift are gathered together, huddled over the schedules. Betty is allocating tills, Louisa is handing out keys, customers are rushing to the tills. They've all got their backs to me. I hand over my till keys to Ayesha and she takes them distractedly. I say goodbye. Nobody hears me.

As I leave the store I see Molly, Katherine and Nelly all with baskets in their hands grabbing some last-minute shopping. We need milk at home, I suddenly remember. I head to the shelf and pick up a bottle. And then I stop. No, today I won't shop at all. I leave it on the meat shelf for a Cog to put away. And then I see Danielle at customer service and we give each other a big smile and a wave. The last person I say goodbye to is also the first person I met here. As I walk out the big double doors I turn one last time to look at the checkouts. At the basket tills there is already another Cog sitting in my chair.

EPILOGUE

During my time at Sainsbury's, the financial crisis became a full-blown recession – our first for almost two decades. Every week brought more job losses and unemployment soared. It now stands at 2.26 million with experts predicting it will hit the 3 million mark by 2010. Interest rates are still at a record low at 0.5 per cent, house-buying activity is low, new car sales continue to dip, there is reduced availability of credit and charities say their donations have fallen.

But since I left there has been talk of the first green shoots of recovery, suggesting that the worst of the recession may now be over. Others believe it is only just starting to bottom out, while many still forecast that it will continue until 2010. At the time of writing, the economy remains fragile and consumer confidence is still low, so for now we are stuck in the mud. Any recovery will be sluggish and the government and the Bank of England have their work cut out.

However, over the past several months I've witnessed first-hand how the supermarkets have adapted swiftly to these hard times and bucked the trend across the rest of the retail industry. From the giants to the discount stores, most have seen a boost in profits. They've offered promotions, played up discounts, catered for consumers trading downwards and seduced each other's customers. Both Sainsbury's and Marks & Spencer have just celebrated big anniversaries, 140 and 125 years respectively, a reminder that – despite some mixed fortunes – they have survived two world wars and several recessions. They will live to tell the tale of this one too. Morrisons and Asda have also been successful in turning economic adversity into corporate triumph, while Sainsbury's has hung on to its customers by promoting and extending its Basics range. All have enjoyed bumper profits and they look set to continue turning this crisis to their advantage by meeting both the needs of their customers and their shareholders alike. The supermarkets are the real winners in this recession. They in turn say they will create thousands of jobs this year in a bid to help boost employment levels in the UK.

Nonetheless things aren't looking too rosy for the ordinary families coping with the stresses of being financially stretched. Latest figures show that food-price inflation is almost four times higher in the UK in any other EU country – and this is translating on to the shop floor: the cost of a basket of twenty-four staple grocery items has reportedly increased by an average of 18 per cent over the last year, but retailers insist that the worst food-price hikes are behind us. Either way, in the few weeks before I left, I saw a sea change, a wartime mindset: the reality of the recession had set in and people were starting to acclimatise. Customers began making cuts, looking for bargains, using their points, digging around for vouchers, switching to cheaper brands, taking food off the bill when the total was too high, and some had taken to shopping around in different stores. This is what people are doing now, and if things take a turn for the worse, they will simply cut back even further. Many of my customers have already started going out less and cooking at home from scratch. Despite the tough times, both the shoppers and the supermarkets have found their feet quickly.

As for my shop-floor colleagues, they are still slogging away.

Trolley Boy continues to marvel customers with his infinite memory bank.

Michelle is still on probation but working hard to make an impression.

Adam is moving from one department to the other, hoping to be moved up to management.

Richard is earmarked for bigger things – today customer service, tomorrow the world.

Rebecca is still working around the clock and delighting colleagues and customers with her dry wit. When I confessed she said, 'It's like *The Secret Millionaire*, without the £10,000 cheque.'

As for the chairs, last I heard there was still no sign of any new ones.

And me? I'm on my best behaviour every time I stop at the supermarket checkouts.

ACKNOWLEDGEMENTS

My thanks to my wonderful literary agent Andrew Gordon for his dogged faith in this, my eagle-eyed and tactful editor Robin Harvie at Harper Collins for running with it and the legendary TV power broker Sue Ayton for her unwavering commitment.

My gratitude to:

My mother for dropping everything at a moment's notice – for me *and* my children – and to my parents-in-law for picking up where she has left off. My brother for always being my first Phone-A-Friend option, my brother-in-law for being a superb sounding-board and Andrew J for his inspired input.

My fine friends: Shariq for being Open All Hours and Parmie for her 'do or die' advice.

My two beloved, gorgeous mini-men whose hilarious quips leave me keeling over with laughter and whose tolerance of my work is truly remarkable in people so little.

Mr Tough Love, my brilliant and beautiful husband, for believing in all my madcap ideas, inspiring me with his and for always being braver than I dare to be.

And finally to the late Professor Cyprion who would have been tickled pink by this.